The Wells-next-the-Sea Branch

via Wymondham and Dereham

by
Stanley C. Jenkins MA

THE OAKWOOD PRESS

© Oakwood Press & S.C. Jenkins 2011

British Library Cataloguing in Publication Data
A Record for this book is available from the British Library
ISBN 978 0 85361 712 9
Second (enlarged) edition 2011, first published 1988

Typeset by Oakwood Graphics.
Repro by PKmediaworks, Cranborne, Dorset.
Printed by Information Press Ltd, Eynsham, Oxford.

County School station in 2010 as restored by the Mid-Norfolk Railway. Shortly after closure of the line to passengers, the station was used by Anglia Television in a TV serial, *Weavers Green*, masquerading as Weavers Green station. In the early 1990s the station was used again for filming, this time disguised as Gare de Nouvion in the penultimate episode of *'Allo 'Allo*. *John Hendy*

Title page: 'J17' class 0-6-0 No. 65586 with the Wells branch goods train near Walsingham, bound for Norwich in the spring of 1960. *Dr G.R. Siviour*

Front cover: 'J15' class No. 65471 climbs towards Dereham with the milk train from North Elmham to Norwich in March 1960. *Dr G.R. Siviour*

Rear cover: A diesel-multiple-unit waits to leave Wells-next-the-Sea station with a passenger service shortly before the station's closure. *Mrs J. Howlett*

Published by The Oakwood Press (Usk), P.O. Box 13, Usk, Mon., NP15 1YS.
E-mail: sales@oakwoodpress.co.uk
Website: www.oakwoodpress.co.uk

Contents

	Historical Summary	4
	Introduction	7
Chapter One	**Origins, Opening and Early Years (1840-1857)**	
	The railways come to Norfolk - Developments in the 1840s -	
	Opening to Dereham - Opening to Fakenham - Formation	
	of the Wells & Fakenham Railway - Problems & Delays	9
Chapter Two	**Early Years of the**	
	Wells & Fakenham Railway (1857-1862)	
	The cost of the railway - Continued difficulties - Opening of	
	the Wells & Fakenham Railway - Early years of the Railway -	
	The end of local control - The West Norfolk branch - Motive	
	power in the early years - A note on early liveries	
	and early signals	21
Chapter Three	**A Norfolk Branch Line (1862-1923)**	
	Victorian developments - An unsuccessful resort? -	
	Locomotives and train services in GER days - Edwardian	
	Wells - World War I - The last days of the GER –	
	A note on tickets	35
Chapter Four	**The LNER Period (1923-1947)**	
	Locomotives and rolling stock in the LNER period -	
	Passenger services - Freight services - Steam railcars on the	
	Wells line - Other developments in the 1930s - World War II	61
Chapter Five	**The Route from Norwich to Dereham**	
	Norwich Thorpe - Norwich Trowse - Hethersett -	
	Wymondham - Kimberley Park - Hardingham -	
	Thuxton - Yaxham	77
Chapter Six	**The Route from Dereham to Wells**	
	Dereham - North Elmham - County School - Ryburgh -	
	Fakenham - Walsingham - Wighton Halt - Wells-next-the-Sea -	
	The Wells harbour branch	111
Chapter Seven	**The British Railways Era and Beyond**	
	Locomotives and rolling stock in the BR era - The East Coast	
	Floods - Dieselization - Closure between Dereham and Wells -	
	Closure between Wymondham and Dereham - A freight-	
	only branch - First steps towards re-opening -	
	The Mid-Norfolk Railway	159
Chapter Eight	**Revival at Wells - The Wells & Walsingham Railway**	
	The first steps - Some details of the line - Narrow gauge	
	locomotives and rolling stock	191
Appendix One	**Promoters, Directors**	
	and other Prominent Personalities	197
Appendix Two	**Signal Boxes and Signalling**	198
	Sources and Bibliography	199
	Index	200

Historical Summary

Companies of Origin (I) The Norfolk Railway

An amalgamation of the Yarmouth & Norwich Railway (incorporated 18th June, 1842) and the Norwich & Brandon Railway (incorporated 16th May, 1844) under an Act of 30th June, 1845. Opened from Norwich to Great Yarmouth on 1st May, 1844, and from Norwich to Brandon on 29th July, 1845, the two sections being linked on 15th December, 1845, to form a continuous route from Brandon (where connection was made with the Eastern Counties Railway (ECR)) to Great Yarmouth. The Norfolk Railway was worked by the ECR from 8th May, 1848. Amalgamated with the Great Eastern Railway (GER) in 1862.

Companies of Origin (II) The Wells & Fakenham Railway

Incorporated 24th July, 1854 (17 and 18 Vict. cap. 180) with Capital of £70,000 in £20 shares and borrowing powers of £23,000). On 13th August, 1859, the company was authorized to extend its line along the Wells quay, and raise additional capital of £3,800 in 6 per cent preference shares, with loans of £1,200 and to convert the debenture debt into stock. By that same Act, the Norfolk Railway was empowered to guarantee interest on the new capital of £3,800, providing that the annual net revenue would so permit. The company was amalgamated with the GER in 1862.

Wells & Fakenham Directors (1857)

>Chairman Sir Samuel Morton Peto, Bart, Somerleyton Hall, Suffolk
>Richard Till (Norfolk Railway Chairman)
>Horatio Bolingbroke, Norwich
>Jacob Watson, 59 Burton Crescent, London
>Hall William Keary, Holkham
>Joseph Springhill Southgate, Wells
>Secretary Mr Hutt, Engineer George Berkeley

Dates of Opening

Wymondham to Dereham, 7th December, 1846 (Goods), 15th February, 1847 (Passengers); Dereham to Fakenham (Norfolk Railway), 20th March, 1849 (Passengers & Goods); Fakenham to Wells (Wells & Fakenham Railway), 1st December, 1857 (Passengers & Goods).

Length of Branch
Wymondham to Wells-next-the-Sea 33 miles 3 chains
(Norwich Thorpe to Wells-next-the-Sea 43 miles 21 chains)

Mode of Operation

Double line block between Wymondham and Dereham North box, with Tyer's No. 6 Tablet between Dereham North box and North Elmham; Train Staff & Ticket system between North Elmham and Wells-next-the-Sea.

Crossing Loops on Single Line

North Elmham, County School, Fakenham. (Walsingham was a staff station, but had no loop, and Ryburgh had a loop but was not a staff station.)

Typical Motive Power

'E4' class 2-4-0s, 'J15' class 0-6-0s, 'D13' class 4-4-0s, 'D15' class 4-4-0s, 'D16/2', 'D12/3' class 4-4-0s, 'F3' class 2-4-2Ts, 'J17' class 0-6-0s.

Dates of Closure

Dereham-Wells, Saturday 3rd October, 1964 (passengers), remaining open for goods until 31st October, 1964.
Wymondham-Dereham, Saturday 4th October, 1969 (passengers).
Fakenham to Ryburgh closed to freight 1979.
Ryburgh to North Elmham closed to freight 1981.
North Elmham to Dereham closed to freight 1989, leaving the Dereham to Wymondham line in an uncertain state of limbo.

Dates of re-opening

Wells to Walsingham as 10¼ inch gauge line on 6th April, 1982.
Wymondham to Dereham as standard gauge preserved line on 1st May, 1999.

'J15' class 0-6-0 No. 65469 runs alongside the banks of the River Tas as it leaves Norwich with empty milk tanks bound for North Elmham in May 1961.   *Dr G.R. Siviour*

'D16/3' class 4-4-0 No. 62564 waits to depart Wells with a passenger train for Norwich on 1st September, 1955.   *H.C. Casserley*

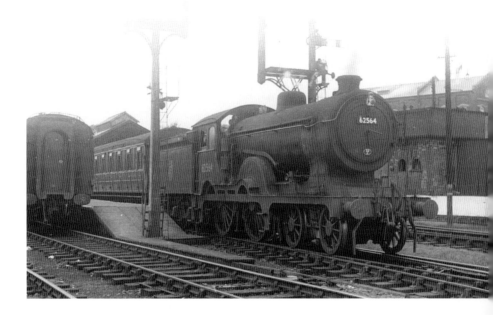

Introduction

Running for 33 miles through remote, yet surprisingly attractive North Norfolk countryside, the branch line from Wymondham to Wells-next-the-Sea was one of the most picturesque routes in East Anglia. The line was opened in stages and had two distinct parts; its southernmost section between Wymondham to Dereham was opened in 1846 and became part of a cross-country route to Kings Lynn just two years later. The line was extended to Fakenham in 1849, and completed throughout to Wells-next-the-Sea in 1857. The section from Wymondham to Fakenham was part of the Norfolk Railway, but the northernmost extremity of the route belonged to the Wells & Fakenham Railway - a small, locally-based company. The Wells-next-the-Sea branch was, from its inception, worked by the Eastern Counties Railway, though it never came under full ECR control, and the owning companies retained their independence until both undertakings became part of the Great Eastern Railway in 1862.

The line ran to the seaside, but it never developed as a true 'seaside branch' because Wells only became a tourist centre in the 1950s and 1960s. It remained a rural branch line, serving local agricultural industries - indeed, much of the route remained *in situ* as part of the British Railways network until the 1980s, albeit as a freight-only branch, rather than as a passenger line. However, the northern end of the route found a new and novel use as a narrow gauge tourist line, and the Wells & Walsingham Railway - the world's longest 10¼ in. gauge line - now occupies much of the former trackbed. Similarly, in 1999, the Wymondham to Dereham section was re-opened as a heritage railway.

Although the former Great Eastern branch lines in East Anglia were, collectively, some of the most interesting branches in Britain, they have not hitherto enjoyed much attention from writers and historians, and when the first edition of this present history was published in 1988 it was the first monograph to appear in print on the Wells-next-the-Sea branch.

The opening of the Wells & Walsingham Railway had focused popular attention on the northern part of the line and, for this reason, the first edition concentrated primarily (though not exclusively) on the former Wells to Fakenham section. Nevertheless, branch train services operated on a Wells-Fakenham-Dereham-Norwich axis, and it was impossible to tell the story of the Wells & Fakenham Railway in complete isolation; for that reason the 'Wells branch' was defined as a dead end branch diverging from the main line at Wymondham - a distance of 33 miles 3 chains.

It was also assumed that further details of the Wymondham to Dereham section would appear in a companion volume dealing with the history of the cross-country route between Norwich and Kings Lynn. The latter publication appeared under the title *The Lynn & Dereham Railway* in 1993. Since that time, there have been several important developments, notably the revival of the Wymondham to Dereham line as a preserved railway.

These welcome developments have served to focus attention on the Wymondham to Wells route as a distinct line, and when an opportunity arose to update the original publication, it seemed sensible to add more details about the lower end of the branch between Wymondham and Dereham. However, as this section is also covered in considerable detail in *The Lynn & Dereham Railway*,

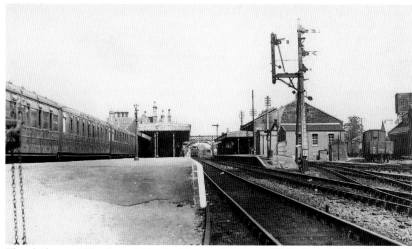

The platforms at Dereham station looking north towards Wells during the LNER era. A Kings Lynn branch train occupies the bay platform (*left*) while an ex-GER locomotive takes water in the far distance.   *Lens of Sutton Collection*

the emphasis must still be on the Dereham to Wells section. This new version of *The Wells-next-the-Sea Branch* contains two new chapters dealing with the route of the line, together with additional information on subjects such as the LNER steam railcars and the role of the railway in the two world wars.

Further details of the Wymondham-Dereham-Kings Lynn cross-country route will be found in *The Lynn & Dereham Railway*, while extra information on the 'other' branch to Wells via Docking and Holkham appears in *The Lynn & Hunstanton Railway*.

Stanley C. Jenkins,
Witney,
Oxon

A Note on Place Names

The correct name of Wells is Wells-next-the-Sea, this being a translation from the Latin Wells-juxta-Mare. However, the LNER called the station Wells-on-Sea, and this name remained in use until British Railways changed the name to Wells-next-the-Sea in 1957. (When first opened in 1857 the station was called simply 'Wells'.) North Elmham was originally called 'Elmham', and Kimberley Park was, until 1923, known as 'Kimberley'.

Chapter One

Origins, Opening and Early Years
(1840-1857)

Wells-next-the-Sea is a small town and seaport, situated on the remote, northern coast of Norfolk, approximately 35 miles to the north-west of Norwich. Recorded in the Domesday Book as 'Quella', Wells may have developed as a haven for nearby Warham after other local creeks had silted up. Although fishing was obviously an important activity, the little town was primarily a trading port, becoming in later years something of a ship-building centre.

Imports, in the Medieval period, probably included lead and building stone destined for use at Binham Priory or Walsingham Abbey, while fish, timber and barley must have formed a considerable proportion of Wells' export trade. By the end of the Middle Ages, 'Wells-juxta-Mare' had emerged as a place of considerable importance, with ship yards, rope walks, wharves, several inns, and no less than three churches.

In earlier times, Wells 'town centre' was situated in the vicinity of St Nicholas's Church, with wharves and other facilities clustered around the original harbour creek. Silting (and possibly a desire to accommodate larger vessels) led to the creation of a new complex of quays and warehouses on a fresh site about ½ mile to the north, and by the 17th century most of the port facilities were concentrated along this new quay. Inevitably, the 'town centre' also moved northwards, with the result that Staithe Street became the town's main thoroughfare, leaving the old High Street to become a residential area.

Unlike most other sea ports, Wells was dominated by a succession of powerful local landlords, and the inhabitants of the little town obviously had to respect the wishes of those who lived in 'the big house' - in this case Holkham Hall, the home of the Coke family. Fortunately, the Cokes were benevolent and improving landlords and, far from retarding economic development, they actively encouraged it.

In 1776 the Holkham estate passed to Thomas Coke (1752-1842), the celebrated 'Coke of Norfolk', who (by the careful application of scientific principles) transformed his barren, sandy estate into an agricultural show-place. Adored by all classes, he was in the vanguard of an agrarian revolution that made British farming the most efficient in the world. When he first came to North Norfolk, it was said that the land was so poor that 'two rabbits could be seen fighting for a single blade of grass'. At that time Holkham rentals averaged just £2,200 a year, yet in a few short years Coke managed to raise this meagre figure to a staggering £20,000 per annum!

The railways come to Norfolk

Although in many ways a remote region, East Anglia has never been regarded as a backward area. On the contrary, its fertile soils and close proximity to Europe ensured that, throughout the Middle Ages, the region was among the most prosperous parts of the country. In the mid-13th century, for example, Norwich was one of our greatest provincial towns, while Lynn was one of the most important ports in the British Isles. In 1377 the tax-paying population of Norwich was 3,952, while the corresponding figure for Kings Lynn was 3,217. These figures suggest that, at the time, Norwich and Kings Lynn must have been the fourth and seventh largest towns in the country.

East Anglia had, since the Reformation in the 16th century, been a staunchly Protestant region, with a long tradition of thrift, sobriety and hard work. These qualities ensured that East Anglians were able to achieve prominence in many walks of life, notably agriculture, banking and politics. Oliver Cromwell (1599-1658), for example, was associated with the district around Ely and Huntingdon, while Admiral Lord Nelson (1758-1805) was born at Burnham Thorpe on the remote north Norfolk coast; these two great figures were, unquestionably, the most famous Englishmen of their day, and their fame will last as long as British history is remembered.

Inevitably, with the rapid development of railways in other parts of the country, local traders, bankers and landowners were eager to share in the advantages of this new and revolutionary form of transport, and as early as the 1820s there were schemes designed to connect Norwich or Cambridge to London. In 1821, for example, the pioneer railway promoter William James (1771-1837) had surveyed a possible 'Engine Railroad from Bishops Stortford to Clayhithe Sluice, with a Branch to Waddon', while in 1824-5 an equally-grandiose 'Norfolk, Suffolk & Essex Railroad' was projected.

If successful, the last-named scheme would have linked London, Norwich and Great Yarmouth, providing a viable nucleus for any future East Anglian railway system. In truth, these 1820s projects were hopelessly premature, but tangible progress was nevertheless made in the following decade, and on 4th July, 1836 two important main line schemes were sanctioned by Parliament. These were the Eastern Counties Railway (6 & 7 Wllm cap. 106), and the Northern & Eastern Railway (6 & 7 Wllm cap. 103).

The Eastern Counties Railway was in effect a revival of the earlier Norfolk, Suffolk & Essex scheme, and like its abortive predecessor, the company hoped to link London with Norwich and Yarmouth. Plagued by financial and other problems, the ECR was forced to abandon its initial aims, and by 29th March, 1843 a much shorter line was in operation from London to Colchester.

Meanwhile, the Northern & Eastern scheme had made considerable progress, and a line between London and Bishops Stortford was in operation by 1842. On 1st January, 1844 the Eastern Counties Railway took over the Northern & Eastern company on a 999 year lease, and although the original Eastern Counties line had still not progressed beyond Colchester, the Northern & Eastern route was ceremonially opened throughout to Cambridge and Brandon on 29th July, 1845.

At Brandon, the ECR line met a line from Norwich, which was opened on the same day by the Norwich & Brandon Railway. The Norwich & Brandon company had been incorporated by Act of Parliament on 16th May, 1844 (7 & 8 Vict. cap. 15), with powers for the construction and maintenance of a railway commencing at Norwich by a junction with the Yarmouth & Norwich Railway, and terminating at Brandon by an end-on junction with an extension of the Northern & Eastern line from Cambridge and Ely. Such schemes were now coming thick and fast, for the 1840s were a time of 'Railway Mania', in which companies were floated in a reckless and completely unco-ordinated manner.

Developments in the 1840s

Other lines promoted at this time included the Lynn & Ely Railway, the Lynn & Dereham Railway, the Lynn & Fakenham Railway and the Eastern Union Railway, together with the Newmarket & Chesterford, the Waveney & Great Yarmouth and the Wells to Thetford railways. Of greater significance, as far as Wells was concerned, was a proposed extension of the Norwich & Brandon line from Wymondham to Dereham, and thence to Wells and Blakeney; this line, which would meet the Lynn & Dereham Railway at Dereham, was a precursor of the later Wells & Fakenham scheme, which eventually succeeded in linking Wells to the Victorian railway system.

Unfortunately the nation was, in 1845, heading towards an economic crisis of unparalleled dimensions, and in the event, many of these railway projects were destined to end in inglorious failure. By 1847 Britain, which was not yet a particularly rich country, was investing far more money in railways than it could earn from exports. Moreover, a series of abysmally wet summers had led to a partial failure of the corn harvest and a total failure of the potato crop.

With so much of the nation's capital tied-up in railway construction schemes a crisis of some kind was perhaps inevitable, but the collapse, when it came, was worse than anyone could have envisaged. Prices spiralled, banks failed, and thousands were thrown out of work; in Ireland and Scotland - even in parts of England - people were starving to death, and against this background of total disaster many of the wild schemes hatched during the Railway Mania were abandoned.

Other more soundly-based projects were hurried to completion, and in these years several important sections of line were opened, including the Eastern Union Railway between Colchester and Ipswich on 15th June, 1846, the Ipswich & Bury Railway between Ipswich and Bury St Edmunds on 24th December, 1846 and an Eastern Union extension between Haughley and Norwich on 12th December, 1849.

In western Norfolk, the Lynn & Ely was opened between Lynn and Downham on 27th October, 1846 and completed throughout to Ely on 25th October, 1847. The Lynn & Dereham line reached Narborough on 27th October, 1846 and Sporle (about 2 miles from Swaffham) on 26th October, 1847. In the meantime the Lynn & Ely, Lynn & Dereham and Ely & Huntingdon railways had amalgamated to form the appropriately-named East Anglian Railway, while the Norwich & Brandon Railway had joined forces in a similar amalgamation with the Yarmouth & Norwich Railway to form the Norfolk Railway Company.

Opening to Dereham

Although few of the Railway Mania schemes in north Norfolk had been immediately successful, a proposed branch to Wells-next-the-Sea was instrumental in persuading the Norwich & Brandon promoters to construct their own branch line from Wymondham to Dereham.

Before starting work on their new Dereham branch, the Norwich & Brandon promoters had to obtain a further Act of Parliament, and in order to save unnecessary expenditure they resolved that a combined Bill would be submitted in the 1845 session. If successful, this would provide powers for branch lines to Dereham and Diss, and for a deviation of the Norwich & Brandon main line. Accordingly, on 6th February, 1845 the *House of Commons Journal* recorded that the Norwich & Brandon Railway had petitioned Parliament for leave to bring in a Bill seeking powers for 'Two branch lines to Diss and East Dereham in the County of Norfolk'. The Bill itself was brought in on 26th February, 1845.

Unfortunately, the Wymondham to Dereham proposal brought the Norwich & Brandon supporters into direct conflict with the promoters of the Lynn & Dereham Railway, who were seeking Parliamentary consent for extensions of their own line. Aware that the proposed Norwich & Brandon branch to Dereham would impede further expansion of the Lynn & Dereham Railway, the Dereham promoters threw their weight behind a rival scheme for a railway from East Dereham to Norwich.

Indeed, the Norwich & Brandon plans were opposed by a wide range of vested interests, among them,

> ... the Governor of the Poor of the City of Norwich ... the Provisional Committee of the proposed East Dereham & Norwich Railway Company ... two owners of property on the line ... Richard Ballard and William Petersen of the City of Norwich, and ... bankers and others of the City of Norwich.

On the other hand, the Bill was strongly supported by petitions from the merchants of Great Yarmouth and from the occupiers of land and inhabitants of a variety of villages along the route of the proposed branch lines.

The Bill was examined by a Select Committee of the House of Lords in July 1845, and having considered the evidence for and against the scheme, the Committee reported in its favour. Finally, on 31st July, 1845, the Act 'For Altering the Line of the Norwich & Brandon Railway & for making a Branch therefrom to East Dereham in the County of Norfolk' received the Royal Assent.

Leaving the Norwich & Brandon main line at Wymondham, the proposed Dereham branch ran north-westwards towards its destination. Although the authorized route was by no means flat, the Wymondham to Dereham route presented no major problems, and the railway builders' task was made easier by the way in which Parliament had consented to the installation of level crossings in lieu of more expensive bridge works. At Kimberley, for instance, the Lords Committee appointed to consider the 1845 Norwich & Brandon Bill had recommended that a level crossing should be allowed, because the proposed crossing would be at 'a first class station at which all trains would stop'.

At Thuxton, the Lords Committee had agreed that a crossing would be installed because 'the road could not be raised without great inconvenience to the public', while at Yaxham the committee suggested (somewhat implausibly) that 'the road could not be raised without great inconvenience, and raising it would preclude the opportunity of giving a small station at the spot'.

Undeterred by the appalling weather and worsening social and economic crisis, the Directors of the newly-formed Norfolk Railway were determined that the branch from Wymondham to Dereham would be completed without delay. In July 1845, George Parker Bidder (1806-1878), the Norfolk Railway Engineer, was ordered to stake out the line between Wymondham and Dereham. Later that same year, the Norfolk Directors decided that they would seek Parliamentary consent for an extension from Dereham to Wells. The contract for construction of the line was awarded to Samuel Morton Peto (1809-1889).

Work on the Wymondham to Dereham line was well advanced by the closing months of 1846, and in November it was reported that some of the Norfolk Railway Directors had recently made an experimental trip along the unfinished branch in company with Samuel Morton Peto. Peto, who had made his fortune as an engineering contractor, was both a builder and a promoter of East Anglian railways - the Norfolk Railway being just one of the many companies in his growing business empire.

The work of construction did not proceed without incident, and on 19th December, 1846 *The Railway Chronicle* reported a bizarre accident that had occurred shortly after the Directors' experimental trip to Dereham. The accident, which had taken place on 8th December, was described as follows by *The Chronicle* reporter:

WYMONDHAM-DEREHAM - A bridge over the line, in the parish of Wicklewood, not being safe from a sinking of one of the buttresses, was ordered to be taken down. The men were at work removing it after dark, and two fires were kept burning upon the crown of the bridge. Late at night, from the removal of the chief supporters, the remaining part of the bridge fell in, and about a dozen labourers fell also upon the line beneath and were mingled with the ruin and fires. Great confusion existed and several of the men, when extricated, were found to be seriously bruised, and burnt.

The fact that Wicklewood bridge collapse had occurred during the hours of darkness suggests that the Norfolk Directors may have been trying to open their line to Dereham before the completion of the Lynn & Dereham route. If this was indeed the case, Samuel Morton Peto and the other Norfolk Railway supporters must have rejoiced when, on 7th December, 1846, their branch was opened for goods traffic between Wymondham and Dereham.

In common with many other East Anglian railway schemes during the 1840s, the Norfolk Railway's new line had been constructed in a phenomenally short space of time, barely 14 months having elapsed since the passage of the Act of Incorporation! The line was not, as yet, open for passenger traffic, the Wicklewood accident having delayed the introduction of passenger services. On 13th February, 1847, however, the railway was inspected by Captain Addington, and he immediately granted permission for the carriage of passengers between Wymondham and Dereham.

Passenger trains commenced running on Monday 15th February, 1847, though at the half-year meeting held on 23rd January the Norfolk Directors expressed 'much disappointment' at the delays that had prevented a much earlier completion of the Dereham branch. These delays were (declared the Directors) 'unavoidable, but their engineers had assured them the works had been retarded by causes over which they had no control'.

The completed railway was a little under 11½ miles in length, and single track throughout. Intermediate stations were provided at Kimberley, Hardingham, Thuxton and Yaxham, and the initial train service consisted of four trains each way.

Thus, by 1848, the first section of the Wells branch had been opened as an 11½ mile branch of the Norfolk Railway. The remaining 21½ miles between Dereham and Wells were not yet built, but with work progressing on an extension to Fakenham, there were hopes that the Norfolk Railway would be able to complete its whole scheme at some future date.

Opening to Fakenham

Many of the lines promoted during the heady days of the Railway Mania were so small that they could not remain viable as independent concerns, and for this reason they tended to amalgamate with each other in order to form larger (and hopefully more profitable) organizations. Inevitably, smaller companies such as the Norfolk Railway and the East Anglian Railway gravitated towards larger, more successful concerns - and in this way the Eastern Counties Railway gradually assumed a position of power throughout East Anglia.

In 1847, the newly-created East Anglian Railway approached the Eastern Counties Board with a view to amalgamation, but negotiations were unsuccessful on that occasion. An amalgamation with the Norfolk Railway was, on the other hand, immediately attractive to the Eastern Counties directorate, and on 8th May, 1848 they assumed control of the entire Norfolk Railway system (including of course the Wymondham to Dereham line).

Curiously, the Eastern Counties took over its smaller neighbour by mutual arrangement, hoping that Parliament would soon consent to a full amalgamation. Perversely, Parliament refused to sanction the proposed amalgamation, and the ECR Directors were unable to take full possession of the Norfolk Railway - which remained in existence as a separate organization. However, the Eastern Counties Railway became responsible for all matters relating to the operation and day to day running of the railway and, by July 1850, all of the Norfolk Railway's locomotives and rolling stock had been purchased by the ECR.

In July 1846 Mr Bidder was asked to lay out a line from East Dereham to Wells, and work was under way on the 12 mile extension by the following September. In August 1846 the engineer reported that the line would be completed in about 12 months, though in the event the underlying economic crisis seems to have caused considerable delays. A single line between Dereham and Fakenham was, nevertheless, ready for inspection in February 1849, the Inspecting Officer being Captain George Wynne.

Sadly, the Inspector was unable to pass the line for public opening because of the weak condition of an underline bridge near Hoe, a little over two miles to the north of Dereham. His inspection report, dated 24th February, 1849, was as follows:

Dear Sir,
    I have to report, for the information of the Commissioners, that I yesterday inspected the Branch Line of the Norfolk Railway between Dereham and Fakenham, a distance of 12 miles 1 furlong. At a distance of two and three quarter miles from Dereham there is an occupation bridge through an embankment 33 feet high, the lateral thrust of this mass of earth had forced out each end of the arch for a length of about four feet, entirely separating it by a fissure several inches wide from the centre part of the arch.
    The east face and the wing walls are worst, and are strongly shored up. The bridge is eighty-four feet in length, and fourteen feet high to the crown of the arch. I cannot recommend the Commissioners to sanction the opening of the line until the under occupation bridge at 2 miles 1 furlong from Dereham has been substantially repaired.
I am, etc.,
Your servant,
George Wynne, Captain, Royal Engineers,
Inspector of Railways

This unforseen problem was soon rectified and, following a reinspection on 24th March, 1849, Captain Wynne was able to report that the Fakenham branch of the Norfolk Railway Company could be opened for traffic between Dereham and Fakenham without danger to the public. The line was, accordingly, opened just six days later on Tuesday 20th March, 1849.

Heading due north from the existing railhead at Dereham, this 12 mile, single track branch followed the Wensum Valley for much of its length, but civil engineering was nevertheless heavy (at least by East Anglian standards) and there were several deep cuttings. Intermediate stations were provided at Elmham and Ryburgh, and the line was single track throughout. All train services were provided by the Eastern Counties Railway, using former Norfolk Railway locomotives and rolling stock.

The line had, apparently, been built as cheaply as possible as a result of the underlying economic crisis, and for this reason its station buildings were timber-framed structures, clad in weather boarding. The original timetable provided four trains each way.

Unfortunately the Norfolk Railway, having remained in being as an independent company, was soon at odds with the Eastern Counties company. The 1848 operating agreement was particularly unsuccessful as far as the branch was concerned, and the Norfolk Railway Directors complained that local services were 'practically useless'. It seems that the Eastern Counties timetable was geared towards main line rather than branch line operation, and in an attempt to remedy this situation the Norfolk Railway Directors undertook to work some local branch services independently of the ECR.

A few of the engines previously sold to the Eastern Counties were therefore transferred back to the Norfolk Railway, the new compromise agreement coming into force in May 1851. Within a few months, however, the ECR had once again assumed control of all train services on the Norfolk Railway.

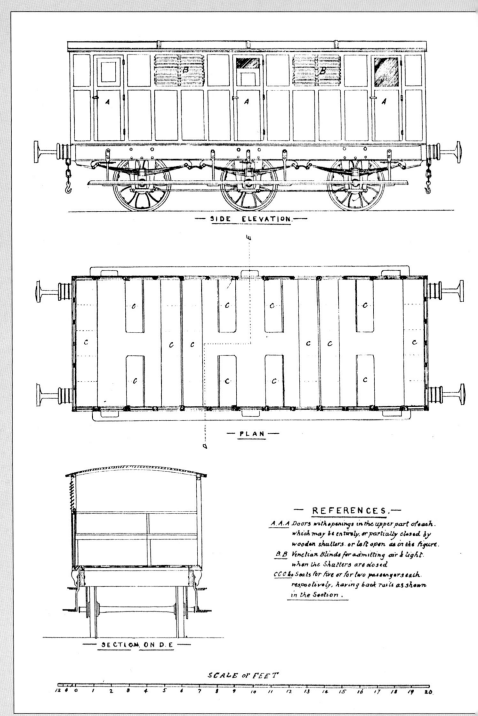

— SIDE ELEVATION.—

— PLAN —

— SECTION ON D.E —

— REFERENCES.—

A.A.A Doors with openings in the upper part of each. which may be entirely, or partially closed by wooden shutters. or left open as in the figure.

B.B Venetian Blinds for admitting air & light. when the Shutters are closed

C.C.C to Seats for five or for two passengers each. respectively, having back rails as shown in the Section.

SCALE of FEET

12 6 0   1   2   3   4   5   6   7   8   9   10   11   12   13   14   15   16   17   18   19   20.

An early Eastern Counties Railway coach similar to those used on the Norfolk Railway *circa* 1840.

Formation of the Wells & Fakenham Railway

The failure of the original Norfolk Railway scheme had obviously caused great disappointment in Wells-next-the-Sea, but the townsfolk still hoped that with a rail link of their own they would be able to develop as a modern sea port, catering for both commercial vessels and an expanded fishing fleet. A railway would also help the Earl of Leicester and his tenants - enabling locally-grown produce to reach wider markets than had hitherto been possible.

There was, therefore, a unanimity of opinion that Wells needed a railway of its own, and when it became clear that neither the Norfolk Railway nor the Eastern Counties Railway was prepared to extend their existing line any nearer than Fakenham, the people of Wells-next-the-Sea decided to form their own, locally-based company as a means of securing the desired rail link.

The decision to form the 'Wells & Fakenham Railway' was probably taken behind the closed doors of Holkham Hall, and it seems clear that Thomas William Coke (1822-1909) was a prime supporter of the scheme. The son of 'Coke of Norfolk', T.W. Coke had succeeded to the Holkham estates on the death of his father in 1842. A dedicated agricultural 'improver', he had already done much to enhance the value of Holkham and the surrounding lands - one of his improvements being the construction of a long 'sea wall' or embankment running due north from Wells Quay, and enclosing an area of reclaimed salt marsh; a rail link to the outside world would be a natural corollary of these improvement schemes.

Other major landowners interested in the new railway included Sir Willoughby Jones and Lord Hastings. Support from the Norfolk and Eastern Counties railways would be essential, and when in the 1850s the Wells & Fakenham promoters held a series of public meetings in the area, they already had the full backing of the Norfolk Railway and several of its Directors.

It was agreed that the new railway would run southwards from Wells to an end-on junction with the existing railway at Fakenham. The proposed line would be 9½ miles long, and follow the Stiffkey Valley for much of its length. An Act for the 'Wells & Fakenham Railway' was obtained on 24th July, 1854 (17 & 18 Vict. cap. 180), the newly-incorporated company having an authorized capital of £70,000. Unfortunately, Parliament had not allowed the Norfolk Railway to subscribe directly, but in practice this apparent obstacle was overcome when a group of individual Norfolk Railway Directors themselves subscribed £30,000.

Local subscribers included the Earl of Leicester, who provided the respectable sum of £10,000, and a group of Wells traders who were able to raise a further £14,000 on behalf of the town itself. Other supporters of the scheme included Sir Willoughby Jones, Sir Samuel Moreton Peto, J.H. Gurney, Hall William Keary, Richard Till, Horatio Bolingbroke, Joseph Springhill Southgate and Jacob Watson of London. The Secretary was Mr Hutt, and the Engineer was George Berkeley.

Some of these gentlemen were, like their patron the Earl of Leicester, local landowners or traders who sincerely believed that Wells needed its own rail link; others were representatives of the Norfolk Railway with little obvious interest in the new line, while one or two individuals may have been speculative investors, seeking a return on their initial outlay. There was nevertheless a 'hard core' of fully-committed supporters, led by H.W. Keary of Holkham, J.S. Southgate of Wells - and of course the Earl himself.

Horatio Bolingbroke and Richard Till were both representatives of the Norfolk Railway, Mr Till being its Chairman. Of greater significance was the interest initially shown by J.H. Gurney - a member of the famous East Anglian banking family - and Sir Samuel Morton Peto. Peto, in partnership with Edward Ladd Betts, had already constructed much of the East Anglian railway system.

As a contractor (rather than a financier or engineer) he had already earned enough money to set himself up as a country gentleman at Somerleyton Hall - just over the county border in Suffolk. Both Morton Peto and J.H. Gurney were representatives of the Norfolk Railway Company, and as well as being major subscribers, they were able to act as a useful link between the Norfolk and Wells & Fakenham companies.

Sadly, Peto was a man who liked to play a leading role in as many projects as he could, and in view of his immense wealth he rapidly insinuated himself into a dominant position on the Wells & Fakenham Board, becoming its Chairman and using the little company as a mere pawn in his own private schemes - which in any case centred on Lowestoft rather than Wells-next-the-Sea.

In retrospect, Peto's apparent duplicity did nothing but harm to the Wells & Fakenham Railway, and one senses that the most-committed Wells Directors such as Joseph Springhill Southgate, Hall William Keary and Richard Till rued the day that Samuel Morton Peto became involved with their modest, but entirely laudable railway scheme. All of this, however, was in the future, and in the meantime Messrs Peto, Keary and Southgate focused their thoughts on the immediate task of constructing their new railway.

With commendable caution the Wells & Fakenham promoters had decided that work would not begin until land had been obtained on reasonable terms, but this was not in the event a major problem, and one assumes that Thomas Coke was able to persuade his fellow landowners that the railway would be a means of improving local agriculture. Happily, the landowners offered 'every facility' to the Wells & Fakenham promoters and there was no difficulty in obtaining possession of land for the stations and track bed. Meanwhile, the Norfolk Railway had agreed to work the branch on unusually generous terms, with only 46 per cent of the gross receipts being paid to the operating company. On the other hand the Norfolk Railway had cleverly persuaded the Wells & Fakenham to agree that compensation might be paid if traffic was lost south of Fakenham as a result of the new link to Wells harbour (where a system of quayside lines was already planned).

The rank and file shareholders were told about their new operating agreement at the half-yearly meeting held at Wells on 15th August, 1855. Peto, in the chair, explained that only 46 per cent would be paid to the Norfolk Railway, and went on to paint a highly-roseate picture of the future. 'The line', he said, 'would pass through a rich agricultural district', while the port of Wells, he claimed, 'possessed great capabilities'.

Moving on to the technicalities of construction, the Chairman told his delighted shareholders that of 87 acres needed for the new railway, no less than 58 had been purchased. A line would be fenced-off 'as soon as the corn was off the ground', and although the station sites had not been finally settled, he assured his listeners that 'there would be one at Walsingham'.

Problems and delays

Having obtained their Act, arranged a favourable operating agreement with the Norfolk Railway, and solved the potentially-thorny problem of land acquisition, the Wells & Fakenham Directors must have assumed that the remainder of their task would be easy, but sadly, this was not to be, and the local company soon found itself at the centre of quarrels that were not of its making. As we have seen, the Eastern Counties Railway had, in the 1840s, emerged as a major force in East Anglian Railway politics.

In the longer term, this ambitious company would ultimately be transformed into the Great Eastern Railway, but in the meantime its devious ways and questionable tactics caused much disquiet. One of the Eastern Counties Board's first actions, on taking control of the Norfolk Railway in 1848, had been the dismissal of most former Norfolk Railway staff - and there were, as we have seen, loud complaints about the way in which the ECR ran its trains. Having paid out dividends from much needed capital, the Eastern Counties soon found itself in dire financial straights, and the company's reputation was not helped by two unpleasant Boardroom revolts (one in 1849 and another in 1856).

The ECR was, by any definition, an exceedingly disreputable organisation - yet this same company was, through its operating agreement with the Norfolk Railway, ultimately responsible for the Wells-next-the-Sea branch! This was clearly a recipe for disaster, and it was perhaps no real surprise that the ECR started to put pressure on the Norfolk Railway over the Wells & Fakenham operating agreement. In 1856 the ECR Directors declared that the operating agreement could not be considered in any way binding until the Board of Trade had given its approval.

This rather high-handed action appeared to be blatant obstructionism, and suspicious minds wondered if the Eastern Counties was jealous of its monopoly at Lowestoft - where huge sums had been spent in the hope that a major international trade could be developed; if Wells was allowed to develop as a rival port the Lowestoft investment would be jeopardized. Significantly, Samuel Morton Peto was one of those attempting to promote Lowestoft and the railways leading to it, and none of these factors boded well for the Wells & Fakenham Railway.

157.—GREAT EASTERN.

Incorporated by 25 and 26 Vic., cap. 223 (7th August, 1862), and comprising the EASTERN COUNTIES, NORFOLK, EASTERN UNION, EAST ANGLIAN, EAST SUFFOLK, and other subsidiary undertakings in connection therewith.

I. EASTERN COUNTIES, which is mainly formed of two arteries—the one to Colchester, and the other to Cambridge ; the first was incorporated by 6 and 7 Wm. IV., cap. 106 (1836), for a railway from London to Norwich and Yarmouth, by Romford, Chelmsford, Colchester, and Ipswich. Owing, however, to difficulties in raising the requisite funds, the original scheme was not carried beyond Colchester, 51 miles from London.

WELLS AND FAKENHAM.—Incorporated by 17 and 18 Vic., cap. 180 (24th July, 1854). The line (10 miles) was promoted by residents in the districts, who determined to obtain possession of the land at reasonable prices before commencing the works. Capital, 70,000*l.* in 20*l.* shares ; power to borrow extends to 23,000*l.* Opened December 1st, 1857. By 22 and 23 Vic., cap. 139 (13th August, 1859), the company was authorised to extend the line along the quay, at Wells, to raise additional capital to the extent of 3,800*l.* at 6 per cent. preference, with loan of 1,200*l.*, and to convert the debenture debt into stock. By the same Act the Norfolk may guarantee interest or dividend on the new capital of 3,800*l.*, provided the annual net revenue will so permit.

Extract from *Bradshaw's Shareholders' Manual.*

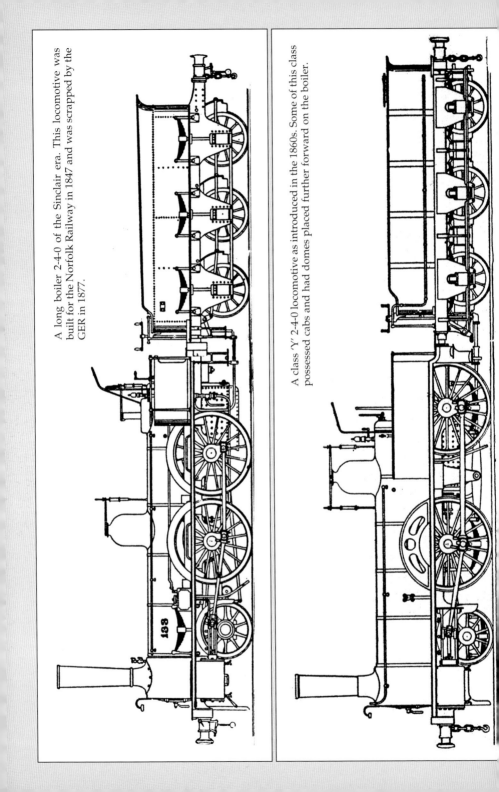

A long boiler 2-4-0 of the Sinclair era. This locomotive was built for the Norfolk Railway in 1847 and was scrapped by the GER in 1877.

A class 'Y' 2-4-0 locomotive as introduced in the 1860s. Some of this class possessed cabs and had domes placed further forward on the boiler.

Chapter Two

Early Years of the Wells & Fakenham Railway (1857-1862)

Undeterred by the problems which now faced them, the Wells & Fakenham Directors pressed on with their scheme, and contracts for construction of the line were signed in September 1855. By 1856 the work had begun in earnest under the direction of George Berkeley (or 'Berkley') - an experienced, though perhaps little-known engineer.

The physical tasks were relatively easy, though not without problems - one of the most testing being at East Barsham, where the authorized route spanned a deep marshy valley. Berkeley's solution was unusual, though by no means unique - he built an American-style timber trestle viaduct as an alternative to an embankment; such structures were cheap to build, and could always be replaced at some later date. Apart from its viaduct, the Wells & Fakenham route necessitated some considerable earthworks, including a deep cutting at Fakenham and a short tunnel at East Barsham (this tunnel was, interestingly enough, one of only two in Norfolk - the other being at Cromer).

The line was said to have been well advanced by the summer of 1856 and, at the half-yearly meeting held at Fakenham on Wednesday 13th August, the Engineer was able to report that the works were progressing satisfactorily, about three-quarters of the earthworks having been completed while Barsham tunnel was in a 'forward state'. The bridges, lodges and stations were being executed so rapidly that the whole of the brickwork would be completed and all of the buildings roofed-in before winter. 'A large proportion of the permanent way materials' had been received and 'a considerable length of trackwork had already been laid'.

The balance-sheet for the period ending 30th June, 1856, showed that the total receipts to that date had amounted to £36,573 8s. 5d., while the total disbursements had been £29,288 11s. 3d., of which £25,97 11s. 3d. had been 'set down as the cost of the Act of Incorporation', while £8,771 9s. had been spent on the purchase of 79 acres and 22 perches of land, including 'three cottages'. Mr Southgate, who was chairing the meeting, replied to a number of questions and offered explanations on one or two matters of detail, and after further discussion the statement of accounts was unanimously adopted. At the end of the meeting, the Chairman stated that the line was 'expected to be opened for traffic in May or June next'.

In the following November, the shareholders were told that the tunnel was nearing completion, while the gatehouses had been roofed-in. At Wells, the terminus was virtually complete, with a 200 ft platform and a station building 'constructed with equal regard for convenience, comfort and neatness'.

The work of construction was accompanied by one or two accidents, one of which took place at Wells when a labourer named William Hubert was crushed by runaway ballast wagons. Later, two navvies who had been 'engaged in sloping the sides of the cutting at Wells through which the tramway is laid' were buried by several tons of debris when the chalk cutting gave way. The men, named Lake and Magness (probably McGuinness), were said to have 'sustained frightful injuries'.

WELLS AND FAKENHAM.

A meeting of this company was held on the 15th instant, at the Crown Inn, Wells; the Rev. J. R. HOPPER, in the chair.—The Chairman said the line was completed and the shareholders very naturally wished to see it opened. The town of Wells was not only suffering from the delay which had taken place. but the shareholders were also losing their interest, In passenger traffic alone he believed they were sacrificing 200l. per week; and it was quite necessary, therefore, that measures should be taken to expedite the opening of the line.—Mr. Gardner said he felt highly dissatisfied with the course pursued by the directors in not opening the line. About three years and a half had now passed since the first call was paid, and the shareholders had still only got a line to look at for their money. He therefore moved—" That this meeting views with great dissatisfaction the repeated delays in opening this line of railway, and, on behalf of the shareholders generally, at once calls upon the directors to explain the cause of such unnecessary postponement."—Mr. Loynes said he had been unable to procure any satisfactory explanation of the delay which had taken place from the resident director. A promise had been made that the line should be opened as soon as the calls were paid up. The shareholders had performed their part, and had a right to know why the opening was delayed.—Mr. Tyrrell said, " hope deferred maketh the heart sick." He believed the hearts of the shareholders had been sick for some time. He begged therefore to move—"That the great delay in not opening this line of railway is highly prejudicial to the interests of this town and district; and that unless steps be immediately taken by the directors to carry out the promise originally made to the shareholders, this meeting will deem it necessary to memorialise the Board of Trade to enforce them to do so."—Mr. Loynes proposed that a letter should be addressed to the directors, calling upon them to state why the line was not opened.—Mr. D. J. Everett expressed his opinion that the directors were entitled to credit for the speedy completion of the line, and that there must be some substantial reason for its not having been opened There was a director present, but perhaps his lips were sealed. He thought that, as the Wells people had subscribed manfully for the line, it was very hard that they should not have a prospect of being remunerated as soon as possible.—A letter to the directors stating the grievances of the shareholders, and expressing their determination, in the absence of satisfactory explanations, to seek the interference of the Board of Trade, was then adopted, and an adjournment to 3d August agreed to.—Mr. Southgate, the director present, having been repeatedly requested to afford some *vivâ voce* explanation, said, as the line was completed, he did not blame the shareholders for demanding the cause of the delay which had taken place. A difficulty had existed between the Eastern Counties directors and the Wells and Fakenham board, but from what he had heard he believed the differences were in a fair way of being settled. Mr. Love, the chairman of the Eastern Counties, with whom he had had an interview, was a thorough man of business; and he felt sure the increase of traffic which the Wells and Fakenham would bring to the Eastern Counties would induce Mr. Love to meet them in an equitable manner.

A press report of the half-year meeting held at Wells on 15th July, 1857.

The cost of the railway

The 9½ mile-long, single track railway was completed by June 1857, the entire project having been accomplished in the creditable time of 20 months. Moreover, the Wells & Fakenham Railway was built at an approximate cost of £70,000 - as had been forecast when the company was incorporated. The company's published accounts provide a valuable insight into how this sum was spent. It is interesting to note, for example, that the Act alone cost over £2,500 - and one wonders how the Directors spent their £750 'fees' (obviously not on travelling because this item is listed separately!). The relevant section of the Wells & Fakenham accounts is reproduced below:

Expenditure to 30th June, 1857

	£	s.	d.
Construction of the railway	31,097	0	10
Permanent way materials	18,456	11	8
Purchase of land	8,950	19	0
Act of incorporation	2,597	11	3
Erection of stations.	4,531	12	9
Engineering & surveying fees	2,091	0	6
Law charges	1,853	4	2
Directors-fees	750	0	0
Salaries & office charges	466	15	5
Compensation to tenants	394	7	4
Travelling expenses	227	16	2
Advertising, printing & stationery	120	15	8
Rates, taxes & auditors' fees	59	7	7
Total Expenditure	*71,597*	*2*	*4*

Although the railway was substantially complete by the Summer of 1857, it could not be opened to traffic until the tedious legal wrangling over operating agreements had been sorted out. Those who had subscribed to the scheme were dismayed to find that trains were not yet able to reach Wells, and the half-yearly meeting held at the Crown Inn, Wells on 15th July, 1857 was a particularly stormy affair. Most Directors failed to appear, and in their absence the chair was taken by the Reverend J.R. Hopper.

Continued difficulties

Opening the meeting, the Reverend gentleman sympathized with the shareholders, stating that their line was complete but not in operation, and in the meantime Wells was suffering as a result of the delay while the shareholders were losing interest. In passenger traffic alone, he believed, they were sacrificing £200 per week, and it was necessary therefore that measures should be taken to 'expedite the opening of the line'.

One by one, the angry shareholders voiced their complaints - much of odium falling upon Joseph Southgate, the only Director brave enough to turn up; a Mr Everett was particularly vociferous, suggesting that there was 'some substantial reason' for the continued delay. Eyeing Mr Southgate, he admitted that the Directors deserved credit for the speedy completion of their line, but the people of Wells had 'subscribed manfully' to the scheme, and it was very hard that they 'should not have the prospect of being remunerated as soon as possible'.

After repeated questioning, Mr Southgate finally spoke to the meeting; he did not, he said, blame them for demanding explanations for the delay that had taken place, but there was a 'difficulty' between the Eastern Counties Directors and the Wells & Fakenham Board. However 'from what he had heard' he believed that these differences would soon be settled. Mr Love, the Eastern Counties Chairman was, he suggested, 'a thorough man of business' who would meet them in 'an equitable manner' when he realised that extra traffic would be brought to the Eastern Counties system once the Wells & Fakenham Railway was open.

At the root of these 'difficulties' was the 46 per cent operating agreement between the Wells & Fakenham and Norfolk companies which the Eastern Counties (as operating company) had no intention of honouring. It was in effect a three-cornered battle between the Wells & Fakenham, Norfolk and Eastern Counties companies - though much speculation centred around the precise role of Sir Samuel Morton Peto.

The Editor of *The Railway Times* was not afraid publicly to accuse Peto of duplicity, and on 29th August, 1857 this influential investors' journal considered the Wells & Fakenham's problems in a leading article. The paper noted that Peto had undertaken 'to secure the working of the line at 46 per cent, the Norfolk being the instrument by which that engagement was intended to be fulfilled'. However, the Norfolk Railway 'by the instrumentality of Sir Morton Peto', was then handed over to the Eastern Counties, and as matters stood, the Eastern Counties Board were under no obligation to work the Wells & Fakenham Railway.

Having in effect accused Peto of double dealing, *The Railway Times* suggested a possible solution to the Wells & Fakenham problem:

> If Sir Morton were called to account by the Wells & Fakenham, the worthy baronet could call the Norfolk to account for breach of the agreement he made in its name and on its behalf ... It is admitted on all hands that the traffic on the Wells & Fakenham cannot be worked at 46 per cent, yet it was on the faith of that representation being carried through that the line was made.
>
> It is obvious therefore that there are other partners to be dealt with than the Eastern Counties, and that it is in no degree surprising that Mr Till of the Norfolk should advise patience in the first instance, and a short agreement with the Eastern Counties in the second, so that the chapter of accidents may be taken advantage of, rather than the original Prospectus should be brought under review.

In the end, the Wells & Fakenham Directors (or rather those who wanted to see the railway in operation) were forced to go cap in hand to the Eastern Counties and accept whatever terms the larger company might offer. There were still three or four loyal Directors willing to stand up for the unfortunate Wells & Fakenham Railway - including Joseph Southgate, Hall William Keary and (perhaps surprisingly) Richard Till of the Norfolk Railway.

Joseph Southgate and H.W. Keary, being local men, were understandably keen to see the railway in operation, but it is harder to see why Mr Till should have fought so hard on behalf of the Wells company - other than perhaps his own sense of honour; a wrong had been done and it was therefore a matter of duty that things should be put right.

Whatever behind-the-scenes 'rescue package' was concocted, the loyal Directors still had to convince their shareholders, and under these circumstances the half-yearly meeting held in August 1857 was expected to be another lively affair. In an attempt to defuse the situation the Directors held this crucial meeting not in Wells but at Fakenham - hoping perhaps that, with the railway not yet in operation, a smaller number of shareholders would be able to attend! If indeed this was the case, their ploy was highly successful, and the meeting was poorly-attended and relatively placid.

The meeting was chaired by Hall William Keary, and the first report was read by Mr Hutt, the company Secretary. Although there was no immediate prospect of opening, the Secretary was able to report at least some progress:

> The Directors have the satisfaction to announce that your line of railway between Wells and Fakenham, with the stations and works, has been completed with the exception of the harbour branch now in progress and a tramway which your Directors, at the earnest solicitation of some of the principal shareholders and merchants of the town of Wells, had undertaken to construct along the quay, but which has not been commenced in consequence of objections raised by one of the owners of property past which it was proposed the intended tram should be carried.
>
> The opening of the main line is now only delayed for the completion of a junction with the lines of the Eastern Counties and Norfolk at Fakenham, and the necessary arrangements for station accommodation there, and for working the line; but your Directors are actively negotiating with the other companies and trust in a short time satisfactorily to effect those objects. Should they be disappointed in this anticipation, your Directors will immediately call a special meeting of the shareholders to consider and determine the course to be pursued. The account of capital received and expended to the 30th June last has already been printed and sent to every shareholder in the usual way.

The Secretary then read a report submitted by George Berkeley, the company Engineer:

> I beg to report that the works on the main line between Fakenham and the passenger station at Wells are complete, with the exception of a short length of about one hundred yards, near the Fakenham station, where possession of the land which is now occupied by the Eastern Counties and used in working their traffic has not yet been obtained. The execution of the works on this land, where possession is obtained, will not occupy more than ten days or a fortnight. The earthworks, etc., on the goods branch to the water-side at Wells are rapidly progressing, and this branch may be completed as soon as the main line can be opened for public traffic.

Hall William Keary apologised for the continued delay in opening the railway, pointing out that the line had been built within its time limit, and would have been in operation had not other matters interfered. Trying to sound optimistic, he emphasised that 'a very excellent line of railway' had been made to 'the seaport town of Wells', and added that negotiations which had been 'long pending' between the Wells & Fakenham and Eastern Counties were at last 'drawing to a favourable conclusion'. He then said a few words on behalf of Richard Till, who had clearly done his utmost to get the railway opened:

> I am glad to see on my right hand Mr Till, the Chairman of the Norfolk, who has throughout conducted the negotiations in a most able manner, and to whom we are much indebted for the position at which we are now arrived. I believe he will be able to explain to you most satisfactorily that nothing has been wanting on our part to fulfil our duties towards you, and that we have taken every step that we could to bring difficult negotiations to a favourable conclusion. I beg to say, as I said before, that if you require any further explanation I am quite sure our friend Mr Till will be most happy to give it.

There were, needless to say, one or two questions - notably from the vociferous Mr Everett who challenged the accounts. Why, he asked 'was something like £3,000 still unpaid on the tenth call?' The Directors replied that this was in fact owed by the Norfolk Railway, but as the Wells & Fakenham was itself in debt to the Norfolk 'it would have been a useless proceeding to have paid the money over under such circumstances'. Finally, Richard Till rose to speak, and the assembled shareholders listened attentively as the Norfolk Railway Chairman delivered a mixture of good and bad news:

> The Chairman has referred to me, in consequence of the disappointment which the proprietors naturally feel when, after having laid out their money in the formation of their railway it is not immediately opened and turned to good account. It is one of those difficulties which frequently present themselves when a small independent company have created a branch and have to deal with an old constituted company who have pretty well the power in their hands.
> We are certainly more than unfortunate with respect to the company with which we have had to negotiate, because that company, prior to the last half year, have been in a state of change and transition, one body of Directors going out and another body of Directors going in.

Mr Till was here referring to the forced resignation of David Waddington (1810-1863), the ECR Chairman; an associate of George Hudson, he had been more interested in railway politics than in running trains, and under his Chairmanship the Wells & Fakenham company stood little chance of getting a fair deal. The Wells Directors clearly hoped that Horatio Love, the new ECR Chairman, would come 'to reasonable and fair terms' vis-à-vis the Wells & Fakenham Railway, and Mr Till seemed relatively optimistic as he continued his speech:

> Of late a better feeling has come over the negotiations … and … I see no difficulty now in coming to a final arrangement with the Eastern Counties. Unfortunately, we first made an arrangement with the Norfolk, who were desirous to receive the traffic and make arrangements which would give us a fair proportion of the advantages which would accrue from the line to both parties.
> Before, however, the line was finished, and before it was ripe for a final settlement of the negotiations, the Norfolk, under a special agreement, made over the whole of their property to the management of the Eastern Counties, for the benefit of the three allied companies. This, as you may easily suppose, has presented a certain amount of difficulty, which would not have occurred if this company had treated only with the Norfolk. But we must take things as they are, and as we find them, and do the best we can.

Things have now come to this - the Chairman of the Eastern Counties has intimated to me that he is authorised to bring the matter to a final close, and this company has done me the honour to authorise me on their part to settle it. The Eastern Counties have appointed their Engineer to settle and arrange with the gentleman appointed by us - that is our Engineer - the terms upon which the junction shall take place, and as far as I am able to understand from our Engineer the matter is approaching very closely to a conclusion.

I should hope within a week there will be an announcement of the terms these two gentlemen recommend; and if they differ, that they will get some third party to decide between them.

A matter affecting the Norfolk, over which the Eastern Counties have no control, has been adjusted in the most friendly way, a proper and efficient person having been appointed as valuer, to settle the sum this company should pay to the Norfolk for possession of their property from the first bridge up to the junction with the Wells & Fakenham line proper.

The only difficulty to be arranged was, that so much of the land as in the occupation and use of the allied companies from the bridge up to the Fakenham station should become the property of this company, that we might have under any circumstances a positive approach which should not be interfered with to the Fakenham station. Then, instead of spending our money uselessly on a building a fresh station, we have to settle the annual amount to be paid for the use of the Fakenham station with respect to our traffic.

There is a third point of more difficulty, namely, the terms upon which the Eastern Counties will work our traffic; but if any confidence is to be placed in the assertions of the Chairman of that company, he is willing to settle the matter upon fair and reasonable terms … if there is any other explanation which I am capable of affording I am quite at your service.

The meeting ended with a question-and-answer session - the main questioner being the irrepressible Mr Everett who seemed particularly concerned with the 46 per cent operating agreement; he was obviously quite right to persist for Mr Till had been unable or unwilling to go into this matter in detail. In fact, there was no hope of the Eastern Counties working the line on anything like favourable terms, and when the matter was finally sorted out the terms were hardly congenial. The Directors must by this time have known that they would have to give way to the ECR - though one feels that they were reluctant to reveal all to their unfortunate shareholders.

Opening of the Wells & Fakenham Railway

As the summer of 1857 turned to autumn, the Wells & Fakenham Directors at last turned their thoughts towards public opening, which was initially planned for 'the end of May or the beginning of June', but was subsequently put back until 1st October, pending the completion of satisfactory working arrangements with the Eastern Counties Railway. On Monday 19th October, 1857, *The Times* was able to report that 'the Government Inspector had passed over the line on Thursday' and, after further delays, the opening finally took place on Tuesday 1st December, exactly six months after the works had been completed. The great day was celebrated in style, and having dipped into their own pockets to provide appropriate festivities, the townsfolk of Wells-next-the-Sea were determined that a good time would be had by all.

Opening day was declared a public holiday, and many hundreds gathered at Wells and along the lineside to witness the arrival of the official 'first train' from Fakenham. The streets of the little town were elaborately decorated with flags, bunting and triumphal arches of evergreens, while 'Mr Widow's Band from Norwich' was hired to provide musical accompaniment. The first train was greeted by tumultuous cheers and a fusillade from the muskets of local Coast Guards. Later, the customary speeches of congratulation were made after a banquet held in the Crown Inn, while the commonalty celebrated outside by the light of bonfires and flaring tar barrels! The celebrations were reported as follows in the *Bury & Norwich Post & Suffolk Herald* on Tuesday 8th December, 1857:

> OPENING OF THE WELLS AND FAKENHAM RAILWAY - This event took place on Tuesday last, and the day was observed at Wells as a general holiday. The terminus was decorated with evergreens and flowers, and a triumphal arch was erected on the line. A procession was formed to receive the first special train, which arrived soon after ten with the Earl of Leicester, Horatio Love Esq., Chairman, and G. Goodison Esq., Deputy Chairman of the Eastern Counties Railway, H.W. Keary Esq., Mr Robertson, Mr J.O. Taylor, and other gentlemen; they were received with enthusiastic acclamation, and a *feu de joie* was fired by the Preventive men. After staying at the station a short time, the above named gentlemen accompanied the noble Lord to Holkham, where they partook of luncheon.
>
> Immediately after their departure, a train of thirteen carriages conveyed a crowded body of excursionists to Fakenham, at which town the station was also decorated and, after staying a short interval, returned to Wells. A dinner afterwards took place at the Crown Inn, at five o'clock, upwards of eighty gentlemen sitting down, and the Earl of Leicester presiding. The Labourers employed upon the line were also provided with a dinner at the Tuns Inn.

Early Years of the Railway

The new railway was worked by the Eastern Counties as a 9½ mile extension of the Norfolk Railway branch from Fakenham. There was an intermediate station at Walsingham, and the ordinary train service provided just four trains each way; one of these was a 'mixed' working conveying both passenger and freight vehicles. At Wells the line terminated away from the quays in the older part of the town, but in 1859 the Wells & Fakenham Directors belatedly completed their short goods branch to Wells quay and, when opened, this useful facility enabled ships to discharge their cargoes directly into waiting railway wagons.

In practice, the ketches, barges and schooners which tied-up at Wells quay tended to compete with the railway - though it was not unknown when vessels were stormbound (or held-up by adverse winds) for shipowners to transfer cargoes onto the railway as a means of ensuring prompt delivery. Corn, destined for export via Wells harbour, may have been sent down to the quays by train - but local farmers would have used their cream or blue-coloured 'Norfolk' wagons for shorter distance journeys. The quayside branch was nevertheless a useful addition to the system, and it obviously attracted at least some extra freight traffic to the Wells & Fakenham Railway.

Sadly, the new railway did not prosper, and although its initial receipts had equalled the 'most sanguine expectations' of the Directors, receipts for the first six months equalled only £1,656 - whereas expenditure totalled £1,774. Moreover, the Eastern Counties railway did nothing to ease the lot of the local company, and the Wells & Fakenham Directors suspected that they were being swindled. At the half-year meeting held at Wells in September 1859, for example, Hall Keary complained that the ECR was working the line at 55 per cent and 'would not co-operate on fair terms'. A revenue account had been rendered by the Eastern Counties, but (he added darkly) it 'had not yet been investigated'.

Six months later the company had still been 'unable to effect any satisfactory arrangement with the Eastern Counties for working the line' and receipts for the half-year ending 31st December, 1859 had amounted to just £1,846; expenses, including interest, had been £1,749 over the same period. Under these unhappy circumstances, the owners of the little railway seem to have lost heart, and when the time finally came to sell-up, Messrs Keary and Southgate probably felt that a heavy load was soon to be lifted from their shoulders. It would at this point be useful to turn once again to the Eastern Counties in order to understand the events leading up to the Great Eastern takeover.

The end of local control

In 1862 the process whereby the Eastern Counties Railway had gained control of its neighbours culminated in an inevitable amalgamation, and on 7th August 1862 an Act (25 & 26 Vict. cap. 223) to 'Amalgamate the Eastern Counties, the East Anglian, the Newmarket, the Eastern Union and the Norfolk Railway Companies' received the Royal Assent. Although in effect the ECR had simply absorbed lines that it already controlled, the company wisely decided to proclaim a distinct break with the past and call itself the Great Eastern Railway - thereby underlining the creation of a new organization that would (hopefully) not be tainted by the abysmal reputation of its immediate predecessor.

These momentous events suggested a solution to the Wells & Fakenham's problems, and the local Directors were only too glad to see their undertaking merged with the Norfolk Railway, the Eastern Counties Railway and other neighbouring companies. In June 1862 Hall Keary and Joseph Southgate announced that the Wells & Fakenham company would be 'transferred to and vested by amalgamation in the Great Eastern Railway'.

The last meeting of the Wells & Fakenham Railway company was held at Wells in the following September, and in a conscious attempt to underline the historic nature of the occasion, the chair was taken by Thomas Coke, Earl of Leicester. It was sad, but entirely appropriate that the man who had done so much for the railway in its early years should have had the last word just eight years later. The Earl stated simply that 'the property would be vested in the Great Eastern, and the proprietors would receive the amount to be allowed for the property in Great Eastern 4½ per cent Preference Stock in accordance with the terms agreed to in the Spring'.

A general discussion followed, but it was generally agreed that the long suffering Directors had secured the best possible terms; the debentures would 'stand in their integrity', although it was noted that 55 per cent was to be written off ordinary stocks. So ended the short, troubled career of the Wells & Fakenham Railway - an innocent victim of a vicious power struggle waged by the likes of Samuel Morton Peto, David Waddington, and other Victorian capitalists whose primary aim was the acquisition of wealth and power at the expense of any who stood in their way.

The newly created Great Eastern Railway soon earned an improved reputation, and although the stigma of its Eastern Counties origins remained for many years the reconstituted company eventually became something of an institution throughout East Anglia - an object of pride rather than derision! This change of ownership is unlikely to have bothered the people of Wells, and their branch line functioned successfully as part of a 43 mile 21 chain route from Norwich. The completed railway was of considerable benefit to East Dereham - which developed as a rural manufacturing centre after the opening of its rail links to Norwich, Wells and Kings Lynn.

Wells itself, however, failed to develop in any material way; as we shall see, the town never became a holiday resort, but more surprisingly, it also failed to prosper as a port. The Great Eastern was not inclined to promote Wells at the expense of its other ports at Kings Lynn, Lowestoft and Harwich, but worse than this, environmental changes along the north Norfolk coast precluded the development of any large scale fishing industry. It had seemed at one time that mussel or oyster fishing might be cultivated off the north Norfolk coast, but storms, and the scouring action of east-west currents seem to have been a major problem. Moreover, Wells had only 9 ft of water at high tide, and its harbour channel was continually shifting - such a port was far from ideal in the age of sail when vessels had no engines to facilitate manoeuvring in an intricate channel.

The West Norfolk branch

In spite of these problems, local squires and landowners still hoped that Wells and the surrounding coastal area could be developed, and to this end the grandly-named West Norfolk Junction Railway was floated in the 1860s. The new line was to run due west from Wells and, if successful it would encourage fishing and tourism in hitherto remote settlements such as Brancaster, Burnham Market and Docking.

At Heacham, the suggested route would join the Lynn & Hunstanton branch - thereby opening up a new route from Wells to Kings Lynn. Supporters of the West Norfolk scheme included Major Humphrey John Hare of Docking, Edward Durrant of Kings Lynn, Edward Self of Kings Lynn, and Lightly Simpson of London. All of these gentlemen were intimately connected with the Lynn & Hunstanton Railway but, as far as can be ascertained, none of them had any obvious links with the Wells & Fakenham company.

A Bill, seeking powers for the 'West Norfolk Junction Railway' was submitted to Parliament in time for the 1864 session, and the scheme received the Royal Assent on 23rd June, 1864. The company was thereby empowered to construct a line from the Lynn & Hunstanton Railway at Heacham, to the

Wells & Fakenham terminus at Wells, a distance of 18¼ miles. Capital of £75,000 in £10 shares was authorized, together with loans of £25,000; a proportion of the capital was subscribed by the GER, which undertook to work the train service between Wells and Heacham in return for 50 per cent of the gross receipts.

The newly obtained Act (27 & 28 Vict. cap. 90) defined the West Norfolk line as follows: 'The Railway, which will be wholly situate in the County of Norfolk, will commence by a junction with the Lynn & Hunstanton Railway at the Heacham Station of that Railway, and terminate in the Parish of Wells-next-the-Sea by two junctions with the Wells & Fakenham line of the Great Eastern Railway'.

The Act provided running powers over the connecting lines at Heacham and Wells-next-the-Sea, and West Norfolk trains would also be allowed to run over the Wells Harbour branch. A further clause stipulated that the Lynn & Hunstanton Railway would 'afford all reasonable and proper facilities' for through bookings and the interchange of traffic at Heacham.

Having obtained their Act, the West Norfolk Junction promoters lost little time in putting their plans into effect. From Wells (where trains would use the Wells & Fakenham station) the authorized route ran due west via Holkham, Burnham Market, Stanhoe, Docking and Sedgeford, following the coast as far as Burnham and then bearing inland for the remaining 11 miles. It was initially proposed that triangular junctions would be provided at both Wells and Heacham, but in the event this part of the plan was not completed.

The first sod was cut on 8th October, 1864 and the work of construction began shortly afterwards. The Engineer for the new line was John Sutherland Valentine (1813-1898), while the contractor was William Smith, who had recently built the Buntingford branch. Although J.S. Valentine was a Derbyshire man by birth, he was intimately connected with the railways of west Norfolk, having already engineered the Lynn & Ely and Lynn & Dereham lines.

It was reported, at the half-yearly West Norfolk Junction meeting held at Kings Lynn in February 1865, that 'the works had been carried on with great expedition'; indeed, progress had been so rapid that the Directors hoped to open their line as far as Holkham before the end of the year. In the event, this forecast was somewhat optimistic, but it is interesting to note that a Royal Special was allowed to work over the uncompleted branch in January 1866; the Royal Train was halted at Burnham Market at which point the Prince and Princess of Wales alighted for the remainder of their journey to Holkham Hall (where they were spending the New Year while their own house at Sandringham was being rebuilt. After many delays, the West Norfolk branch was opened for public traffic on 17th August, 1866, thereby opening-up a second route to Wells-next-the-Sea and effectively doubling the amount of traffic handled at Wells.

There were, in general, four trains each way between Wells and Heacham, rising to five on Saturdays and market days; most services terminated at Heacham, but there was usually one through working to Hunstanton, which continued northwards after reversal at the junction. Freight services consisted of one return working between Kings Lynn and Wells.

These modest services remained unchanged for many years, the amount of traffic offering itself being so small that additional trains would have been superfluous. Receipts were correspondingly low, but unlike the Wells & Fakenham, the West Norfolk company struggled on as an independent concern until 1874 - when it was merged with the Lynn & Hunstanton Railway to form the 'Hunstanton & West Norfolk Railway'. (The Hunstanton & West Norfolk company was itself sold to the GER in 1890.)

Motive power in the early years

It is impossible to say, with any degree of accuracy, which classes of locomotive were used on the Wells branch during its very early years, but it is nevertheless possible, by a process of elimination, to suggest the kind of engines which might have appeared. When in 1848 the Norfolk Railway first placed itself under Eastern Counties control, the company possessed just 37 locomotives - most of which were of the ungainly 'long boiler' type. Built by Stephensons, Jones & Potts and other specialist manufacturers, they included several 0-6-0 goods engines, some 2-2-2s, and a class of ten 2-4-0s.

It is reasonable to assume that most of these engines remained on their own section long after the ECR takeover - the usual practice being for elderly main line locomotives to be demoted to secondary duties when more modern motive power became available on 'top link' services.

It is tempting to conclude that former Norfolk Railway 'long boiler' 2-4-0s worked on the Wells branch around the time of its opening; as tender engines, they would have the necessary fuel capacity for the 87 mile round journey between Wells and Norwich, while their 5 ft 7 in. wheels would have been ideal for passenger duties. Numbered from 130 to 139 in the ECR locomotive list, they had 15 inch by 22 inch outside cylinders and weighed 23 tons 12 cwt. Some members of the class were later rebuilt by the ECR, receiving new boilers, stove pipe chimneys and simple weather boards in place of their earlier open cabs.

The Norfolk Railway also owned three small 2-2-2Ts which had been built specifically for branch line duties, and may therefore have been used on some shorter distance services. Built by E.B. Wilson at the Railway Foundry, Leeds, they had 10 inch by 17 inch inside cylinders, fluted safety valve covers and unusually slender chimneys; probably too small and under-powered for everyday use, they were scrapped at an early date.

Although these suppositions are entirely plausible, recorded locomotive history on the Wells branch really begins with the advent of Robert Sinclair's 'Y' class 2-4-0s. Built in batches between 1859 and 1866 there were eventually 110 of these versatile machines at work on the GER, and although originally designed for freight duties they were also used as passenger engines. The 'Y' class engines had 17 inch by 24 inch cylinders and 6 ft 1 in. coupled wheels; their weight, in full working order was approximately 54 tons, and the locomotives were numbered in sequence from 307 to 416.

The 'Y' class were rebuilt and modified in a number of ways in the course of their lives, some being fitted with leading bogies to become 4-4-0s, while others remained 2-4-0s. The 4-4-0 rebuilds were intended for main line use, whereas the 2-4-0s remained at work on local passenger and freight services in Norfolk and elsewhere on the Great Eastern system. Ernest Ahrons recalled that No. 328 worked for many years on cross-country services between Norwich, Wymondham, Dereham and Hunstanton, while other members of the class could often be seen in use as shunting engines - this expedient being necessary because the Great Eastern Railway had very few shunting engines during the Victorian period.

The relatively long journey between Wells and Norwich dictated the use of tender locomotives rather than tank engines, and for most of its life the branch was worked by various types of 2-4-0 locomotive. These engines were turned at the end of each journey, using a 41 ft 11 in. diameter turntable outside Wells engine shed (this was later replaced by a 45 ft diameter table so that 4-4-0s could be used). There were usually at least two engines shedded at Wells to work the morning up services to Norwich and Heacham respectively; on occasions, however, there could be three or even four locomotives in the cramped sub-shed at the end of each day's operation.

A note on early liveries and early signals

The range of paints available in mid-Victorian years was severely limited in comparison with later periods, and for this reason the predominant colours used on external structures were buff and either brown or green. By analogy with other Victorian lines, the Wells & Fakenham would probably have painted its structures in a two tone livery incorporating buff (sometimes described as 'stone') and brown. If green was used it would have been a drab mixture known usually as 'Holly Green'.

The constraints governing station colours applied also to locomotives, and it comes as no surprise to find that Eastern Counties and Great Eastern locomotives were adorned - if that is the right word - in a sombre green colour, relieved only by black and red (later white) lining.

In common with other ECR lines the Wymondham to Wells branch would originally have been signalled with simple, slotted post semaphores, which were probably supplied by Messrs Stevens & Co. of Darlington Works, Southwark Bridge Road, London. These were worked independently by railwaymen turning a handle near the base of the post, and signal boxes as such did not appear until the later Victorian period. There were, in many cases, two semaphore arms on each post - one for up and the other for down trains, and the operating handle also turned a rotating spindle which, in turn, rotated an oil lamp showing either red or blue-green.

GER Johnson 'No. 1' class 2-4-0 No. 30 stands besides the tiny water tower at Wells. The headcode suggests that the locomotive is about to work through to Norwich. The 'No. 1' class was introduced in 1867 and were known as 'Little Sharpies' (the early batches had been built by Sharp, Stewart & Co. of Manchester). The final locomotive of the class to be withdrawn was scrapped in 1913. *Canon Charles Baynes*

GER Holden 'T26' class 2-4-0 No. 492 at Wells. The 'T26s' were first introduced in 1891 and they were to give many years service. The engines were reclassified as 'E4' by the LNER and all survived into British Railways days, the first withdrawal not taking place until 1954. BR No. 62785 (ex-GER No. 490) was the last 'E4' to be withdrawn (in 1959), it was saved for posterity and is now part of the National Collection and it currently resides at Bressingham Steam Museum near Diss in Norfolk. *Canon Charles Baynes*

Chapter Three

A Norfolk Branch Line
(1862-1923)

Much of the East Anglian railway system had been built piecemeal by a bewildering variety of independent companies, but after the formation of the Great Eastern Railway in 1862 the network developed in a more rational way. The emphasis shifted from the internecine and unregulated competition of the 1840s towards a more rational approach, and in the next few years several more towns and villages were connected to the main system by small (often locally-promoted) branch lines.

These lines were usually worked by the Great Eastern Railway - an arrangement which was of benefit to all in so far as the small towns and villages concerned obtained their vital rail links while the GER gained several useful additions to its system. The Norwich to Cromer branch was a typical, locally-based branch line; promoted by the East Norfolk Railway, it was opened from Whitlingham Junction, through Wroxham to North Walsham on 20th October, 1874 and extended northwards to Gunton on 29th July, 1876. Completion to Cromer was accomplished on 26th March, 1877, on which date Great Eastern trains began running to yet another Norfolk seaside town.

Victorian developments

The appearance of the Eastern & Midlands Railway (later the Midland & Great Northern Joint (M&GN)) prompted a further bout of inter-company rivalry at the end of the 1870s, resulting in further additions to the local railway system. The history of the Eastern & Midlands is complex, but briefly, this competitive cross country-route originated in the 1860s when three local companies had amalgamated to form the 'Midlands & Eastern Railway' - thereby bringing a 36 mile branch from the Great Northern at Bourne under unified management; in this way the Great Northern was able to reach Kings Lynn in opposition to the GER.

Meanwhile, the opening of a Midland-backed line from Peterborough to Sutton Bridge had brought a third company into the arena, while further east the Lynn & Fakenham railway and other non-GER interests were actively promoting a tenuous chain of local railways which, when completed at various times between 1877 and 1883, effectively carried the Midlands & Eastern route from Kings Lynn to Great Yarmouth.

On 1st August, 1882 the lines east of Kings Lynn were amalgamated as the Eastern & Midlands Railway, and a year later the Eastern & Midlands absorbed the earlier Midlands & Eastern and Peterborough & Sutton Bridge lines. The end result of these complicated amalgamations was a lengthy 'main line' from the GNR at Bourne, extending eastwards across Great Eastern territory to Great Yarmouth, with branches from Sutton Bridge to Peterborough and from Melton Constable to Norwich; a third branch was later opened between Melton Constable and Cromer.

Understandably alarmed at this blatant threat to its East Anglian heartlands, the Great Eastern promoted new lines of its own - one of which was a short branch running westwards from the East Norfolk line at Wroxham towards Aylsham, Parliamentary sanction for the proposed line being obtained in 1876. It was later agreed the branch would be extended westwards to join the Wymondham to Wells branch near Broom Green.

The authorized route followed the Bure Valley north-westwards for the first eight miles from Wroxham to Aylsham, and then proceeded westwards across rolling farmland with an average elevation of around 150 ft above mean sea level. The undulating nature of the surrounding terrain would necessitate numerous cuttings and embankments, and there would be a small viaduct across the River Bure on the approaches to Buxton Lamas.

A classic 'political' line, this new section of railway served no obvious economic need. Running for 23 miles 51 chains through sparsely-populated countryside that yielded little or no originating traffic, it was opened in stages, reaching Buxton Lamas on 8th July, 1879 and Aylsham on 1st January, 1880. Although part of the nominally-independent East Norfolk Railway, the new line was clearly the Great Eastern's response to the Lynn & Fakenham Railway - which was itself being built in stages just a few miles to the north.

The Great Eastern route was pushed westwards to reach Cawston on 1st September, 1880, and Reepham by 2nd May, 1881. Finally, on 1st May, 1882, the line was completed throughout to its junction with the Wymondham to Wells branch.

The completed line was a single track route with intermediate stations at Coltishall, Buxton Lamas, Aylsham, Cawston, Reepham and Foulsham. There was no station at Broom Green, where the new branch converged with the Wells route. Instead, the 'junction' was established at County School - a new station that had been opened by the GER to serve the adjacent Norfolk County School. Aylsham, Cawston and the other stations en route to County School were substantially constructed of brick, while the formation was wide enough to accommodate a second line of rails if traffic was sufficient to justify such a facility in the years ahead.

Meanwhile, the rival Lynn & Fakenham Railway (L&F) had itself been opened to traffic, though there was no connection whatsoever between the Great Eastern and Lynn & Fakenham routes at Fakenham - the two stations being on opposite sides of the town.

In 1880 the Lynn & Fakenham obtained Parliamentary consent for a branch from the L&F line at Melton Constable to the coast at Blakeney, and in answer to this further attack on its monopoly in north Norfolk the Great Eastern put forward its own scheme for an extension from Wells to Blakeney. Neither of these lines were ever built - though the Lynn & Fakenham project eventually materialized in a slightly different form as the Eastern & Midlands Railway Cromer branch. Later, at the end of the 19th century, there was talk of a new GER line from Wells to Holt, but again this interesting scheme was abandoned, and Wells was destined to remain the terminus of the line until its closure in 1964.

The growth of East Dereham brought much extra traffic to the southern half of the Wells branch, and for this reason the GER Directors decided that double track would be installed between Wymondham and Dereham. The necessary work was put in hand in the early 1880s, and the additional trackwork and associated signalling was inspected in November 1882. In connection with this scheme, the Great Eastern rebuilt the intermediate stations at Kimberley, Hardingham, Thuxton and Yaxham, new platforms and additional station buildings being provided in each case.

North of Dereham, however, the Wells-next-the-Sea route remained single, the main crossing loops being at County School and Fakenham. Two freight trains, or one freight and one passenger train, could cross at North Elmham, but the loop at Ryburgh was not used for passing purposes (except possibly in emergencies). Similarly at Walsingham, the sidings could have been used for passing in emergencies, but the operating authorities frowned on this practice, and Great Eastern working timetables dictated that Walsingham was 'not to be used as a crossing station'.

Other developments in the last quarter of the 19th century included the elimination of Barsham tunnel. The tunnel - which may have been cheaply-constructed with inadequate lining - was replaced by an open cutting with substantial retaining walls.

Meanwhile, at Dereham, the continued growth of through traffic on the Norwich to Kings Lynn cross-country route was resulting in considerable congestion, and it seemed sensible, therefore, to construct an avoiding line between Dereham South and Dereham West junctions, thereby reducing the amount of traffic needing to reverse in the confines of the passenger station. The new curve, which was inspected by the Board of Trade in June 1886 and brought into use shortly afterwards, was designed primarily for freight traffic, and ordinary passenger services continued running into Dereham station on the old alignment.

An unsuccessful resort?

In general, development was rapid around a newly-opened seaside resort, and in some places the railway companies themselves took a lead in laying out streets and building guest houses. This happened, for, example at Hunstanton where the Lynn & Hunstanton Railway built an entire resort on a 'green field' site. Elsewhere, speculative builders moved in to accelerate resort development, and in this way Cromer was transformed from a small fishing village to become one of the most fashionable watering places in East Anglia. (Significantly, Lord Suffield - a major landowner in the Cromer area - was Chairman of the East Norfolk Railway Company.)

Curiously, such development did not occur at Wells, and while neighbouring Hunstanton and Cromer were enjoying unprecedented growth, the little port stubbornly refused to 'develop' as a conventional resort. The reasons for this are complex, but not hard to find. In the Victorian period, seaside resorts were usually upper middle class residential towns, catering for permanent or long-stay patrons rather than day trippers.

Typically, a Victorian or Edwardian gentleman would purchase a villa or book rooms for use during the summer, and at the start of the season his wife, children,

A photograph looking north from Polka Road towards Wells station *circa* 1904. Judging from the number of wagons in the yard the town and harbour are providing plenty of goods traffic. This view shows the 13-arch brick-built train shed that afforded passengers some shelter. The tall building beyond the station was Dewing & Kersley's granary and this was served by a private siding.

Oakwood Collection

nanny and servants would migrate *en masse* to the chosen resort. The head of the family might stay in London during the week and travel to the seaside at weekends, or (if there was a good train service) he could commute - and in this way the most popular resorts became long-distance commuter towns in their own right.

The GER, and other railway companies, were only too glad to see this development taking place, and they arranged prestige morning up and evening down expresses for their high class patrons. By 1910, the Great Eastern was providing restaurant car facilities to and from Clacton, Hunstanton, Cromer and its other top resorts, and such facilities did much to enhance the prestige of the resorts concerned.

Obviously, the price of property would increase in these successful resorts, and this, together with the actual cost of travelling, made long-distance commuting an expensive business. It followed that, if a Victorian family was going to take up residence by the sea, the heavy cost involved would have to be weighed against environmental and health factors, and in this context resorts with attractive cliff scenery, dry sandy or gravel soils, mild climates and 'healthy' air were preferred.

An ideal resort for holidays or permanent residence might be from 50 to 100 miles from London, have cliff scenery and a health-giving climate. Sadly, Wells (a low-lying marshland town, 144½ miles from Liverpool Street) did not fulfil any of the above requirements, and it was not even by the sea - being about a mile away from the nearest beaches!

It seems that, as far as GER resorts were concerned, 140 miles was the maximum distance for long distance commuting, but an ideal distance was something under 100 miles from London. Only ultra-rich and successful Victorian businessmen or professional people could afford to commute from places above 100 miles from London, but the resorts concerned tended to have above-average scenic attractions which made the long and expensive daily journey worthwhile (Cromer being the classic example).

This point is underlined forcibly by the following table, which shows that Wells, even if it had the requisite scenic attractions, would have been further from London than any other Great Eastern resort town.

Distances from Liverpool Street of GER seaside resorts		
Town	*Date of rail link*	*Distance*
		(by usual route)
Southend-on-Sea	1st October, 1889 (GER)	41½ miles
Southminster	1st June, 1889	45½ miles
Harwich	15th August, 1854	70¾ miles
Clacton-on-Sea	4th July, 1882	71 miles
Felixstowe Beach	1st May, 1877	85¾ miles
Aldeburgh	12th April, 1860	99¼ miles
Hunstanton	3rd October, 1862	112¼ miles
Yarmouth	1st May, 1844	128 miles
Mundesley-on-Sea	1st July, 1889	136¼ miles
Cromer	26th March, 1877	141¾ miles
Wells-next-the-Sea	1st December, 1857	144½ miles

(NB Yarmouth not connected with London until 15th December, 1845.)

A further point which might be made with reference to the table, is that Wells was one of the first East Anglian seaside towns to acquire a rail link - but this made no difference to its popularity (or lack of it) as a resort town.

Another factor which may have impeded resort development was the attitude of the Earl of Leicester - who as resident landlord could veto any plans put forward by outside developers. A paternalistic landlord of the old sort, Thomas Coke was probably interested in estate development rather than resort promotion, and one senses that this somewhat shy and retiring man would not have welcomed large scale resort development on his own doorstep.

He was, it seems, happy to encourage the railway as a means of 'improving' his beloved Holkham estate, and to this end he had actively promoted both the railway and the port of Wells. If, by building an embankment to enclose neighbouring marshland he also created an attractive 'promenade', then so much the better. Townsfolk, farm tenants (perhaps even the occasional day trippers from Norwich) were welcome to visit the Earl's seaside lands, but when it came to building large hotels and laying out wide boulevards to encourage speculative building - in other words any kind of large scale development - the old Earl was less than enthusiastic. Furthermore, he was destined to live to a ripe old age (87) and in that long lifetime he never lost his firm, but benevolent grip on Holkham and Wells.

Locomotives and train services in GER days

The original train service of four trains each way persisted for several years. In 1862, there were up trains from Wells at 7.00, 9.15 am, 1.50 and 6.00 pm, arriving in Norwich at 9.10, 11.30 am, 4.20 and 8.15 pm respectively. On Mondays, the first up working left Wells at the earlier time of 6.00 am, and arrived in Norwich at 8.00 am. In the down direction, northbound services left Norwich Thorpe at 7.00 am, 12.20, 3.20 and 7.50 pm, while the Sunday service consisted of two trains in each direction between Norwich Thorpe and Wells.

Study of the timetable suggests that the Norwich to Wells route was regarded as the 'main line', while the Lynn & Dereham line was worked as a branch, with a service of connecting trains between Dereham and Kings Lynn. There was, at that time, no south-to-west avoiding line at Dereham, and for this reason all through workings to or from Norwich and Kings Lynn had to reverse in the platforms at Dereham. There was, nevertheless, one through train in each direction, which left Norwich at 9.00 am and reached Dereham at 9.45 am before going forward to Kings Lynn. In the up direction, the balancing service left Dereham at 6.30 pm, and reached Norwich by 7.15 pm.

The frequency of services had been increased to six up and six down workings by the end of the century. Trains ran through from Norwich Thorpe to Wells, taking from 1 hour 40 minutes to 2 hours for the 43 mile 21 chain trip, and there were additional services between Norwich, Wymondham and Dereham, which continued (after reversal at the latter station) through to Kings Lynn.

The West Norfolk branch was served by four trains each way between Heacham and Wells, but GER timetables did not encourage London travellers to use this route. Ironically, the distance from Liverpool Street to Wells via Heacham and the West Norfolk line was only 128¼ miles, and this compared very favourably with the 158½ miles via Norwich. However, the GER seemed reluctant to utilize the Heacham route to the full (perhaps because the busy Hunstanton branch could not have accommodated extra traffic between Heacham and Kings Lynn).

Instead, the company made some small attempt to offer an improved service via Dereham and Wymondham - from where, on 2nd May, 1881, a 'cut-off' had been opened between the Cambridge and Ipswich main lines; this cut-off shortened the distance between Wells and Liverpool Street to 144½ miles. Diverging south eastwards from Wymondham, the 'cut-off' line was double track throughout, with an intermediate station at Ashwellthorpe; it joined the Ipswich line some 32 chains north of Forncett station, thereby providing a short-cut for any future Wells to London through traffic.

As we have seen, Wells-next-the-Sea did not attract Victorian holidaymakers - at least not in any appreciable quantity - and the new Forncett line was used mainly as a freight and diversionary route. Nevertheless, for travellers wishing to reach London in a hurry, the GER provided a 1.50 pm afternoon service from Wells, which missed out certain intermediate stops *en route* to Wymondham and terminated at Forncett at 3.08 pm. This provided a connection with the 2.55 pm express from Norwich Thorpe, allowing through travellers to reach London by 6.00 pm.

In the reverse direction it was possible, by leaving Liverpool Street on the 5.00 pm express, and changing at Forncett, to be in Wells by 9.15 pm. The Forncett connections enabled through travellers to reach Wells in a little over four hours, but these times would clearly have been improved if trains had run non-stop to Wells. However, there was no point in running non-stop at a time in which so little traffic was offering itself. Wymondham, Dereham and Fakenham were, in any case, more important destinations, and the Forncett connections were probably designed for Dereham travellers rather than for people making the through journey to Wells-next-the-Sea.

London travellers willing to study their timetables carefully might have found some reasonably-fast journey times via Heacham and the Hunstanton line, and although the infrequent services between Wells and Heacham may have forced many travellers to use the longer Forncett route, the West Norfolk line was a useful, though perhaps under-valued, alternative route to the capital. In 1909, for example, the 8.10 am service from Wells to Heacham provided a 25 minute connection, giving travellers ample time to catch the 9.10 am express from Hunstanton to Liverpool Street.

Overall time for the 128½ mile journey to London was 4½ hours and clearly, if the Great Eastern had wanted to run a fast through train between London and Wells, the Heacham route would have offered many possibilities - although as pointed out above, such a service would not have served Dereham or other intermediate stops which were, in GER eyes, more important than Wells itself. (An added advantage of the Heacham route was the fact that through services were available from Hunstanton to St Pancras.)

The Wroxham to County School line was originally worked as a largely self-contained route, and passengers wishing to travel through to Foulsham,

NORWICH, DEREHAM, FAKENHAM, AND WELLS.

UP TRAINS.

Mls from Wells.	FROM	WEEK DAYS													SUNDAYS			

	Wells .... dep.
7	Walsingham ....
44	Fakenham ....
62	Ryburgh ....
171	North Elmham ....
214	Dereham {arr. / dep.}
234	Yaxham ....
264	Thurton ....
271	Hardingham ....
304	Kimberley ....
32	Wymondham {arr. / dep.}
37	Hethersett ....
124	Trowse ....
44	Norwich .... arr.
671	Cromer .... arr.
604	Lowestoft ....
724	Yarmouth (Vauxhall) ....
1024	Ely ....
1004	Cambridge ....
74	Peterborough ....
904	Ipswich ....
147	LONDON {St. Pancras / Tel pool St.}

Netherset, Kimberley, Thurton, Yaxham, North Elmham, and Ryburgh.—The Trains although noted to call will stop only at these Stations when required to take up down Passengers. Passengers wishing to alight are requested to intimate the same to the Guard at the preceding stopping Station. Passengers wishing to be taken up should be at the Station Five Minutes before the time named in the Table.

Calls at Kimberley to take up Passengers for Norwich only. Passengers from Stations between Wells and Kimberley for Junction to London, and intermediate Stations. Parliamentary from Stations between Wymondham and London. Horses and Private Carriages are not conveyed by this Train for stations between Wymondham and London. Will call when required to take up or set down Passenger. Passengers wishing to alight must intimate the same to the Guard at the preceding stopping Station.

Mixed Trains.—These Trains being Goods Trains with Passenger Carriages attached for the general convenience of the Public, the same punctuality cannot be observed as with ordinary Passenger Trains. Horses and Private Carriages are not conveyed by these Trains.

Public timetable for up trains, 1882.

NORWICH, DEREHAM, FAKENHAM, AND WELLS.

DOWN TRAINS.

WEEK DAYS. — **SUNDAYS.**

Miles from Norwich	FROM		
	LONDON { Liverpool St. dep.		
	{ St. Pancras		
	Ipswich .... dep.		
	Peterborough		
	Cambridge		
	Ely		
	Yarmouth (Vauxhall) ..		
	Lowestoft		
	Cromer		
—	Norwich .... dep.		
1	Trowse		
6¼	Hethersett		
10¾	Wymondham { arr. dep.		
14	Kimberley		
14¾	Hardingham		
17¼	Thurton		
19½	Yaxham		
21¾	Dereham { arr. dep.		
26	North Elmham		
31½	Ryburgh		
33½	Fakenham		
38¼	Walsingham		
44½	Wells .... arr.		

Notes:

¶ Hethersett, Kimberley, Thurston, Yaxham, North Elmham, and Ryburgh.—The Trains although noted to call will stop only at these Stations when required to take up or set down Passengers. Passengers wishing to alight are requested to intimate the same to the Guard at the preceding stopping Station. Passengers wishing to be taken up are at the Station Five Minutes before the times named in the Table.

P From Yarmouth on Mondays only.

Q From Lowestoft at 7.35 a.m. on Mondays.

R Calls at Yaxham when required to set down Passengers.

Fakenham Market.—On Thursdays the Train leaving Fakenham for Wells at 4.10 p.m. will start at 5.0 p.m.

● Will call when required to take up or set down Passengers. Passengers wishing to alight must intimate the same to the Guard at the preceding stopping Station.

Mixed Trains.—These Trains being Goods Trains with Passenger Carriages attached for the general convenience of the Public, the same punctuality cannot be observed as with ordinary Passenger Trains.

Public timetable for down trains, 1882.

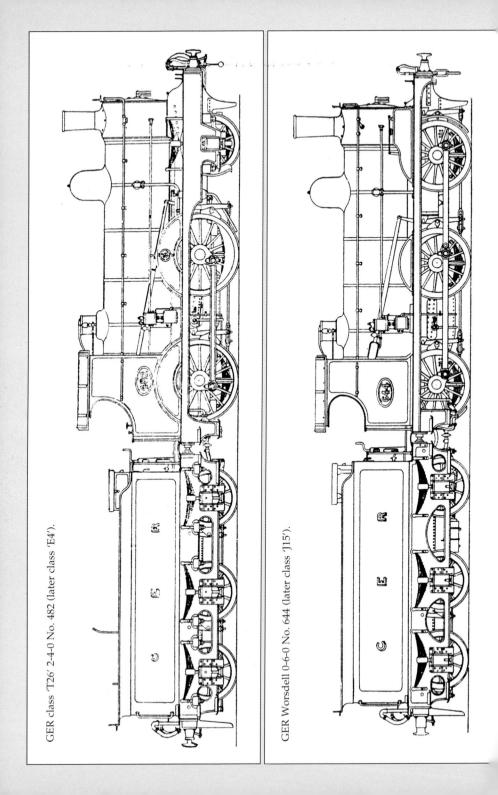

GER class 'T26' 2-4-0 No. 482 (later class 'E4').

GER Worsdell 0-6-0 No. 644 (later class 'J15').

NORWICH, DEREHAM, FAKENHAM AND WELLS.

Junction with Cambridge Main Line at Wymondham.

DOWN TRAINS.

Reference to other Trains	DOWN TRAINS.	WEEK DAYS.	SUNDAYS.	NOTES.

Down stations:
Yarmouth (Vaux.) dep. · Lowestoft · Cromer · NORWICH (Thorpe) dep. · Hethersett · Trowse · Wymondham arr. · Wymondham dep. · DON / St. Pancras dep. · Ipswich · Cambridge · Peterborough dep. · York · Doncaster · Lincoln · Ely · Wymondham · Kimberley · Hardingham · Thuxton · Yaxham · Dereham arr. · Dereham dep. · North Elmham · County School · Ryburgh · Fakenham · Walsingham · WELLS arr.

UP TRAINS.

Up stations:
WELLS dep. · Walsingham · Fakenham · Ryburgh · County School · North Elmham · Dereham arr. · Dereham dep. · Yaxham · Thuxton · Hardingham · Kimberley · Wymondham arr. · Wymondham dep. · Ely · Lincoln · Doncaster · YORK · Peterborough arr. · Cambridge · Ipswich · LON / St. Pancras · DON / Liverpool St. · Wymondham · Hethersett · Trowse · NORWICH (Thorpe) arr. · Cromer · Lowestoft · Yarmouth (Vaux.) arr.

NOTES.

A Arrives at Fakenham at 2.10 p.m.
B On Mondays leaves Cromer at 7.0 a.m.
O Calls at Hethersett on Tuesdays when required to take up Passengers.
B On Mondays, Thursdays, & Saturdays during June will leave Lowestoft at 7.0 p.m.
F Calls at Yaxham on Mondays when required to set down Passengers.
H Passengers for Trowse, Norwich, Cromer, Yarmouth, and Lowestoft by this train change at Wymondham.
J Horses and Private Carriages are not conveyed by this train between Wymondham and London.
K On Thursdays during June will arrive at Cromer 3.43.
L Calls at Hethersett on Tuesdays when required to set down Passengers.
Lowestoft 4.43 p.m.
M From Lowestoft on Saturdays only.
P During June will arrive at St. Pancras at 12.48 p.m.
S Fakenham Market.— On Thursdays this Train for Wells will leave Fakenham for Wells at 5.0 p.m.
T On Mondays only, Passengers for Ipswich and Liverpool St. to leave via Forncett, and arrive at Ipswich 9.3, and Liverpool Street at 10.45 a.m.
U On Saturdays leaves at Ipswich 9.3, and Liverpool St. leaves.
V On Thursdays during May will arrive at 3.29 p.m. commencing 1st June.
W From Wells and Walsingham on Saturdays only Week-day at 3.26 p.m.
X From Wells and Walsingham on Saturdays only. Horses and Private Carriages not conveyed by these Trains.
+ To Lowestoft on Tuesdays and Saturdays only. Will commence running 1st June.

NORWICH, DEREHAM, FAKENHAM AND WELLS.

Junction with Cambridge Main Line at Wymondham.

DOWN TRAINS.

WEEK DAYS. — SUNDAYS.

- Yarmouth (Vaux.) — dep.
- Lowestoft (Central) — ,,
- Cromer — ,,
- NORWICH (Thorpe) — dep.
- Trowse — ,,
- Hethersett — ,,
- Wymondham — arr.
- LON. { Liverpool St. — dep.
- DON. { St. Pancras — ,,
- Cambridge — ,,
- Wymondham —
- Peterborough — dep.
- YORK — ,,
- Doncaster — ,,
- Lincoln — ,,
- Ely — dep.
- Wymondham — arr.
- Kimberley —
- Hardingham —
- Thuxton —
- Yaxham —
- Dereham — { arr. / dep.
- North Elmham —
- County School —
- Hoe —
- Walsingham —
- Fakenham —
- WELLS — arr.

UP TRAINS.

WEEK DAYS. — SUNDAYS.

- WELLS — dep.
- Walsingham — ,,
- Fakenham — ,,
- Ryburgh — ,,
- County School — ,,
- North Elmham — ,,
- Dereham — { arr. / dep.
- Yaxham —
- Thuxton —
- Hardingham —
- Kimberley —
- Wymondham — dep.
- Ely — ,,
- Lincoln —
- Doncaster —
- YORK —
- Peterborough —
- Cambridge — arr.
- Ipswich —
- LON. { St. Pancras — arr.
- DON. { Liverpool St. — ,,
- Wymondham —
- Hethersett —
- Trowse —
- NORWICH (Thorpe) — arr.
- Cromer — ,,
- Lowestoft (Central) — ,,
- Yarmouth (Vaux.) — ,,

NOTES.

B Arrives at Fakenham at 2.17 p.m.

B Calls at Hethersett at 9.30 a.m. when required to take up Passengers.

CO Calls at Hethersett at 8.29 a.m. on Tuesdays when required to take up Passengers.

D During October will leave Cromer 8.45 p.m.

H Commencing 2nd November will leave Yarmouth at 9.15 a.m.

F Calls at Yarham at 8.0 p.m. on Mondays when required to set down Passengers.

G Passengers for Trowse, Norwich, Cromer, Yarmouth, and Lowestoft by this Train change at Wymondham.

H Horses and Private Carriages not conveyed by these Trains.

J Horses and Private Carriages are not conveyed by this Train for Stations between Wymondham and London.

K To Lowestoft on Mondays only, and will run during October only.

L Calls at Hethersett at 6.16 p.m. on Tuesdays when required to set down Passengers.

M On Saturdays arrives at Lowestoft 4.32 p.m.

N From Lowestoft on Saturdays only.

P During October will arrive at Lowestoft 9.55 a.m.

R Calls at Thurton at 9.23 p.m. when required to set down Passengers from March and Stations beyond.

S Fakenham Market.—On Thursdays this Train will leave Fakenham for Wells at 5.50 p.m.

T On Saturdays leaves Cromer at 5.58 p.m.

U On Saturdays leaves Cromer at 5.24 p.m.

V On Mondays, Thursdays, and Saturdays during October will arrive at 3.30 p.m.

W On Saturdays leaves Wymondham at 5.21 p.m.

Z From Wells and Walsingham on Saturdays only.

Y During October will leave Cromer at 8.50 a.m.

Z On Saturdays leaves Cromer at 5.52 p.m.

Public timetable for October 1908.

Aylsham or the other stations en route to Wroxham normally had to change trains at County School. The 1908 timetable provided six up and six down workings on this very rural line. In the up direction, the first train apparently left Foulsham at 7.20 am (although in practice this service may have started its journey as an unadvertised working from Dereham).

Further up trains left County School at 9.25 am, 12.05, 2.30 and 5.30 pm, while the last eastbound service of the day departed from Reepham at 8.05 pm. In the down direction, trains left Wroxham at 7.42, 11.51 am, 2.11, 4.32, 7.12 and 9.35 pm. The 7.12 pm ex-Wroxham ran only as far as Reepham, from where it returned as the 8.05 pm up service, while the 9.35 pm from Wroxham terminated at Foulsham.

This basic pattern of operation remained fairly constant for many years. The branch continued to be served by around half a dozen trains each way, but trains began to run to run through from Dereham to Norwich around the time of World War I, thereby providing local travellers with an alternative, albeit circuitous, route to the county town; in later years, the Wroxham to County School line became known as the 'round the world' route!

Wells was served by three freight services, two of which ran via Dereham while the third travelled via Heacham and the West Norfolk branch. One of the Dereham workings started its journey at Norwich in the early hours of the morning, and returned from Wells at around 11.00 am. In the meantime, a second goods train had left Beccles, and, travelling via Forncett and Wymondham, it reached Wells in the early afternoon. The West Norfolk freight left Kings Lynn at 10.47 am, and arrived at Heacham by 12.25 pm. Gaining the West Norfolk branch this third train then pursued its leisurely course through the north Norfolk countryside, reaching Wells in the early afternoon.

Freight traffic on the Wroxham to County School line was normally conveyed by an early morning working which, in the later Great Eastern period, left Norwich around 5.50 am and made its leisurely way along the line from Wroxham, shunting as necessary at the wayside stations and finally reaching Dereham at 12.14 pm. In the eastbound direction, the returning goods service left Dereham at 12.45 pm on Saturdays, 3.02 pm on Thursdays, and 2.55 pm on all other days of the week.

The Wells branch was worked for many years by the famous 'No. 1 Class' or 'Little Sharpie' 2-4-0s, the first five of which had been delivered to the GER in 1867. Built by Neilson, Reid & Co., they had originally been designed for the North British Railway; the initial (and later) batch had 5 ft 7 in. coupled wheels, and 16 inch by 22 inch inside cylinders. The type was so successful in Great Eastern service that three further engines were built at Stratford, and these became the prototypes of the 'No. 1 Class', of which 40 were constructed between 1867 and 1872. Thirty of the new engines were constructed by Sharp, Stewart & Co., and a further 10 were built at Stratford.

The 'No. 1 Class' proper weighed 47 tons in working order, and they had a boiler pressure of 140 lb. per square inch. The first five engines were numbered in sequence from 125 to 129, and the remaining 40 'No. 1 Class' 2-4-0s were numbered in random batches between 1 and 161.

The 'No. 1' class engines were widely used on local passenger and freight duties throughout East Anglia, and in this capacity they enjoyed a long

GER 'T26' class No. 488 is being prepared for duty at the coaling stage at Norwich. These engines worked on the Wells branch for many years. *Real Photographs*

Norwich Trowse, *circa* 1900, showing the original Swing Bridge Junction signal box, with a train approaching. *Lens of Sutton Collection*

association with the Wymondham to Wells line. Engine No. 115 was stationed at Dereham for much of its life, while Nos. 6, 26, 31, 33, 34 and 49 were based at Norwich at various times. Nos. 30, 117 and 126 were stationed at Wells, and on 21st January, 1881 the latter engine was involved in a collision at Norwich while working a early morning up service.

When new, the 'No. 1 Class' locomotives were painted in a dark green livery with brown underframes, but in the 1880s (by which time paint technology had increased the range of paints available to Victorian railway companies) Great Eastern engines started to appear in the attractive Royal Blue livery that became the GER's trademark. Many of the 'No. 1 Class' had by then been rebuilt with characteristic Holden boilers and, with their tall stove pipe chimneys and smart blue livery, they were attractive little engines, well-suited to light branch line duties.

In 1902, Wells-based 'No. 1 Class' 2-4-0 No. 117 became a local celebrity when it was elaborately decorated to mark the coronation of King Edward VII. Driver Woodhouse and fireman Houseago decided to show their patriotism by adorning their engine with flags, drapes, garlands, flowers and ornaments, though the end result might have been (to modern eyes) rather excessive. No. 117 worked a normal diagram on Coronation Day, becoming the centre of attraction at every station between Wells and Norwich!

Edwardian Wells

Having stagnated for over half-a-century, Wells appeared quaint and picturesque even in the Edwardian era, and G.W. Potter, arriving by train in about 1909, noted that the station was 'on a very small scale throughout' in relation to 'modern day stock'. Writing in *The Railway Magazine*, he gave an interesting description of the town as it appeared at that time:

Although the town is called Wells-next-the-Sea to distinguish it from Wells in Somerset, it is a considerable distance from the sea, and except by a stretch of the imagination can hardly be termed a seaside resort. The tiny station lies inland; and when one has traversed the narrow and quaint little streets of the town and descended to the broad quay with its lines of railway, at which the boats are loading or unloading, only the first part of the journey to the shore has been accomplished.

Speaking generally, the quay here runs east and west, but at its western termination the creek turns straight out to sea in a northerly direction. By its side is a high earthen rampart, forming a very pleasant promenade, and furnished with seats. On the one hand a view is obtained eastwards in the direction of Blakeney, and on the other are seen low-lying pasture lands intersected by broad water channels, bounded on the seaward side by a long line of dark green firs and pines.

A lifeboat house stands at the junction of land and sea, and refreshment rooms are provided in a sheltered nook. Otherwise one looks back to the distant town of Wells-next-the-Sea, and lazily makes conjectures about the length of the promenade, the distance the crew would be compelled to travel should their services be required to man the lifeboat, and the genius who first gave the more or less appropriate title of Wells-next-the-Sea to this quaint little Norfolk seaport town.

The two-road wooden engine shed at Dereham *circa* 1914. A 'T26' class 2-4-0 is standing on the north-to-west curve. Some of Dereham's extensive agricultural factories can be seen in the background, and Dereham Central signal box is at left. *National Railway Museum*

Dereham West Junction, looking west, with London Road level crossing in the distance. The structure visible on the extreme right was a granary and the sidings seen to the left were part of the engine shed. *National Railway Museum*

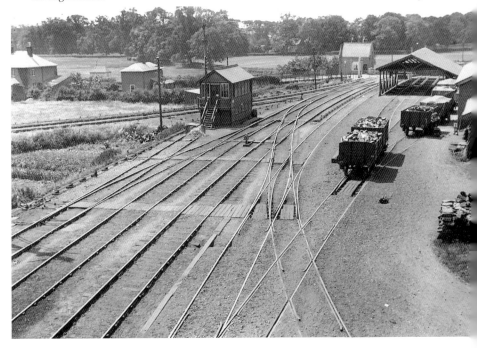

Other writers echoed these thoughts, the general impression being that Wells was a quaint old seaport with few formal attractions. This was not necessarily a condemnation, and if Wells did not attract conventional Edwardian holidaymakers it had already gained favour with lovers of the quiet and the picturesque; in the longer term Wells did have a future as a holiday resort, and it had clearly been 'discovered' by the end of the 19th century. In the meantime, the GER had done very little to encourage an influx of tourists, and the Wells branch in 1900 was not very different from the Wells branch of 1857.

The somnolent pace of local life was rudely shattered on 26th August, 1912, when (not for the last time) Norfolk was paralysed by severe flooding. On that memorable day, 6 inches of rainfall fell in a period of 12 hours and the normally-tranquil River Stiffkey was transformed into a raging torrent which washed away part of the embankment at East Barsham and destroyed bridge No. 1724 at nearby North Barsham. A freight train had been crossing the bridge when it collapsed, but fortunately the bulk of the train reached safety before the failure occurred.

Meanwhile, the Norwich to Ipswich main line had been obstructed at Flordon, and in the next few days Norwich to London trains were diverted via the Forncett route - which played an important role in emergencies such as this. The Wymondham to Forncett line was itself closed for a few hours, but it was soon re-opened for the diverted main line trains, which were able to run through to Norwich via Wymondham from Wednesday 28th August. This situation pertained until 2nd October, 1912, when the main line was finally re-opened throughout between Forncett and Norwich.

Writing in the 1929 *Railway Magazine*, J.F. Gairns recalled that during the great floods of 1912 trains to and from London and Ipswich had used the Wymondham to Forncett line, reversing at Wymondham in order to continue their journeys to Norwich. The writer even remembered 'being conveyed this way by the Norfolk Coast Express, which was thus reversed at Wymondham in order to make its otherwise non-stop journey between Liverpool Street and North Walsham'.

World War I

On 4th August, 1914 the Imperial German army marched into Belgium, and at midnight Britain declared war; the ensuing conflict cost 1,114,789 British lives and brought to an end the halcyon Edwardian era in which railways had played a central role in society and the economy.

In common with other East Anglian lines, the Wymondham to Wells route was intimately connected with the Great War by reason of its geographic position on the eastern side of England. It was thought at one stage that the Germans might mount a sudden attack upon the flat beaches and open spaces of East Anglia, and to counteract this perceived threat, Norfolk was heavily-garrisoned throughout the 1914-18 war, not only by soldiers, but also by naval airmen of the Royal Naval Air Service, who were entrusted with the task of protecting the British homeland against enemy air attack.

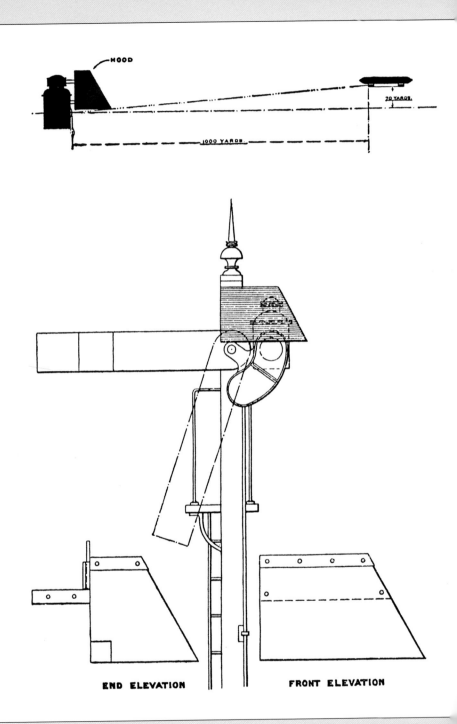

This is how GER signal lamps along the east coast were screened against Zeppelin raids during World War I. Inset: The angle of visibility of a shielded signal lamp relative to the Zeppelins.

There were fears of a German naval attack, and indeed on 25th April, 1916 an enemy squadron ineffectively shelled Lowestoft. In the event, the main threat to East Anglia came, not from the sea but from the air, and from 1915 until 1918 enemy Zeppelins flew across Norfolk more or less at will. The first raid occurred on 19th January, 1915 when the airship L4 dropped bombs near Hunstanton and on Kings Lynn.

Thereafter, the nightly raids took place with considerable frequency and, despite improved ground defences and a nightly 'blackout', Dereham was bombed by a Zeppelin raider in 1915. In a later raid, on the night of 19th October, 1917, a small force of Zeppelins flew southwards over Wells-next-the-Sea and Holt before parting company in the vicinity of Dereham. One airship then circled above Wymondham, dropping its bombs in the immediate vicinity, while another appeared to fly back and forth between Thetford and Bury St Edmunds, and in the course of these wanderings it dropped another bomb near Thetford.

It remains a matter of conjecture why the German airship commanders should have expended their lethal cargoes in such a wasteful fashion, but the most plausible explanation is that they were simply lost! Lacking navigational aids for accurate night operations, the Zeppelins were forced to rely on dead reckoning, chart reading and other traditional methods. The railway system was itself a superb navigational feature, especially on moonlit nights, and many of the raiders obviously attempted to follow convenient railway lines in the course of their nocturnal attacks.

The British defenders soon realised that the Germans were relying on visual navigation, and a strict blackout was quickly imposed as a means of further confusing the Zeppelin crews. It was also realized that railway signal lamps could be of immense use to the enemy, and to eliminate this source of assistance, the GER fitted hooded shields to signal lamps in the threatened areas. As British air defence measures became more sophisticated, the Zeppelins were forced to fly at hitherto unknown altitudes of 20,000 ft or more.

The Great Eastern Railway was, from 1915 onwards, called upon to play an important role on the anti-Zeppelin campaign. Railwaymen were expected to keep a sharp lookout for nightly raiders and when a 'Zepp' was spotted its position was immediately telegraphed to London, where the GER had established a civilian-manned 'Military Office' to deal with wartime traffic and all other matters requiring liaison with the military authorities. In order to ascertain the progress of Zeppelin raids, the railway company devised a method of plotting airship positions with coloured pins carrying time-labels.

In the days before effective road transport, railways were expected to play a vital role in the British defensive system - and in the event of an invasion lines such as the Wells branch would have been used to transport men, horses and equipment to threatened coastal areas. A concomitant of this vital defensive function was the appearance of rail-mounted guns and mobile armoured trains - one of the latter being stationed in north Norfolk. Built by the London & North Western Railway at Crewe this curious assembly consisted of a Great Northern 0-6-2T marshalled between two bogie infantry wagons and two gun-carrying vehicles.

The whole train was encased in steel plate, and it could be driven either from the locomotive or from push-pull type control positions at each end of the gun

NORWICH, DEREHAM AND WELLS.

Single Line between Dereham and Wells.

DOWN WEEK DAYS.

Miles from Norwich	See page		1 Engs.	2 Engs.	3	4 Eng.	5 Pass.	6 Gds.	7 Pass.	8 Gds.	9 Pass.	10 Eng.	11 Pass.	12 Pass.	13 Pass.	14 Gds.	15 Gds.	16 Gds.	17 Gds.	18 Pass.	19 Pass.	20 Pass.	21 Gds.	22 Gds.	23 Pass.	24 Pass.	25 Cars.	26	27	28 Pass.
—	Forncett	dep.											10 33												2 25				
—	Yarmouth	"							7 27																3 8				
1 0	Trowse	arr./dep.						4 30/4 35	6 37/6 37	8 6/8 11				10 48						1 0					3 17				
6 16	Hethersett	"							6 52	8 28				10 56						1 15					3 32				
10 18	Wymondham	arr./dep.						5 15/5 29	7 8/8 8	8 34/8 37				10 59			11 25	11 35		1 25					3 40/3 44				
13 77	Kimberley	"							7 10	8 44				11 6						1 32					3 51				
15 60	Hardingham	"							7 14	8 49				11 10						1 38					3 55				
17 10	Thuxton	"							7 20	8 53				11 15						1 41					3 58				
19 59	Yaxham	"							7 31	8 59				11 21						1 47					4 0				
21 51	Dereham	arr./dep.	4 30			5 47/7 7	7 30/7 37	9 4/9 20				9 35/9 39	11 35/11 52	12 16/12 18				1 52/2	1 56	2 3			4 11/4 20					4 42
26 14	North Elmham	arr./dep. (See note)		4 29		5 56/6 0	7 10/7 11		7 44/7 45	9 27/9 28		9 57/9 58	12 1/12 3	12 23/12 24						3 24/3 25			4 25/4 26			1 34			4 49/4 50
27 57	County School	arr./dep.	4 32			6 4/6 12	7 15/7 18		7 49/7 50	9 32/9 33		10 1/10 10	12 8/12 11	12 30/12 32					2 10/2 17	2 17	2 28/2 30			4 31/4 38		4 40			4 54
31 21	Ryburgh	"				6 16	7 67		7 67	9 40		11 55						2 22					4 43					
33 62	Fakenham	arr./dep. (See note)	4 43			6 26/6 30	7 28/7 30		8 6/8 14	9 45/9 47		10 20/10 23	12 0/12 2						2 24/2 34		2 34			4 44/4 54					
38 58	Walsingham	arr./dep. (See note)	4 55			6 38			10 0/10 7	9 51		12 7							2 35/2 45	2 35	2 45			4 55					
43 21	Wells	arr./dep.	5 3			6 30			11 0/11 15	10 0		12 13/12 23							2 45					5 3					
—	See page		134			134	134		107	134		134	134			107	107	134	134	134	134		107					134

6 To shunt at Dereham for 7, and at Fakenham for 8 and 9. Calls at Kimberley, Hardingham and Yaxham, to detach only and attach traffic for stations beyond Dereham, and to leave brake fish at those stations when required.

14 Calls at Kimberley, Hardingham and Yaxham to attach traffic for King's Lynn and Aylsham line stations and leave empty B.W.'s.

15 To call at Kimberley, Hardingham and Yaxham when required to leave brake goods and attach traffic for King's Lynn and stations beyond Dereham, and at Hardingham and Yaxham to detach empty B.W.'s.

16 Due to arr. Kimberley 12.50 and Thuxton 1.47. To shunt at Hardingham for 18.

17 To call at North Elmham, when required for brake goods for East Norfolk line only.

17 & 22 To call at North Elmham, when required, for brake goods for East Norfolk line only.

Nth. Elmham.—A passer train must not be arranged to cross another passer train at this station.

Walsingham.—Trains must not be arranged to cross at this station. No down goods or ballast train is to exceed 20 loaded trucks and the brake on leaving Walsingham for Wells.

Working timetable, down trains, for January 1917.

NORWICH, DEREHAM AND WELLS.

Single Line between Dereham and Wells.

DOWN WEEK DAYS.

Station		31 Gds.	32 Pass. (SO / NS)	33 Eng. NS	35 Pass. 128	36 Pass.	38 Pass.	40 Pass.
See page					128	128		
		p.m.	p.m. p.m.	p.m.	p.m.	p.m.	p.m.	p.m.
Forncett	dep							
Yarmouth					5 47	5 3		
Norwich (Thorpe)	arr					6 5		9 0
Norwich (Thorpe)	dep		5 20		6 20			9 0
Trowse	dep				6 28			9 13
Hethersett	dep				6 30			9 21
Wymondham	arr	5 38	5 40 / 5 40		6 37			9 27
Wymondham	dep	*			6 41			9 34
Kimberley	dep	*	5 47 / 5 51		6 42			9 38
Hardingham	dep	*	5 52 / 5 56		6 46			9 39
Thuxton	dep	*	6 2		6 52			9 43
Yaxham	dep	*	6 7 / 6 10	6 10	6 57			9 49
Dereham	arr		6 9		7 2			9 54
Dereham	dep	7 24	6 16 / 6 17		7 9		8 24	9 58
North Elmham (see note)	arr	7 42	6 21		7 10		8 31	10 5
North Elmham	dep	7 49	6 22		7 14		8 32	10 6
County School	arr	7 57	6 29		7 15		8 36	10 10
County School	dep				7 22		8 38	10 11
Ryburgh	dep	8 15	6 34		7 27			10 18
Fakenham	arr	8 25	6 35		7 28			10 23
Fakenham	dep	8 35	6 45		7 38			10 24
Walsingham (see note)	arr	9 25	6 46		7 39			10 34
Walsingham	dep	9 35	6 56		7 49			10 35
Wells	arr	9 55	7 18					10 45
To		King's Lynn	King's Lynn	(For 7.25 p.m. up goods.)			Norwich	
See page		619					134	

(Columns 29, 30, 34, 37, 39, 41–51 carry no times.)

SUNDAYS.

Station		1 Eng. (For 4.45 p.m. ex Wells)	3 Pass. 129	4 Pass.
		p.m.	p.m.	p.m.
Forncett	dep		6 0	
Yarmouth	dep		6 52	7 0
Norwich (Thorpe)	arr			7 0
Norwich (Thorpe)	dep			7 16
Trowse	dep			7 25
Hethersett	dep			7 28
Wymondham	arr			7 36
Wymondham	dep			7 40
Kimberley	dep			7 41
Hardingham	dep			7 45
Thuxton	dep			7 52
Yaxham	dep			7 57
Dereham	arr			8 0
Dereham	dep	3 30		8 9
North Elmham		3 39		8 9
County School	arr	3 43		8 13
County School	dep			8 14
Ryburgh	dep			8 21
Fakenham	arr	3 55		8 26
Fakenham	dep			8 27
Walsingham	arr	4 15		8 37
Walsingham	dep			8 38
Wells	arr			8 52

34 To call at Kimberley, Hardingham, Thuxton and Yaxham, if required, to detach only, and at County School to leave or take in brake goods. To shunt at Dereham for 36, and on Saturdays where required for 32.

— **36** May work from Norwich not exceeding 4 trucks of cattle for West Norfolk line stations, if the trucks are fitted with Westinghouse brake pipes.

— **40** May work cattle from Wymondham for Dereham or Fakenham, if the trucks are fitted with W'house brake pipes, but trucks for both stations must not be attached at one time.

North Elmham.—A pass. train must not be arranged to cross another train at this station. No down goods or ballast train is to exceed 20 loaded trucks and the brake on leaving Walsingham for Wells. Down road traffic for Coleman's Sdg. to be detached at Walsingham, & worked back 1.40 & 3.30 p.m. ex Wells.

Walsingham.—Trains must not be arranged to cross at this station.

Working timetable, down trains, for January 1917.

WELLS, DEREHAM AND NORWICH.

Single Line between Wells and Dereham.

Walsingham.—Trains must not be arranged to cross at this station.

North Kimham.—A passenger train must not be arranged to cross another passenger train at this station.

UP WEEK DAYS.

From	1	2	3	4	5	6	7	8	9	10	11	12	13	14	15	16	17	18	19	20	21	22	23	24	25	26
	Pass.	Eng.			Gds. ex King's Lynn 5.15 a.m.	Pass. ex Norwich 7.0 a.m.	Pass.	Pass.	Pass. ex Norwich 9.30 a.m.	Pass. ex King's Lynn 10.18 a.m.	Pass.	Gds. ex Norwich 5.50 a.m.	Gds. ex Norwich 5.50 a.m.	Gds. ex Norwich 5.50 a.m.	Eng.	Pass. ex Norwich 11.50 a.m.	Gds.	Pass.	Pass. ex Norwich 2.22 p.m.	Exp. Cattle Gds. Class B.	Pass.	Eng. 12.30 p.m. ex Dereham.	Eng. For 7.0 Dereham to Norwich.			Gds.
See page					106	134			134	106		134 N8	134	134		134			134	80		80	80			N8
Wells .... dep.	5 55																									
Walsingham (see note) arr.	6 4																									
Walsingham (see note) dep.	6 5																									
Fakenham ...... arr.	6 14																									
Fakenham ...... dep.	6 15																									
Ryburgh						8 20																				
County School arr.						8 26			10 48																	
County School dep.	6 27					8 27			10 50										3 37							
North Elmham arr.	6 31					8 30			10 54										3 41							
North Elmham (see note) dep.	6 32					8 31			10 55										3 42							
Dereham .... arr.	6 40					8 36			11 3										3 50							
Dereham .... dep.	6 42	7 0			6 50	10 0				11 11					12 30											
Yaxham	6 47				7 40	10 27								10 45												
Thurton	6 53					10 33								10 51												
Hardingham	6 57				8 5	10 37								10 54												
Kimberley	7 5				8 25	10 42								10 55												
Wymondham ... arr.	7 10	7 30				10 48								12 55												
Wymondham ... dep.	7 19	7 8			8 40	10 51			11 28					13 17												
Hethersett						11 0																				
Trowse .... arr.					9 5																					
Trowse .... dep.	7 31				9 15																					
Norwich (Thorpe) arr.					9 30	11 15			11 28	11 44							2 18									
Yarmouth																			2 30							
Forncett																										

Notes:

5 Calls at Yaxham to detach traffic or attach cattle for Trowse.

— 7 On Wednesdays may work 1 truck cattle (2 on Fridays and Sats.) from Fakenham to Norwich, if truck is fitted with Westinghouse brake pipes. The Yarmouth and Axle traffic to go forward from Norwich by goods train.

— 10 Runs via Dereham South Curve.

15 On Sats. to perform yard shunting at Wymondham, leaving there for Norwich 4.46 p.m.

17 To shunt at Fakenham for 18. Calls at Yaxham and Hardingham if required to detach or attach cattle and traffic for stations on E.U. Line or W.V. branch. On Sats. calls at Kimberley if required to attach traffic for stations on E.U. Line and W.V. Branch.

12 and 13 To shunt at County School for 14.

12 and 13 To shunt at County School for 14, leaving there for Norwich 4.46 p.m.

20 To call at Coleman's Siding (between Walsingham and Fakenham) when required. To shunt at Walsingham for 21. London cattle worked by this train between Wells and Dereham to be brought into Dereham next engine. To call at County School when required to leave brake goods.

— 21 Will not convey horses and private carriages for stations between Wymondham and London.

23 To run to Dereham attached to 19.

26 To shunt at Wymondham for 34, and on Thursdays where required for 27.

Working timetable, up trains, for January 1917.

WELLS, DEREHAM AND NORWICH.

Single Line between Wells and Dereham.

UP WEEK DAYS.

From		27 Pass. Th.O a.m.	28 Pass. 4.20 p.m. ex Norwich 134 p.m.	29	30	31 Gds. .80 p.m.	32 Gds. NTh.S p.m.	33 Gds. Th.O p.m.	34 Pass. 3.35 p.m. ex Peterboro' 106 p.m.	35 Pass.	36 Gds. TO p.m.	37 Gds. p.m.	38	39 Gds. NS p.m.	40 Pass. 7.0 p.m. ex Norwich 106 a.m.	41 Pass. ex Peterboro'	42 Eng. E. of 6.15 pm ex Heacham & 6.65 p.m. ex Norwich p.m.	43 Pass. 8.28 p.m. ex Norwich 134 p.m.	44	45	46 E. of 5.5 p.m. ex Wymondham and 9.0 ex Norwich p.m.	47	48	49	50 Pass. p.m.	51	52 Eng. Eng. of 7.0 p.m. ex Norwich p.m.	53	54
Wells .... dep.							3 30	3 25							8 35						11 10				4 45		9 10		
Walsingham (see note) {arr. dep.			5 5				3 43 3 51	3 40 3 48							8 44 8 45		8 45				11 30 11 33				4 54 4 56		9 20		
Fakenham .... {arr. dep.		5 0					3 51 4 55	4 23 4 33		6 6					8 54 8 55		8 56 9 7				11 33				5 4 5 6		9 35		
Ryburgh ...... {dep.		5 3	5 35					5 25		6 13					9 0			9 42							5 16				
County School {arr. dep.		5 11 5 12	5 30					5 45		6 19 6 21					9 6 9 7		9 24	9 43			11 42				5 22 5 25		9 42		
North Elmham (see note) {arr. dep.		5 16 5 17	5 40 5 41					5 50 5 55		6 25 6 30					9 11 9 12			9 47 9 48			11 46 11 51				5 29 5 34		9 46		
Dereham .... {arr. dep.		5 25 5 26	5 49				6 20 7 55	6 30 7 30	6 35 6 43	6 38	7 15			7 25	9 20	9 34 9 39		9 50			11 55				5 42 5 46		9 55		
Thuxton .... {arr. dep.							7 47		6 49				**			9 48									5 53 5 59				
Hardingham						7 30 7 32	8 0 8 10						**												6 3				
Kimberley							8 14 8 33		7 0		7 55					9 59									6 5				
Wymondham .... {arr. dep.		5 43 5 44				8 38 9 15	8 40 9 15		7 9 7 15		8 10		8 0 10 5			10 1									6 11 6 17				
Hethersett							9 27		7 27		9 05														6 33				
Trowse .... {arr. dep.						10 30 10 40	9 40 9 55		7 36				10 30 10 45																
Norwich (Thorpe) {arr. dep.		6 0				11 5	10 0		7 43 8 32		9 05		11 5			10 17									6 47				
Yarmouth																													
Forncett																													

SUNDAYS. (columns 49–54)

34 Class B. To shunt at Wymondham for 41. Runs into and out of Crown Point sidings.

32 To call at Coleman's siding (between Walsingham and Fakenham) when required and shunt at Dereham for 35.

33 To call at Coleman's siding (between Walsingham and Fakenham) when required and shunt at Dereham for 35. To call at County School when required for brake goods.

=34. On Saturdays to cross at County School 34 down, leaving there 6.23 p.m. and run 2 minutes later to Norwich. Due to arrive Yaxham 6.47, Thuxton 6.54, and Kimberley 7.7 p.m.

39 To work from Dereham important M.C. traffic and tramships, also Trowse cattle off 3.30 p.m. ex Wells. To call at Hardingham, if required, for London and N.C. traffic, meat and market goods, that station to advise Dereham what they have to go on. Dereham to arrange and advise guard and driver. To shunt at Wymondham for 32, 33 & 41. Engine to perform shunting at Wymondham.

42 To run into and out of Crown Point siding.

42 To run from County School to Dereham attached to 42.

= 50 Due to run past Ryburgh 5.13, Yaxham 5.50, and Kimberley 6.9 p.m.

North Elmham.—A passenger train must not be arranged to cross another passenger train at this station.

Walsingham.—Trains must not be arranged to cross at this station.

Working timetable, up trains, for January 1917.

wagons; for offensive armament the train was equipped with naval-type 12 pounders and rapid-firing maxim machine guns. Based on the M&GN at North Walsham, the armoured train could be rushed to any threatened part of the coast, and it was frequently seen on patrol on coastal lines such as the West Norfolk branch.

In general, the war resulted in a gradual reduction in services, but the Wells branch retained a relatively 'full' train service throughout the war. In 1917, for example, there seven trains each way, with up services from Wells at 5.55, 9.25, 10.48 am, 12.50, 3.17, 5.43 and 8.35 pm. In the opposite direction, down workings left Norwich at 6.37, 8.11, 10.33 am, 1.00, 3.17, 6.05 and 9.00 pm. Some of these services were self-contained workings between Norwich and Wells, while other were apparently combined workings that conveyed portions for both Wells and Kings Lynn between Norwich and Dereham.

As mentioned earlier, Wroxham to County School branch trains began working to and from Dereham during World War I. At the eastern end of the route, the train service was similarly extended to Norwich, and the line thereby formed a circuitous alternative route for people travelling between Norwich, Dereham and Wells. The January 1917 GER working timetable shows six up and six down services between Dereham and Norwich, with up trains from Dereham at 7.03, 9.50 am, 12.16, 2.17, 4.42 and 8.24 pm. The return workings left Norwich at 7.00, 9.30, 11.50 am, 2.22, 4.20 and 8.28 pm.

Local railways remained in a state of readiness until the early months of 1918, but as the war approached its end the anti-invasion precautions were scaled-down; by August, it was clear that Germany was on the point of defeat. The Zeppelin raids nevertheless continued almost to the bitter end, and on 5th August, 1918 the 'monster' airship L70 appeared over north Norfolk. On this occasion the Germans were unlucky and a British aeroplane managed to destroy the raider; mortally wounded, L70 fell into the sea off Wells, and in the next few days hundreds of people thronged local beaches hoping to see the wreck.

The destruction of Zeppelin L70 was, for local people, a fitting conclusion to the Great War, which ended with an Armistice in the following November.

The last days of the GER

The bitter struggle against Imperial Germany had left all railways in a run-down condition, and recovery was not helped by a coal strike in 1920/21. In spite of these problems, the Wells branch was still served by seven trains each way. The January 1921 timetable provided four morning and three afternoon workings between Wells and Norwich, balanced by three morning and four afternoon services in the opposite direction. Additional short distance workings ran between Wells and Dereham on Saturdays only, while the cross-country service between Norwich and Kings Lynn provided many extra workings on the southern part of the branch.

The post-war freight service was similar to that in operation before 1914, with minor variations in arrival and departure times. The West Norfolk branch was still served by four trains each way, with good connections for London available at Heacham; most West Norfolk services still terminated at Heacham, but one or two workings continued through to Hunstanton after reversal. (In 1921 the 10.12 am and 12.55 pm departures from Wells both worked through, but in later years only the later train served Hunstanton directly.)

Locomotives seen at Wells in the early 1920s were mainly 'T26' or 'Intermediate' 2-4-0s, which had replaced the long-serving 'No. 1 Class' engines just before World War I. The 'T26s' were superficially similar to the rebuilt 'No. 1 Class' - but of considerably greater dimensions. Goods services were often worked by Worsdell 'Y14' class 0-6-0s - the standard GER mixed traffic type. Larger engines were rarely used, and most Norwich to Wells and West Norfolk branch services were handled by these two familiar Great Eastern locomotive classes. All passenger trains were, in 1921, still formed of archaic short-wheelbase stock.

Deferred maintenance and lack of regular cleaning had an adverse effect on the once-smart GER trains during the 1914-18 conflict. Some engines retained their famous blue liveries throughout the war, but, as an economy measure, the Great Eastern started to paint its locomotive fleet in an austere grey livery that needed less cleaning and polishing than the flamboyant colour schemes of earlier years. In practice, pre-Grouping locomotives were normally given several coats of nondescript grey paint known as 'lead colour' before their distinguishing liveries were applied, and it seems that the wartime GER grey livery was basically this grey undercoat, without the normal topcoats and varnish.

A note on tickets

Before leaving the Great Eastern period, it would be fitting to make at least some mention of that company's fascinating multi-coloured ticket system. Briefly, tickets issued at Wells and other GER stations were coloured in accordance with a directional colour code. In the up direction, the relevant colours were yellow, blue and buff for first, second and third class bookings respectively; the corresponding 'down' colours were white, red and green.

Tickets for through bookings to St Pancras, for example, would have been coloured buff, with a broad blue stripe. In later years, this system was simplified; GER second class tickets were abolished (outside the London area) in 1893, and directional colours were abandoned in 1914 - thereafter, first and third class tickets became plain white and plain buff respectively.

In 1923 the independent life of the Great Eastern Railway came to an end, for the Government had decided (as an alternative to nationalization) that the main line railway companies would be grouped into four main regional organizations; the necessary Act of Parliament was passed in 1921 and a few months later the Wymondham to Wells branch became part of the London & North Eastern Railway.

NORWICH, WYMONDHAM, DEREHAM, FAKENHAM AND WELLS.

WEEK-DAYS.   **SUNDAYS.**

(Down direction)

Stations:

- LONDON (Liverpool St.) dep
- Cambridge
- Ely
- Wymondham — arr
- LONDON (Liverpool B.) dep
- Ipswich
- Forncett
- Wymondham — arr
- NORWICH (Thorpe) — dep
- Trowse
- Hethersett
- Wymondham
- Kimberley
- Hardingham
- Thurton
- Yaxham
- Dereham
- North Elmham
- County School
- Ryburgh
- Fakenham
- Fakenham
- WELLS — arr

WEEK-DAYS.   **SUNDAYS.**

(Up direction)

Stations:

- WELLS — dep
- Walsingham
- Fakenham
- Ryburgh
- County School
- North Elmham
- Dereham
- Yaxham
- Thurton
- Hardingham
- Kimberley
- Wymondham
- Hethersett
- Trowse
- NORWICH (Thorpe) — arr
- Forncett
- Ipswich
- LONDON (Liverpool St.)
- Wymondham — dep
- Ely
- Cambridge
- LONDON (Liverpool St.)

Thursdays only.

Notes:

A Via Norwich.

B Calls at Thurton 10.1 p.m. when required to set down passengers only.

D Arrives Fakenham 7.15 a.m.

E Arrives Fakenham or Kimberley 8.5 a.m. when required to set down passengers only.

MO Mondays only.
NM Not Mondays.
NS Not Saturdays.
SO Saturdays only.
TO Tuesdays only.
X Via Trowse.

For service between Dereham and King's Lynn, see page 56.

For service between County School and Wroxham, see page 63.

Passenger timetable for 3rd October, 1921.

Chapter Four

The LNER Period
(1923-1947)

The London & North Eastern Railway (LNER) was the poorest of the 'Big Four' main line companies created at the Grouping, and although in 1908 the Great Eastern, Great Central and Great Northern companies had contemplated a voluntary merger, many East Anglians felt a pang of regret when the once-proud Great Eastern Railway became part of such a ramshackle amalgamation.

The LNER lavished money on new locomotives and rolling stock for its prestigious East Coast Main Line, but the branch lines of East Anglia did not benefit from this new investment, and much of the former Great Eastern system was obliged to struggle on with elderly Victorian equipment that should, perhaps, have been renewed before World War I. This was particularly unfortunate as far as the Wells-next-the-Sea branch was concerned, for this remote and very rural route had been starved of investment even in the Great Eastern period.

Locomotives and rolling stock in the LNER period

For administrative purposes, the Great Eastern, Great Northern and Great Central systems became the LNER Southern area, and this geographically distinct area was placed under its own General Manager. Otherwise, the former Great Eastern system was more or less undisturbed by the Grouping, and ordinary travellers would probably have been blissfully unaware that a significant change of ownership had in fact taken place! The one obvious change put into effect in the months following the 1923 Grouping concerned the liveries of locomotives and rolling stock.

In Edwardian days the Wells branch trains, with their blue locomotives and smart teak coaches, had made an attractive sight in the rolling landscape of north Norfolk; after 1923 they were, arguably, slightly less pleasing to the eye. Coaches had been painted crimson red during the last years of Great Eastern ownership, but this livery was replaced in the LNER period by a drab overall brown mixture that was sometimes called 'teak brown'. However, it was extremely difficult to remove the red paint from former GER coaches, and the 'teak' was in most cases, brown paint; true varnished teak (either real or 'scrumbled') was confined to new or main line vehicles.

The coaches used on local services during the 1920s were exclusively six-wheelers, but bogie vehicles appeared once a week in the form of a Tuesdays-only through portion from Liverpool Street. Bogie coaches were used in greater numbers during the 1930s, though older short-wheelbase stock was still used on school services and for strengthening purposes. Another innovation, at this time, was the introduction of an LNER steam railcar on certain off-peak services - there was for example, a Thursdays-only market day trip from Dereham to Fakenham.

An unusual view of Wells shed on 29th June, 1936. 'E4' class 2-4-0 No. 7472 stands on the short loco siding, while to the left, the goods siding passes through the engine shed to reach the goods shed at the rear.   *H.C. Casserley*

'F3' class 2-4-2T No. 8088 at Norwich shed in 1933. This locomotive was withdrawn in November 1947, shortly before the nationalization of Britain's railways.   *Real Photographs*

One small, but important, change carried out under LNER auspices concerned the numbering system for locomotives and rolling stock. In the case of locomotives, the former Great Eastern classes were renumbered in the 7XXX or 8XXX series, the GER numbers being increased by 7,000+. The Great Eastern wagon fleet was renumbered in the 600,000+ series, while all GER passenger vehicles were initially given an 'E' prefix. In 1925, the 'E' was replaced by a 6 which denoted all stock from the GER operating section.

The LNER also introduced a new alpha-numeric engine identification system based upon locomotive wheel arrangements. This new classification system was both logical and simple, in that large Pacifics were given an 'A' prefix, 4-6-0s received a 'B' prefix, 4-4-2s received a 'C' prefix, 4-4-0s received a 'D' prefix, and so on. As there was usually more than one engine type with a particular wheel arrangement, these basic notations were further sub-divided by the addition of numerals denoting each class.

Locomotives seen on the Wymondham to Wells branch in the 1920s and 1930s included Holden's famous 'Intermediate', or 'T26' class 2-4-0s, which became class 'E4' under the LNER classification scheme. These engines had first been introduced in 1891 for mixed traffic duties, and a hundred examples were built at Stratford works between 1891 and 1902. The 'T26' class engines had 5 ft 8 in. coupled wheels, and 17½ inch by 24 inch inside cylinders. The 'E4' class worked both Norwich to Wells and Wells to Heacham services, becoming, in many ways, the 'classic' Wells branch locomotive type. Some examples recorded on the line during the LNER period included Nos. 7415, 7422, 7457, 7472, 7486 and 7492.

Another class seen in the LNER period were the familiar Worsdell 0-6-0 mixed traffic engines, which became the LNER 'J15' class; they worked both passenger and goods services on the Wells line. Although these engines had been introduced by T.W. Worsdell as far back as 1883, they remained in production until 1913, no less than 289 being constructed for goods and mixed traffic work. Other ex-Great Eastern six-coupled locomotives, including 'J17' and (to a lesser extent) 'J19' class 0-6-0s appeared in increasing numbers throughout the 1930s.

'Claud Hamilton' 4-4-0s appeared sporadically in the years before World War II, and by the later 1930s it was possible to see 'D15s', 'D16/2s' and 'D16/3s' at work on the branch. Another class of ex-GER 4-4-0s used in the 1930s were the 'T19' rebuilds, which became 'D13s' under the LNER classification system. These were probably the first 'large' locomotives seen at Wells, and their appearance caused considerable excitement for youthful 'spotters'! Some examples recorded on the Dereham and Wells route during the LNER era included Nos. 7707 and 8030.

Tank engines, in the form of Holden 'F3' class 2-4-2Ts, had started to appear on the Norwich to Wells route towards the end of World War I. Originally designed for main line stopping services, these locomotives were mechanically-similar to the 'E4' class 2-4-0s, with 5 ft 8 in. coupled wheels and 17½ inch by 24 inch cylinders. They often hauled the remaining through services from London which, in LNER days, ran on Tuesdays only via Forncett and Wymondham.

Former Great Northern Railway 4-4-0s were introduced into the area towards the end of the 1930s. These 'foreigners' undoubtedly added an element of

Two views of ex-North Eastern Railway 'J21' class 0-6-0 No. 300 at Dereham on 29th June, 1936. Six 'J21s' were sent to Norwich shed in 1935 to balance six 'E4' class 2-4-0s that had been sent to Darlington. The 'E4s' successfully worked passenger duties over the Pennines previously performed by 'D23' 4-4-0s from Darlington to Penrith and Tebay via the Stainmore route. Although the 'J21s' had much in common with the ex-GER 'J15' class, both having been designed by T.W. Worsdell, they were not popular with Norwich crews and only stayed in Norfolk for around 18 months.   *(Both) H.C. Casserley*

variety to an otherwise mainly Great Eastern scene, but the newcomers were said to have been feeble performers and local train crews seem to have preferred their 'own' GER engines, claiming that the Ivatt 4-4-0s were unsuitable for service on heavily-graded lines. The ex-GNR engines were typically employed on light cross-country and branch line services, and it was perhaps unfortunate that this took them onto the Wells-next-the-Sea branch, with its 1 in 77, 1 in 80 and 1 in 81 gradients!

Among the former Great Northern engines transferred to East Anglia were Ivatt 'D1' class 4-4-0s Nos. 3059 and 3060, which were allocated to Norwich and sub-shedded at Dereham as replacements for withdrawn 'D13' 4-4-0s. Other non-Great Eastern locomotives seen in Norfolk during the LNER period were former North Eastern Railway 'J21' class 0-6-0s such as No. 300, which was photographed by H.C. Casserley on 29th June, 1936 while working the 7.16 pm service from Dereham to Norwich via County School.

Passenger services

The train service provided by the LNER was little different to that offered in the Great Eastern era, and there were still only half a dozen workings each way between Norwich Thorpe and Wells. The March 1938 timetable, for instance, showed five up and six down workings, with various additional services on Mondays and Saturdays. In the up direction, southbound workings left Wells at 7.33, 9.07 am, 12.48, 3.16 and 5.54 pm, while down services departed from Norwich Thorpe at 6.20, 8.17, 10.38 am, 1.04, 3.10 and 6.38 pm. An additional up service left Wells at 5.52 am on Mondays only, and a short-distance Monday-only down service ran from Dereham to Wells at 8.40 pm.

The through Forncett service no longer ran from Wells - though it was still possible for through travellers to make use of this 'short cut' to London by changing at Dereham and Forncett. The Dereham to Wymondham portion of the line (which was of course shared by Norwich to Wells and Norwich to Kings Lynn services) was served by about 10 workings each way, including some steam railcar trips.

As in Great Eastern days, Wells was also served by four up and four down services on the West Norfolk branch from Heacham, while the section of line between Dereham and County School was traversed by around half a dozen trains each way on the 'round the world' cross-country route between Dereham, Aylsham, Wroxham and Norwich.

In 1938, up West Norfolk workings departed from Wells at 7.18, 10.08 am, 1.35 and 5.15 pm, while in the down direction the corresponding eastbound branch services left Heacham at 8.15, 11.51 am, 3.23 and 6.16 pm. An additional evening train left Wells at 5.40 pm, and returned from Heacham at 6.41 pm on Saturdays only. There were no Sunday trains, and indeed Sunday services never became an established feature of operations on the West Norfolk line. In general, West Norfolk branch trains worked out and back trips from Wells to Heacham, but there were also one or two through workings to and from Hunstanton which reversed at Heacham in order to complete their journeys.

NORWICH, WYMONDHAM, DEREHAM, KING'S LYNN, and WELLS-ON-SEA.

Miles	Down.	Week Days.																	Sundays.				
		mrn	mrn	mrn	mrn	mrn Z		aft	aft T	aft	aft S	aft S	aft	aft	aft	aft S			aft				
	Norwich (Thorpe) ....dep.	6 20	7 56	8 17	1038	1124	..	1 4	..	3 10	..	3 55	5 30	6 38	7 40	9 15	..	..	7 9	..	..	..	..
1	Trowse..................	6 24	8 0	8 21	1042	..	..	1 8	..	3 14	..	..	5 34	6 42	7 44	..	..	..	..	..	..	..	..
6¼	Hethersett..............	6 34	8 10	Dd	1053	..	..	1 19	..	3 25	..	..	5 45	6 53	7 55	9 26	..	..	7 20	..	..	..	..
10¾	Wymondham 874 ..arr.	6 42	8 18	8 39	11 1	1140	..	1 27	..	3 34	..	4 13	5 53	7 1	8 2	9 33	..	..	7 27	..	..	..	..
—	860London A 874..dep.	..	..	5 0	5 56	8‡15	..	10 3		‡1225	..	1225	2 40	3 40	5 16	5 49	..	..	3 33	..	..	..	..
—	Wymondham ....dep	6 44	8 20	8 41	11 8	1141	..	1 29	..	3 38	..	4 15	5 54	7 3	8 9	9 34	..	..	7 29	..	..	..	..
14	Kimberley Park B........	6 51	8 27	..	1110	..	..	1 36	..	3 46	..	4 22	6 1	7 10	8 16	9 41	..	..	7 36	..	..	..	..
15½	Hardingham	6 56	8 32	8 51	1115	..	..	1 41	..	3 52	..	4 27	6 6	7 15	8 21	9 46	..	..	7 41	..	..	..	..
17¾	Thuxton................	7 0	8 36	..	1119	..	..	1 45	..	3 57	..	4 31	6 10	7 19	8 25	9 50	..	..	7 45	..	..	..	..
19¾	Yaxham.................	7 6	8 42	..	1125	..	..	1 51	..	4 4	..	4 37	6 16	7 25	8 31	9 56	..	.	7 51	..	..	..	..
21¼	Dereham..............arr.	7 11	8 47	9 1	1130	1158	..	1 56	..	4 9	..	4 42	6 21	7 30	8 36	10 1	..	..	7 56	..	..	..	..
—	Dereham...........dep	7 25	..	9 6	1133	12 4	..	2 1	..	4 16	..	4 47	One class only.	7 33	Stop	..	..	..	..	..	..	..	..
25¼	Wendling...............	7 32	..	9 14	1140	..	..	2 8	..	4 24	..	4 54		7 40		..	..	..	..	..	..	..	..
28¼	Fransham	7 37	..	9 20	1145	..	..	2 13	..	4 31	..	5 0		7 45	..	..	..	..	..	..	..	..	..
29¾	Dunham	7 41	..	9 25	1149	..	..	2 17	..	4 37	..	5 4		7 49	..	..	..	..	..	..	..	..	..
33¾	Swaffham 879	7 53	..	9 37	1158	1222	..	2 26	..	4 47	..	5 12		7 58	..	..	..	..	..	..	..	..	..
39¼	Narborough & Pentney..	8 2	..	9 46	12 6	1230	..	2 34	One class only.	4 57	..	5 21		8 6	..	..	..	..	..	..	..	..	..
43	East Winch.[1081,1082	8 9	..	9 53	1213	1236	..	2 41		5 6	..	5 27		8 13	..	..	..	..	..	..	..	..	..
45	Middleton Towers..[882,	8 13	..	9 58	1217	..	..	2 45		5 11	..	5 32	..	8 17	..	..	..	..	..	..	..	..	..
48¼	King's Lynn 881, arr.	8 21	..	10 4	1224	1245	..	2 51		5 20	..	5 38	..	8 24	..	..	..	..	..	..	..	..	..
89¼	881Cambridge......arr.	9 52	H	1144	..	..	..	4 37		6 57	..	6 57	..	12Y51	aft	..	..	..	..	..	..	..	..
145¼	881London (Liv.St.) "	1119	H	2 5	..	..	..	6 10		8 20	..	8 20	..	2Y40	M	..	..	..	..	..	..	..	..
—	Dereham.............dep.	7 17	..	9 9	1134	..	..	2 0	3 2	4E21	435	4 46	..	7 34	8 40	10 5	..	..	8 0	..	..	..	..
26¼	North Elmham...........	7 29	..	9 17	1142	..	..	2 8	3 10	4E29	443	4 54	..	7 42	8 48	1013	..	..	8X13	..	..	..	..
27¾	County School..........	7 34	..	9 22	1147	..	..	2 14	3 15	4E34	447	4 59	..	7 47	8 53	1020	..	..	8 18	..	..	..	..
31½	Ryburgh................	7 42	..	9 29	1154	..	..	2 21	3 22	4E41	..	5 6	..	7 54	9 0	1027	..	..	8 25	..	..	..	..
33¾	Fakenham C 1082.......	7A58	..	9 37	12 1	..	..	2 28	3 27	4E47	..	5 13	..	8 0	9 7	1033	..	..	8 31	..	..	..	..
38¼	Walsingham.............	8 9	..	9 48	1212	..	..	2 39	..	4E58	..	5 25	..	8 11	9 18	1044	..	..	8 45	..	..	..	..
40¼	Wighton Halt*	8 14	..	9 53	1217	..	..	2 44	..	5E3	..	5 30	..	8 16	..	1049	..	..	8 50	..	..	..	..
46½	Wells-on-Sea 878 ....arr.	8 21	..	10 0	1224	..	..	2 51	..	5E10	..	5 37	..	8 23	9 28	1056	..	..	8 57	..	..	..	..

Miles	Up.	Week Days.																	Sundays.				
		mrn	mrn	mrn	mrn	mrn S	mrn S		aft	aft	aft T	aft Z	aft	aft E	aft S	aft		aft	aft				
	Wells-on-Sea ....dep.	5m52	..	7 33	9 7	..	1137		B1248	3 16	..	..	..	5 54	6 8	..	..	..	450	..	..	..	..
2¼	Wighton Halt*	..	..	7 39	9 13	..	1143		B1254	3 22	..	..	..	6 0	6 14	..	..	..	456	..	..	..	..
4¼	Walsingham.............	6m2	..	7 45	9 19	..	1148	..	1B0	3 28	..	..	..	6 7	6 21	..	..	..	5 3	..	..	..	..
9½	Fakenham C 1082	6m12	..	7 55	9T37	..	12 2	..	1B10	3 38	418	..	..	6 20	6 33	..	..	..	514	..	..	..	..
12	Ryburgh................	6m17	..	8 0	9 42	..	12 7	..	1B15	3 43	424	..	..	6 25	6 38	..	..	..	520	..	..	..	..
15½	County School 886......	6m24	..	8 7	9 49	..	1214	..	1B22	3 50	434	..	6 3	6 32	6 45	750	..	..	527	..	..	..	..
17	North Elmham	6m29	..	8 12	9 57	..	1222	..	1 30	3 55	439	..	6 8	6 37	6 50	755	..	..	536	..	..	..	..
21½	Dereham (above).....arr.	6m37	..	8 20	10 5	..	1230	..	1 38	4 8	447	..	6 16	6 45	6 58	8 3	..	..	544	..	..	..	..
—	Miles 881London (L.S.)dep.	..	..	..	..	5 56	..	..	8 30	1155	..	..	..	2 40	2 40		..	5 49	..	..	..	..	..
—	881Cambridge "	..	..	..	..	8P18	..		P1020	1 22	..	1P27	..	4 5	4 15		..	7 15	..	..	..	..	..
—	King's Lynn.....dep.	..	..	7 20	9 4	1030	..	..	1245	3 14	One class only.	4 5	..	5 48	6 3	One class only	..	8 49	..	..	..	..	..
—	3¼ Middleton Towers....	..	..	7 27	9 11	..	..	..	1251	3 20		..	..	5 54	6 9		..	8 56	..	..	..	..	..
—	5¼ East Winch..........	..	..	7 32	9 16	..	..	..	1256	3 25		..	..	5 59	6 14		..	9 1	..	..	..	..	..
—	8¼ Narborough&Pentney	..	..	7 38	9 22	1043	..	..	1 2	3 31		4 18	..	6 5	6 20		..	9 8	..	..	..	..	..
—	14¼ Swaffham 879	..	..	7 52	9 37	1054	..	..	1 13	3 43		4 29	..	6 17	6 32		..	9 21	..	..	..	..	..
—	18½ Dunham.............	..	..	8 0	9 45	11 2	..	..	1 21	3 51		4 37	..	6 25	6 40		..	9 29	..	..	..	..	..
—	19¾ Fransham	..	..	8 4	9 49	..	..	..	1 25	3 55		..	..	6 29	6 44		..	9 33	..	..	..	..	..
—	22¼ Wendling........[886	..	..	8 10	9 55	1110	..	..	1 30	4 0		4 45	..	6 34	6 49		..	9 39	..	..	..	..	..
—	26¼ Dereham (above) arr.	..	..	8 17	10 2	1116	..	..	1 36	4 6		4 51	..	6 40	6 55		..	9 46	..	..	..	..	..
—	Dereham.............dep.	6 41	6 57	8 23	1011	1120	1232	..	1 41	4 13	448	4 55	6F36	6 49	7 2	825	..	9 51	547	..	..	..	..
23½	Yaxham.................	6 46	..	8 28	1016	1125	1237	..	1 46	4 18	..	..	..	6 54	7 7	830	..	9R56	552	..	..	..	..
26	Thuxton................	6 52	..	8 34	1022	1131	1243	..	1 52	4 24	..	..	6F45	7 1	7 13	836	..	..	559	..	..	..	..
27½	Hardingham	6 56	7 7	8 38	1026	1135	1247	..	1 56	4 28	..	..	6F49	7 5	7 17	840	..	..	6 3	..	..	..	..
29¼	Kimberley Park B [874	7 1	..	8 43	1031	1140	1252	..	2 1	4 33	..	..	6F54	7 11	7 23	845	..	..	610	..	..	..	..
33	Wymondham 862..arr.	7 7	7 16	8 49	1041	1146	1258	..	2 7	4 39	5 6	5 11	7F2	7 17	7 29	851	..	1010	617	..	..	..	..
147	862London (L.St) 874arr	10n23	1023	1235	2V14	..	4‡57	..	5 19	8 20	820	8 20	11F38	11N24	11N24	..	..	2 40	941	..	..	..	..
—	Wymondham........dep.	7 9	8F9	8 52	1044	1147	1259	..	2 10	4 42	5 7	5 12	..	7 20	7 31	852	..	1012	619	..	..	..	..
37	Hethersett.............	7 20	8F18	9 1	1053	..	1 8	..	2 19	4 51	..	..	..	7 29	7 40	9 1	..	..	628	..	..	..	..
42¼	Trowse...............[884	7 29	8F26	9 9	11 1	..	1 16	..	2 27	4 59	..	..	..	7 37	7 48	9 9	..	1025	..	..	..	..	..
43¾	Norwich (Thorpe) 882 arr	7 33	8F30	9 13	11 5	12 8	1 20	..	2 31	5 3	525	5 28	..	7 41	7 52	913	..	1029	638	..	..	..	..

A Liverpool Street.
A Arrives at 7 47 mrn.
B Station for Hingham (3 miles).
B 5 mins. later on Sats.
C Over ¾ mile to Mid. & G. N. Joint Station.
Dd Stops at 8 32 mrn. when required to take up for beyond Dereham.
E or E Except Saturdays.
F One class only.
H Arr. Cambridge 11 54 mrn. and London (L. St.) 2 9 aft. on Sats.

M or m Mondays only.
N King's Cross Station.
n Arr 10 18 mrn Mons.
P Via March.
R Stops when required to set down.
S Saturdays only.
T Thurs. only.
T Arrives at 9 28 mrn.
V 5 mins. later on Sats. Passengers can arrive 2 10 aft., via Norwich.
X Arr. 8 7 aft.
Y Via March except on Sats.
Z Tues. only.

* Passengers to or from Wighton (Halt) must travel in the compartment next to the guards van.
‡ Via Norwich.

Other Trains

Norwich and Wymondham.......862
Dereham and County School.....886
Norwich and County School. . ..886

Bradshaw's timetable for March 1938.

The July 1939 working timetable reveals that the pattern of operation on the neighbouring County School to Wroxham route had changed little since the Great Eastern period. There were five up and six down passenger workings on weekdays, all of these being through workings between Norwich and Dereham. In the up direction, there were departures from Dereham at 6.34, 8.37, 11.46 am (Saturdays-only), 11.50 am (Saturdays-excepted), 4.35 (SO), 4.50 (SX) and 7.16 pm. Down workings left Norwich Thorpe at 6.25, 9.45 am, 2.20, 4.49, 6.17, 8.34 (SX) and 9.07 pm (SO). An additional down service left Norwich at 11.52 am on Thursdays only.

An interesting feature of summer 1939 timetable was the provision of a Sunday through train from Dereham to Great Yarmouth via County School, Aylsham and Wroxham. This left Dereham at 8.35 am and returned from Yarmouth at 7.55 pm, allowing people from the towns and villages along the line to spend a whole day by the seaside before returning home in the evening; the train finally arrived back in Dereham at 9.58 pm.

Freight services

Freight services on the Wells branch comprised two up and two down goods workings between Wymondham, Dereham and Wells. One of these pick-up services generally ran through from Norwich to Wells, while the other ran between Wymondham and Wells, in connection with a branch freight service between Beccles, Forncett and Wymondham; the through freight service to Beccles no longer ran.

Freight carried on the line was mainly coal or fertiliser inwards, and agricultural products outwards, and the goods rolling stock use on the branch reflected this range of traffic. In earlier years open wagons had predominated, and a typical Norwich to Wells freight train might have included GER 7-plank coal wagons, 5-plank general merchandise vehicles and 10 ton ventilated vans. Agricultural machinery was brought into the area on flat 'engine wagons', while fish traffic from Wells was conveyed in the Great Eastern's special fish vehicles.

An unusual source of traffic at this time was fish bait, and in 1931 it was reported that large numbers of lug worms were being gathered at Wells and sent to Yarmouth, Lowestoft and Southwold by passenger train; these unfortunate creatures were packed in wooden boxes and conveyed in the guard's compartments of ordinary trains - up to 10,000 worms being dispatched each week during the winter months.

Most intermediate stations were equipped with cattle docks, end-loading bays, coal wharves and goods sheds, while some stations had fixed yard cranes capable of lifting containers, timber, drain pipes and other types of freight from rail to road vehicles. In addition, several stations had private industrial sidings for dealing with the area's important agricultural products, one of these 'lineside industries' being at Ryburgh, where the maltings were among the biggest in Norfolk.

There were also rail-connected granaries, malt houses or other installations at Wells, Fakenham, Dereham, Hardingham and Yaxham, together with a dairy at

North Elmham. The following table (compiled with the aid of the 1938 *Railway Clearing House Handbook of Stations*) gives some indication of the freight facilities available between Wymondham and Wells-on-Sea:

Goods and passenger accommodation on the Wymondham-Wells branch

Station	Accommodation	Crane
Wymondham	G P F L H C	1 ton
Kimberley Park	G P	–
Hardingham	G P F L H C -	–
Thuxton	G P	–
Yaxham	G P L H	1 ton 10 cwt
Dereham	G P F L H C	6 tons
North Elmham	G P F L H C	1 ton
County School	G P	–
Ryburgh	G P F L H C	1 ton
Fakenham	G P F L H C	3 tons
Walsingham	G P F L H C	1 ton 10 cwt
Wighton Halt	P	–
Wells-on-Sea	G P F L H C	1 ton 10 cwt

Key: G = Goods; P = Passengers & Parcels; F = Loading docks for cars, furniture, portable machines, etc.; L = Livestock; H = Horse boxes & prize cattle vans; C = Carriages & motor cars by passenger train.

Goods traffic on the West Norfolk branch was usually conveyed by a daily pick-up working from Kings Lynn to Wells, and in 1913 this service reached Heacham at 12.25 pm, after running non-stop over the Lynn & Hunstanton line as far as the junction. The train then proceeded along the West Norfolk line, calling as required at intermediate stations. The return working left Wells at 3.07 pm, and again called en route at every station or siding as required.

A second West Norfolk goods working reached Heacham from Hunstanton at 1.05 pm, and this service ran as far as Docking (arr. 1.50 pm); other goods and cattle trains ran as required. As in the case of passenger services, the pattern of goods train operation on the West Norfolk branch changed very little and by the 1930s there were still two goods trains each way. One of these ran through from Kings Lynn, while the other was a short distance working from Hunstanton to Docking which ran on an as required basis.

Freight traffic on the Wroxham to County School line was conveyed by two trains from Norwich, one of which left at 5.00 am and travelled outwards to Wroxham, from where it continued westwards along the County School branch at 7.13 am. The second train left Norwich at 8.10 am, reaching Dereham later in the morning and then forming a 2.25 pm afternoon freight service from Dereham to Wroxham. On arrival at Wroxham the engine carried out shunting work in the yard before finally returning to Norwich as a special when necessary. On Wednesdays the 2.25 pm was double-headed by two engines as far as Reepham, so that a special cattle train could be arranged as necessary from Reepham to Dereham.

Steam railcars on the Wells line

In 1925, the LNER acquired two Sentinel steam railcars, for use on branch lines in East Anglia, and following successful trials a further 22 vehicles were purchased. Further Sentinel railcars were subsequently obtained, together with a numerically-smaller batch of 11 Clayton vehicles. The later Sentinel railcars were 58 ft 6 in. long, their power bogies being driven by 6-cylinder steam engines developing approximately 120 horse power.

The Sentinel and Clayton railcars were visually similar, although the Clayton cars could be easily distinguished because they featured coupled driving wheels and a projecting coal bunker at the driving end. When first introduced, at least some of the railcars sported full LNER 'varnished teak' livery, while in their declining years the surviving vehicles were painted in the company's drab 'carriage brown' livery. A few cars were painted in a red and cream colour scheme, although, in general, the examples seen in and around Norwich carried standard green and cream railcar livery. All of the LNER steam cars were named, most of the names being derived from long-defunct stage coaches.

In practice, the LNER steam railcars worked complex diagrams, involving trips over the Dereham and Aylsham routes, with occasional forays along the Norwich & Brandon main line. A typical railcar duty involved return journeys from Norwich Thorpe to Attleborough, and from Norwich to Dereham, with a trip around the circuitous Aylsham route via Wroxham, County School and Dereham. Railcars also worked the 5.30 pm evening down service from Norwich Thorpe to Dereham, and the balancing 8.25 pm return working. The steam cars did not normally run through to Wells - Fakenham being the northern limit of their regular operations.

In the early 1930s, Norwich shed had two railcar diagrams, one of which started at 8.26 am and finished at 10.36 pm, and involved journeys to Aylsham, Wymondham, Dereham, Attleborough and Acle. The second diagram included trips to Attleborough, Lowestoft, Dereham and County School, while on Thursdays and Saturdays one of the steam cars made a return trip from Dereham to Fakenham at 3.02 pm, returning at 4.18 pm. This service normally called intermediately at Ryburgh, County School and North Elmham, though on the return journey to Norwich it ran non-stop between Dereham and Wymondham, arriving back in Norwich by 5.25 pm.

The LNER steam railcars were well-liked by the travelling public, who appreciated their rapid acceleration and smooth riding. The steam cars were electrically-lit, and steam-heated, and could carry parcels and luggage in addition to their normal complement of seated and standing passengers. Steam railcars employed in the Norwich area at various times included Clayton cars Nos. 43302 *Chevy Chase* and 61999 *Transit*, and Sentinel vehicles Nos. 51908 *Expedition* and 51909 *Waterloo*.

The coaches used on local services during the mid-1930s were still predominantly six-wheelers, most branch line trains and main line stopping services being composed mainly of short-wheelbase stock. It was therefore decided that ex-North Eastern Railway bogie coaches would be transferred to the GER section (and other parts of the LNER system), the coaches concerned

Sentinel-Cammell steam railcar No. 51909 *Waterloo* entered traffic in January 1929 and was allocated to Norwich shed. In May 1930 it was transferred to Hitchin on the Great Northern section.   *Real Photographs*

being a mixture of elliptical-roofed stock and clerestory vehicles. Over 200 vehicles were transferred over a five year period between 1935 and 1939, and these transfers enabled the short-wheelbase coaches to be belatedly withdrawn.

Other developments in the 1930s

Apart from the progressive introduction of bogie passenger stock, the LNER made one or two other changes and improvements during the 1930s. Wells station, for example, was substantially rebuilt, with a new connection between the Wells & Fakenham and West Norfolk portions of the terminus. Hitherto, the only connection between what were in effect two separate stations had been a single crossover. The new connection supplemented this by diverging southwards from the West Norfolk line and rejoining the Fakenham line near the signal box. The passenger station was rebuilt at about the same time, with new platforms, improved lighting and an extended overall roof (*see Chapter Six*).

Another innovation was the opening of Wighton Halt to serve the village of Wighton (roughly midway between Wells and Walsingham). This simple, passenger-only stopping place appeared in the timetables in 1924. One small alteration carried out in the 1930s was a change of name from 'Wells' to 'Wells-on-Sea' - presumably in an attempt to prevent confusion with the Great Western station at Wells in Somerset.

The main development at this time was not, however, initiated by the LNER, but by certain 'High Church' elements within the Church of England. Until the Protestant Reformation, Walsingham had rivalled Canterbury as a centre of Christian pilgrimage, but in the 1530s the monasteries were abolished, and the Shrine of 'Our Lady of Walsingham' was dismantled - its 'graven images of silver and gold' being symbolically burned at Smithfield. Thereafter, the Church of England remained visibly Protestant in its forms of service, and only in the 19th century did incense, stained glass, plaster saints, genuflection and other supposedly 'Catholic' practices become acceptable to Anglican worshippers.

At its most extreme, 'High Church' Anglicism developed into a form of Anglo-Catholicism which was, in most respects, identical to traditional Catholicism. Inevitably, Anglo-Catholics were eager to repair what they saw as the 'damage' of the Reformation, and with this thought in mind an Anglican shrine was opened at Walsingham in 1931. Walsingham pilgrimages became so popular that in 1938 the original shrine was enlarged to accommodate the growing number of visitors.

Meanwhile, the Roman Catholics had established a shrine of their own in the historic 'Slipper Chapel' at Houghton St Giles, and in 1934 no less than 12,000 people travelled to Walsingham for a service at the restored shrine. For the first time in its history, the Wells branch became an important excursion destination, and in the next few years special trains were run to Walsingham from London and other large cities (further details of Walsingham and 'Slipper Chapel Halt' will be found in the next chapter).

Unfortunately, this renewed interest in Walsingham did not contribute towards a sudden growth in holiday traffic to Wells, and the LNER never treated the little town as a seaside resort. In 1931, for instance, the company's annual publicity material featured a map of Eastern England together with the slogan, 'LNER for the DRIER SIDE'. Significantly, Wells-on-Sea was omitted from this map through the neighbouring resorts of Hunstanton, Sheringham and Cromer were clearly marked. Only in terms of excursion traffic could Wells claim to be a 'holiday' resort, and at the height of summer there was a considerable flow of day trippers from Dereham and Norwich.

Like most branch lines, the Wells branch served the surrounding area in perfect safety for over a century, but on 27th May, 1931 Fakenham was the scene of an accident which could easily have been disastrous. The platform layout at that station included a dead-end bay on the down side which could be used by services starting or terminating journeys between Fakenham and Norwich. On the day in question the bay was occupied by the 9.06 am Wells to Norwich service, consisting of an 'E4' class 2-4-0 and a train comprising bogie vehicles and six-wheeled coaches.

Owing to a points failure, the turnouts were set for the bay, when another 'E4' heading the 8.17 am Norwich to Wells working ran past two down home signals at danger and crashed into the stationary train. The locomotives involved in the collision were Nos. 7457 and 7486, and although not badly damaged both were subsequently scrapped (one assumes that their age made repairs unworthwhile). Fortunately, the down working had been slowing prior to stopping in the platform at Fakenham station, but this slow speed could not prevent the death of one person and injuries to a further 12 passengers and three staff.

Class 'E4' 2-4-0 No. 7492 at Dereham on 29th June, 1936.   *H.C. Casserley*

'D13' class 4-4-0 No. 8030 takes water at Wells on 29th June, 1936. This type, classified 'T19' by the Great Eastern, were originally built at Stratford works as 2-4-0s between 1886 and 1897. Many of the class were rebuilt as 4-4-0s between 1905 and 1908. No. 8030 was withdrawn from service in November 1938.   *H.C. Casserley*

World War II

At lunchtime on Sunday 3rd September, 1939, the people of Wells, Dereham and the rest of Britain turned on their wireless sets to hear Prime Minister Neville Chamberlain announce that Great Britain had declared war on Nazi Germany following Adolf Hitler's brutal invasion of Poland. Many listeners expected the skies to fill with Luftwaffe bombers within the first few days, but in reality the first few months of World War II were so uneventful that people began to speak derisively of a 'Phoney War'. For railway travellers, a reduction in services, the nightly 'blackout', and the sight of uniformed servicemen hurrying to join their ships or units were the only signs that there was a 'war on'.

The sudden and unexpected Fall of France in June 1940 dispelled any illusions about the gravity of the situation, and with the British Empire standing alone against an armed and largely hostile Europe, London, Bristol, Belfast and other large cities were, for a short time, subjected to nightly air attacks of varying severity. It was feared that invasion was imminent and elaborate preparations for the defence of the British homeland were put into effect. Thousands of concrete pillboxes were erected as part of a series of 'stop lines' and, with a broad swathe of land from Sussex to the Wash declared an emergency area, the people of north Norfolk found themselves in the 'front line'.

Road signs and station nameboards were taken down, beaches were mined, and obstructions were placed in fields and open spaces to impede airborne landings. All able-bodied males were encouraged to join the Local Defence Volunteers (renamed the Home Guard in July 1940) and - at a time when invasion was thought to be imminent - these part-time soldiers could be seen guarding beaches, railway bridges and other installations in the area.

Less visibly, a secretive force of elite Home Guard 'Special Units' was preparing to wage guerrilla warfare on the event of a successful landing. Consisting mainly of local farmers, poachers, gamekeepers and other specialists, the Special Units had made elaborate plans and, although these preparations are still secret, there can be little doubt that the Wells branch would itself have become a target for sabotage as soon as it fell into enemy hands. (It is rumoured that the large embankment at East Barsham would have been blown up to sever the line at a particularly inconvenient place.)

It was at this critical phase of the war that armoured patrol trains were brought into play in order to counteract Britain's acute shortage of conventional guns and armoured vehicles and, like other coastal lines, the Wells-next-the-Sea branch was patrolled regularly by one of these hastily-assembled units. The train consisted of former GER 'F4' class 2-4-2T No. 7189 flanked by two low-sided general purpose wagons and two LMS steel 20 ton coal wagons. The locomotive and coal wagons were protected by ½ inch steel plate and the entire train was camouflaged.

Offensive armament consisted of rifles, machine guns and naval 6-pounders - the latter being mounted in the armoured wagons in such a way that a 240 degree arc of fire was possible ahead and astern of the train. When on patrol, the train carried a crew of 26, including gunners, wireless operators and locomen. There were in all a grand total of 12 such trains, together with several 'spares', each one being given a distinguishing letter of the alphabet. Train 'G' was allocated to the North Norfolk area, and in July 1940 it started to patrol the area between Kings Lynn and Great Yarmouth, making regular trips along the Wells branch and the West Norfolk line.

The train was stationed, for much of the war, at Heacham, from where it made regular patrols to both Hunstanton and Wells-next-the-Sea. It was while on one of these patrols that Train 'G' collided with a rake of stationary coaches at Wells with such force that the locomotive broke its buffer beam. It is interesting to recall that, for at least part of its wartime career, Train 'G' was manned exclusively by Polish Army officers, who (like their fellow countrymen in the RAF) welcomed any chance to participate in the allied war effort after the tragic defeat of their own country in 1940.

Basing their estimates on the known casualty figures resulting from Zeppelin raids in World War I, government 'experts' had predicted that the Germans would drop no less than 950 bombs a day during the first months of the war, poison gas and fire bombs being used in conjunction with high-explosive bombs to ensure the total destruction of cities such as London and Birmingham in a series of 'knock-out blows'.

Happily, pre-war fears of a 'knock-out' blow were wildly inaccurate, and although at certain periods of the war the Luftwaffe did indeed turn its full attention to London or other major British cities, it emerged that the destructive capabilities of the dreaded Nazi airforce had been greatly over-estimated. The Germans were simply not equipped to wage a sustained bombing campaign over a well-defended island nation such as Britain - and in particular, they lacked four-engined heavy bombers capable of dealing really destructive blows on civilian or military targets.

Historians now agree that Hitler never seriously intended to invade Britain, but on the other hand he hoped that the threat of invasion, coupled with heavy air attacks, would force Britain into an armistice so that the Germans could invade Russia. As we now know, the attack on Russia went ahead in June 1941, leaving Britain undefeated in the West, and able to bomb Hitler's Europe from the air. As far as the Wells branch was concerned, this second phase of the war was dominated by a vast build-up of British air power in East Anglia and, like other local lines, it carried a heavy traffic in RAF (and later USAAF) personnel to and from local aerodromes such as RAF Langham and RAF North Creake.

The construction of these aerodromes was an epic task that recalled the building of the railways back in the 1840s. Each airfield required vast amounts of cement, tarmac, concrete, bricks, corrugated iron and other building materials. Bomber stations were typically equipped with three runways and a perimeter track, the runways being laid out in a roughly triangular pattern. There were normally at least two hangars, and on wartime aerodromes these would normally be steel-framed prefabricated structures of the 'T2', 'B2' or 'Bellman' type.

Many of the local airfields were bomber stations; North Creake, for example, was a Bomber Command support station operating Stirling and Halifax heavy bombers. This aerodrome was opened as a satellite for RAF Foulsham in November 1943. It was situated on a low hill about two miles to the north-west of Walsingham station and its facilities included three concrete runways, two steel-framed 'T2' hangars and a 'B1' maintenance hangar. RAF North Creake became a full station in 1944, and at the time of the D-Day invasion its aircraft allocation comprised Stirling III heavy bombers of 199 Squadron, 100 Group, Bomber Command.

RAF Little Snoring, some three miles to the north-east of Fakenham station, was a very similar Bomber Command establishment with three concrete runways, two 'T2' hangars and a single 'B1' hangar. The airfield was opened as another satellite of RAF Foulsham in July 1943, but became a full station just one month later. The resident units in June 1944 were Nos. 23 and 515 squadrons, flying Mosquito twin-engined light bombers. Langham, in contrast, was a Coastal Command station equipped with Beaufighters. Other local aerodromes included RAF Sculthorpe, RAF Foulsham, RAF Swanton Morley, RAF Wendling and RAF Shipdham - all of which were conveniently situated within a mile or two of the Wymondham to Wells line.

As in World War I, British military planners assumed that the enemy might launch an attack on the flat beaches around East Anglia, and to deter such attacks the entire coast line was defended by coast artillery batteries. These normally consisted of two 4.7 inch or 6 inch guns in twin gun houses, together with their associated magazines, battery observation posts, guard rooms and domestic buildings. The batteries were sited at roughly 12 mile intervals, some typical examples being located at High Cape, to the north-west of Wells, and Cley Eye to the east. Both of these batteries were equipped with 6 inch BL guns, firing 100 lb. shells up to a range of 12,600 yards.

With so many legitimate military targets in the immediate vicinity it was perhaps inevitable that the Luftwaffe would bomb the area, and on one of these enemy raids - on August Bank Holiday Monday 1941 - Ryburgh railway station was hit. The target on this occasion, was probably Little Snoring airfield rather than the railway - though the latter must have made an ideal navigational feature for the enemy pilots. In fact the Germans managed to inflict considerable damage not just to railway property but also to the adjoining maltings; the remains of the station were afterwards demolished.

Norwich, too, was badly hit during a series of German air raids which inflicted damage on the historic city centre. Norwich, in fact, suffered damage to several of its ancient buildings, the churches of St Julian, St Michael-at-Thorn, St Paul's and St Benedict's being damaged by fire or blast, while Norwich Thorpe goods station lost part of its overall roof.

Quite apart from any physical damage inflicted by these air raids, they obviously caused delays and disruption to ordinary train services at a time when the railways were struggling to carry extra traffic. Trains were, at this time, packed with service personnel from all over the British Isles, and the accents of Northern England, the Midlands, Ireland, Scotland and Wales could be heard in every train and on every station, interspersed with the distinctive yet familiar Norfolk drawl. Commonwealth accents could be heard too, for there were numerous Canadian, Australian and New Zealand airmen in the area; indeed, there was quite a concentration of Antipodean airmen around Wells, and by 1944 RAF Langham had one Royal Australian Airforce and one Royal New Zealand Airforce Squadron!

The railways had been taken into government control at the start of the war, and every effort was made to restrict unnecessary civilian travel. Timetables were drastically cut and, although there were large numbers of special freight and passenger trains for military purposes, ordinary travellers were offered a severely restricted train service. On the Wymondham to Dereham section, the pre-war service of 10 up and nine down trains was reduced to six trains each way by May 1943. The Wymondham to Forncett branch, in contrast, lost its passenger trains altogether, public services being withdrawn with effect from 11th September, 1939.

The May 1943 timetable shows five trains each way between Norwich and Wells. In the up direction, trains left Wells at 7.14, 9.55 am, 1.10, 3.14 and 6.00 pm, while in the opposite direction the corresponding down workings departed from Norwich Thorpe at 7.25, 10.05 am, 12 noon, 4.45 and 6.38 pm. The timetables suggest that most of the through services between Norwich and Kings Lynn had been withdrawn, although the Wroxham to County School branch trains still ran through to Dereham - resulting in an enhanced train service over the Dereham to County School section.

The locomotives employed on the Wells line during World War II consisted of the usual ex-Great Eastern 'D13' 4-4-0s, 'E4' 2-4-0s, 'J15' 0-6-0s, 'J17' 0-6-0s and 'F3' 2-4-2Ts, together with the former GNR 'D2' 4-4-0s. Many of these locomotives were fitted with canvas screens, which could be lowered at night to eliminate footplate glare, and thereby reduce the threat of air attack. Similar blackout precautions were put into effect at stations and goods depots - all platform lamps being masked or extinguished, while carriage lights were dimmed.

In physical terms the war produced few changes, the extensive track layouts at most intermediate stations being adequate for the needs of most wartime traffic. Apart from the influx of military personnel, the Wymondham to Wells line carried large amounts of building materials, most of which, as we have seen, was used to build runways or other military installations. Dereham became an important marshalling centre during the peak of airfield construction, and additional sidings were installed for this important wartime traffic; at one period Dereham was handling no less than 75 wagon loads of construction materials each day.

The end of the war in Europe was followed by the election of Mr Attlee's Labour government, and on 1st January, 1948 a nationwide fanfare of locomotive whistles heralded the demise of the 'Big Four' main line companies and the birth of BRITISH RAILWAYS - the new, nationally-owned railway organization; as in 1923, an era had come to an end.

Chapter Five

The Route from Norwich to Dereham

Having outlined the history of the Wells-next-the-Sea branch from its inception until dawn of the British Railways era, it would now be appropriate to examine the stations and other infrastructure of this interesting East Anglian rural line in greater detail. The following sections will therefore take readers on an imaginary guided tour of the railway from Norwich Thorpe to Wells. Generally speaking, the topographical details that follow are correct for the early British Railways period around 1950; by that time, the stations had reached their final form and there would be no further changes until the general run-down of the system during the 1960s.

Norwich Thorpe

Wells trains commenced their journeys at Norwich Thorpe, where the station, opened in 1844, had been the original western terminus of the Yarmouth & Norwich Railway. Trains from Brandon and Ely shared the station from 15th December, 1845, by which date the Yarmouth & Norwich and Norwich & Brandon companies had combined to from the Norfolk Railway Company. The Eastern Union Railway opened a separate terminus at Norwich Victoria in 1849, but the station known to present day railway travellers as Norwich Thorpe became the city's main terminal station after the formation of the Great Eastern Railway Company in 1862.

In its original form, the first Yarmouth & Norwich Railway station had consisted of a series of low, barn-like train sheds, and an Italianate facade of modest architectural pretension featuring a tall, campanile-type tower and an arched loggia. This original station was subsequently adapted for use as part of an enlarged goods depot.

The station was rebuilt and partially re-sited in 1886, as a result of which it acquired new platforms and an impressive brick and stone station building of decidedly 'Central European' appearance. Designed by W. Ashbee, the Great Eastern Railway architect, this stylish two-storey building features a large, centrally-placed dome, with a projecting *porte-cochère* in front, and long wings on either side. The first storey is 'rusticated', while engaged pilasters and elaborate fenestration contribute further baroque atmosphere to this distinctive building. Part of the roof structure was damaged by enemy action in World War II, but this air raid damage was belatedly rectified when the station was refurbished in 1999.

Behind its towering dome, the new station was an essentially-simple affair, with three double-sided platforms providing six platform faces. Platforms 1, 2, 3 and 4, on the west side of the station, handled most of the traffic, while the fifth platform was much shorter than Nos. 1-4, and its outer face was closed off by a brick wall, so that in practice Norwich Thorpe had just five passenger platforms. In 1955, British Railways increased the capacity of the station by

Although it occupied the approximate site of the original Norfolk Railway terminus, Norwich Thorpe station was relatively modern, and dated from 1886 (the original terminus then became a goods yard). The station was bombed by the Luftwaffe in World War II, and evidence of the resulting damage can be seen in this *circa* 1958 view. Remarkably, the damaged roof seen here was not fully restored until 1999.   *Lens of Sutton Collection*

An earlier view of Norwich Thorpe station, taken *circa* 1921.   *Photomatic*

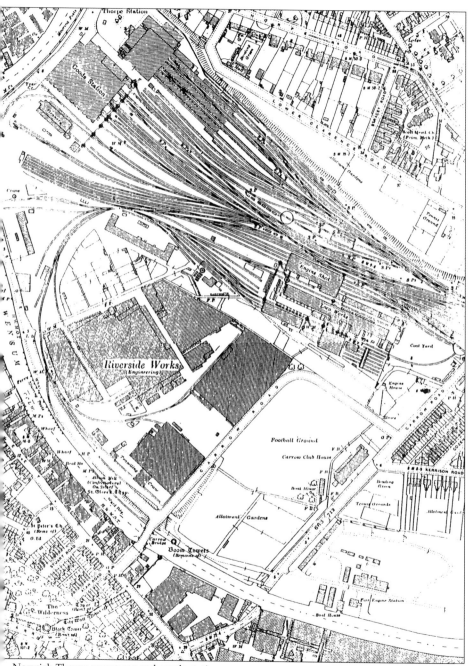

Norwich Thorpe passenger and goods stations.

Reproduced from the 1906, 25″ Ordnance Survey Map

An atmospheric photograph of Norwich Thorpe during the 1950s. An ex-Great Northern Railway 0-6-0 stands in platform 5, while an ex-LMS 2-6-4T blows off steam in platform 3.
Douglas Thompson

'Claud Hamilton' 4-4-0 No. 62604 awaits the 'right away' at Norwich Thorpe during the early 1950s.   *Douglas Thompson*

demolishing the wall behind platform 5 to create a sixth platform. At the same time, platforms 5 and 6 were extended by 70 ft, a new engine spur and ashpit being constructed, while new water columns were also provided.

A triangular junction at the southern end of the station enabled through passenger and freight workings to avoid the station entirely, and this avoiding line (known as the Wensum Curve) was regularly used by prestige trains such as the Norfolk Coast Express on its exacting summer schedules.

Norwich Thorpe was signalled from separate passenger and goods boxes, which were known as Norwich Passenger Station box and Norwich Goods Yard box respectively. In 1923, the Passenger Station box was equipped with a 125-lever frame, whereas the Goods Yard cabin contained a 62-lever frame. Further signal boxes, known as Norwich Thorpe Junction and Wensum Junction, controlled the northern and eastern ends of the Norwich triangle, while Trowse Swing Bridge Junction box controlled the southern corner of the triangle, where the Wensum curve converged from the Yarmouth direction.

Much of Norwich's freight traffic was handled in the goods sidings at Norwich Victoria, but Norwich Thorpe was, until recent years, a busy freight centre in its own right. The area to the west of the passenger terminus was occupied by a large goods station, which incorporated parts of the original pre-1880s passenger station. Other goods facilities were available at Norwich Trowse, the most important forms of traffic handled at the latter station being livestock and private siding traffic to Messrs Colman's vast mustard works, which was served by its own siding connections from Trowse goods yard.

Norwich Thorpe station was flanked by an array of parallel loops and sidings on its west side, while Norwich Motive Power Depot (32A) occupied a restricted site to the south of the platforms. In Great Eastern days the shed could accommodate up to 15 tender locomotives and 21 tank engines, but in LNER days the shed was greatly expanded, and in the BR period the allocation was over 120 locomotives. As one might expect, indigenous Great Eastern classes were always well-represented, and in the early 1950s the shed housed over 20 'Claud Hamilton' 4-4-0s, eight 'E4' class 0-6-0s and large numbers of ex-GER 0-6-0s.

Large passenger locomotives allocated to Norwich at various times during the British Railways period included 'B17' class 4-6-0s and 'Britannia' 4-6-2s such as Nos. 70000 *Britannia*, 70008 *Black Prince*, 70009 *Alfred the Great*, 70010 *Owen Glendower*, 70013 *Oliver Cromwell* and 70036 *Boadicea*.

Norwich Trowse

Leaving Norwich Thorpe, Wells branch trains initially headed south-eastwards to Thorpe Junction, at which point the line divided, with one line continuing due east towards Whitlingham Junction and Great Yarmouth, while the other route curved south-westwards towards Norwich Trowse station. Norwich Thorpe Junction was the setting for an accident on 21st January, 1881, when the 6.30 am train from Wells to Norwich over-ran the signals and collided with an eastbound Norwich to Great Yarmouth working headed by Sinclair 'Y' class 2-4-0 No. 375.

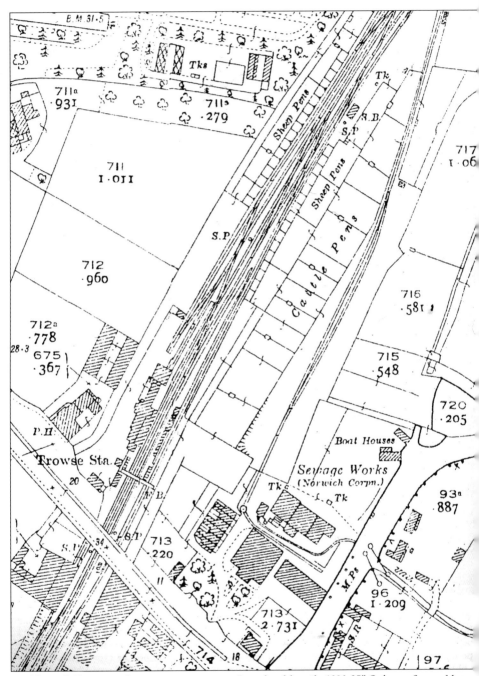

Norwich Trowse station.   *Reproduced from the 1906, 25″ Ordnance Survey Map*

Before reaching Norwich Trowse station, trains crossed the River Wensum on Trowse swing bridge. When opened in December 1845 this structure was the most impressive engineering feature on the Norfolk Railway system. The original single track bridge, designed by George Parker Bidder (1806-1878), was 188 ft long and fabricated mainly from cast-iron components that had been supplied by Messrs Grissell of the Regents Canal Iron Works in London. The bridge consisted of five spans, the moving centre span being pivoted at its centre of gravity so that it could be swung open.

The swinging span was 108 ft long, and when rotated on its centre bearing it formed two openings, each of which was 44 ft in width. The swinging span was supported by a foundation plate and a massive centre post, lateral stability being ensured by a system of cast-iron piles. The cast-iron spans of the moving section were supported by four massive, wrought-iron struts, which were themselves attached to a pair of huge cast-iron 'A' frames on each side of a square carriage frame. The fixed approach spans on the east and west sides of the swinging span were formed of cast-iron girders resting on iron piles. Each of these subsidiary openings had a clear span of 20 ft.

The original Norfolk Railway bridge was replaced by a more modern structure in 1904, this second bridge being a double track structure, with an electrically-operated moving span. In the early days, the original single track bridge had been worked by a so-called 'Bridgeman', who wore a distinguishing armlet and acted as pilotman by riding on the engine of each train that crossed the bridge - his presence giving the driver authority to proceed.

In addition to the Bridgeman, the first bridge was protected by primitive signals, although interlocking and new signalling was carried out in the early 1870s. In November 1872 McKenzie & Holland were awarded a contract for resignalling in the Norwich area at a cost of £4,265. Several new signal cabins were erected in connection with these schemes, including a new cabin at Trowse Swing Bridge which was inspected by the Board of Trade Inspector in August 1874. The first box was a hipped roof Great Eastern 'Type One' cabin, and as such it was one of the company's first standardized signal box designs.

The Great Eastern carried out another resignalling scheme during the 1880s, as a corollary of the new works at Norwich Thorpe. The original hipped-roof box at Trowse Swing Bridge Junction was replaced by a brick and timber cabin with a gable roof. The LNER carried out a comprehensive survey of GER lever frames shortly after the 1923 Grouping, and this interesting document contains much useful data; as far as Trowse Swing Bridge Junction was concerned, the post-Grouping survey reveals that the signal box was equipped with a 25-lever Dutton frame.

From Trowse Swing Bridge, the route continued south-westwards into Norwich Trowse station, which was just one mile from Norwich Thorpe, and the terminus of the line from Brandon until the completion of the first swing bridge in December 1845. It is likely that, when first opened, Trowse station may have featured staggered up and down platforms on either side of a level crossing - though the crossing was abolished in 1881 when a replacement overbridge was brought into use. The original Norfolk Railway station building was described in a contemporary account an 'as edifice in the Elizabethan style, built of white brick and flints worked by the men from Brandon'.

A Swindon '120' class dmu (car No. 53708 leading) crosses the Trowse swing bridge on 19th September, 1983, forming a cross-country service to Peterborough via Thetford and Ely.

Brian Morrison

Norwich Trowse station (closed) looking towards Norwich Thorpe. The downside station building incorporates a mixture of Norwich & Brandon and GER fabric. *Lens of Sutton Collection*

Norwich Trowse was aligned from north-east to south-west, the main station building on the down, or eastbound side. Three platforms were provided, the up side being arranged as an island with tracks on each side. For most of its operational life the station functioned as a two platform stopping place, the outer platform face on the up side being fenced off, the track behind it being used as a goods line. Latterly, however, all three platforms were used for passenger traffic, the down platform being designated platform 1, while the two platforms on the up side became platforms 2 and 3 respectively.

The main station building consisted of an attractive range of buildings, with a two-storey station master's house arranged at right angles to the platforms, and two single-storey flanking wings containing the usual public facilities. This distinctive structure was constructed of grey brickwork with a steeply-pitched slated roof and ornamental bargeboards. Its architectural details suggested that the building may have been an enlarged version of an original Norfolk Railway structure, and if this is indeed the case, it seems likely that the two-storey cross wing may have been a Great Eastern addition to the earlier structure.

Trowse station was surrounded by a multiplicity of goods sidings, though in reality the volume of ordinary goods traffic handled was relatively small. On the other hand, livestock and private siding traffic was very important. The station handled large numbers of cattle in connection with Norwich market, for which purpose the goods yard was equipped with extensive cattle loading pens. Of equal if not greater importance, Trowse was the site of a private siding connection to Messrs Colman's famous mustard works, which generated large amounts of traffic. Other private sidings served the nearby power station, sewage works, Trowse Mills, Laurence Scott Electromotors and an industrial estate.

Cattle traffic remained important at Trowse for several years, wagons being received in train loads until this form of traffic finally ceased in the mid-1960s. Livestock pens were provided on both sides of the line for cattle and sheep traffic. Colman's famous mustard works was situated to the north of the station, the internal factory system being linked to the main line via the down sidings; a short branch diverged eastwards from the works sidings to reach saw mills, and a timber yard - a short tunnel being necessary so that this private line could pass beneath the main Norwich & Brandon route.

There were two signal cabins at Trowse, Trowse Yard box on the up side having a 45-lever frame, while Trowse Lower Junction box on the down side was equipped with a 47-lever frame. Both frames were of McKenzie & Holland origin. A further cabin was provided to the north of the station at Trowse Swing Bridge Junction. Trowse Yard and Trowse Lower Junction boxes were closed in November 1986, while Trowse Swing Bridge Junction box was reduced to the status of a bridge control cabin.

In operational terms, Trowse Lower Junction box was particularly important in that it controlled the connection to Trowse Upper Junction and the Liverpool Street main line - this connection being used by London trains, while trains to Cambridge, Dereham and Wells continued south-westwards beside the Rivers Yare and Tas, and thence into a deep cutting. The link between Trowse Lower and Trowse Upper junctions was 1 mile 2 chains in length, and it was opened by the Eastern Union Railway in 1851.

Hethersett station on 23rd April, 1963, some 6¼ miles from Norwich. Hethersett was served by most Dereham trains in GER and LNER days, though in the BR period many trains passed through this wayside station without stopping.   *Douglas Thompson*

Hethersett station, post-closure, *circa* 1972, showing signal box, level crossing and former station building.   *Lens of Sutton Collection*

Norwich Trowse was closed to regular passenger traffic in 1939, but its platforms and other facilities were retained for occasional use during emergencies or engineering work. At other times, the station was used by football excursions when Norwich City were playing at home - the station being conveniently close to the Carrow Road football ground.

Hethersett

Turning onto a westerly heading, Wells branch trains passed beneath the Ipswich main line, an impressive, six-arched brick viaduct being provided at this point. Beyond, the double track line continued along more or less dead level alignments for about two miles, after which up trains were faced with a 1 in 129 ascent, which continued for a little under two miles towards Hethersett. There was an intermediate block post at Eaton Crossing, an 11-lever signal cabin having been erected on the down side in 1885; this box remained in use until 1965. Beyond, the double track route continued for a further 2½ miles to Hethersett, some 6 miles 15 chains from Norwich Thorpe.

Hethersett was a simple, two-platform wayside station, with staggered up and down platforms separated by an intervening level crossing. The up platform was situated on the Norwich side of the level crossing and there was a small goods yard on the up side of the running lines.

The main station building was on the up (westbound) platform. This single-storey, hipped-roof structure was of traditional Norfolk brick-and-flint construction, though its original appearance was somewhat obscured by a disproportionately-large platform canopy which, from its appearance, had obviously been added in Great Eastern days. Despite its comparatively restricted dimensions, this small building contained domestic accommodation for the local station master and his family, together with the usual booking office and waiting room facilities.

The down platform was equipped with a simple wooden waiting room. This diminutive timber-framed structure was of typical Great Eastern design, and from its late-Victorian appearance, it probably dated from the 1890s; significantly, in October 1892 the GER Way & Works Committee had authorized an expenditure of £200 on a 'waiting room' at Hethersett.

Hethersett's goods facilities originally consisted of a single dead-end siding, entered by means of a connection that was trailing to the direction of up trains. From this siding, a short spur extended westwards behind the up platform. The 1938 *Railway Clearing House Handbook of Stations* reveals that the station could, at that time, handle coal and mineral traffic, together with horse boxes and prize cattle vans - there was, however, no cattle dock or yard crane.

The station was signalled from a standard GER gable-roofed signal cabin beside the level crossing on the down side of the line. Photographic evidence shows that an all-wood box was in use at the end of the Victorian period, the box in question being a typical Great Eastern 'Type Seven' cabin with 9-pane windows. This structure was later rebuilt with a brick locking room - the brickwork being built-up around the timber structure as a sort of external

Reproduced from the 1906, 25" Ordnance Survey Map

Wymondham station and junction.

protective layer; this work was presumably undertaken as an Air Raid Precaution measure during World War II.

Interestingly, Hethersett signal box was badly damaged by fire during the pre-Grouping period, and the later 'Type Seven' cabin was presumably a replacement structure. The circa-1923 post-Grouping LNER survey of Great Eastern section lever frames indicates that Hethersett signal box had a 15-lever McKenzie & Holland 'Soldier' pattern frame at the time of the survey; this was later increased to 18 levers in connection with the installation of intermediate block signals. Additional levers were also needed in connection with a rail-connected oil fuel depot, which was opened at Hethersett during World War II to supply the many aerodromes that had been constructed in the immediate vicinity.

Hethersett had a staff of around half a dozen under a class four station master. These included one porter and three signalmen during the British Railways period. In 1881 the station master was James Stone, while in the later GER period, around 1917, the station master was Mr C. Chissell.

Hethersett's chief claim to fame centres on its role in a popular uprising known as Kett's Rebellion. In 1549 Robert Kett, a Wymondham tanner, became the leader of a mass protest against enclosures which quickly turned into an insurrection; the insurgents are said to have met under an oak tree at Hethersett, where they swore to reform abuses in both church and state. Edward VI's government soon restored order, over 3,000 rebels being cut down at the 'Battle of Mousehold Heath', while Robert Kett was hanged from the walls of Norwich Castle.

Wymondham

From Hethersett, the Norwich & Brandon line continued generally south-westwards on a series of rising gradients, the steepest of which was at 1 in 101. After two miles, trains reach Ketteringham level crossing, where the railway crossed a minor road. There was formerly a signal box here, on the down side of the line, and this controlled a crossover between the up and down lines, as well as the level crossing. The LNER survey revealed that the box contained a 10-lever McKenzie & Holland 'Soldier' frame. Ketteringham box was abolished in British Railways days, around 1960.

Spinks Lane, roughly 8½ miles from Norwich Thorpe, was the site of a long-closed stopping place; it appeared in the 1845 public timetable, but had disappeared by 1866 and may well have faded into obscurity long before that date. From this point, the line falls at 1 in 192 towards Wymondham, where the branch to Dereham and Wells-next-the-Sea diverged north-westwards from the Norwich & Brandon main line.

Wymondham station was 10 miles 18 chains from the start of the journey at Norwich. It was opened by the Norwich & Brandon Railway on Tuesday 29th July, 1845, with regular public services commencing on the following day. In its original form the station was similar to other intermediate stopping places on the Norwich & Brandon route, the likelihood being that staggered up and down

An Edwardian view of the main station buildings at Wymondham. The attractive, brick-and-flint buildings were similar to others on the former Norfolk Railway.

Lens of Sutton Collection

A general view of Wymondham station, looking west, in British Railways days.

Lens of Sutton Collection

platforms were originally provided with the up (westbound) platform being sited further along the line towards Ely than its counterpart on the up side. The two platforms were separated by an intervening level crossing, which was abolished in 1877 when the station was resignalled and reconstructed.

In fact, Wymondham's track layout was altered on at least five occasions between 1877 and 1917, and in this context it is interesting to consider the possibility that the station may have been designed as a three-platform junction, affording cross-platform interchange facilities between the Forncett branch and the Norwich to Ely main line. The 25-inch Ordnance Survey map of 1882 clearly shows that the up platform was at that time an island with tracks on either side, although the trackwork on the south side appears to be in an incomplete state (presumably because the survey was undertaken while the Forncett branch was still under construction). A platform extension was authorized in 1898.

In later years the outermost platform face was fenced off, and for most of its life the station functioned as a two-platform stopping place, the 'third line' behind the up platform being used as a goods loop. The 1906 Ordnance Survey map shows that the outer platform face was no longer continuous, the up side waiting rooms having been built on a projection at the rear of the main up platform. There remains a possibility, however, that three platform faces had been available for a very short period, which may have lasted from the opening of the Forncett branch in 1881 until the layout at Wymondham was altered in 1903.

The main station building was on the down side, and there was an additional building on the opposite platform. The up and down sides of the station were linked by a footbridge, and there were extensive goods sidings on both sides of the running lines. The station building was an interesting brick-and-flint structure reflecting Norwich & Brandon practice at larger intermediate stations. A two-storey station master's house adjoined the main building at its eastern end, and there was an accretion of later GER additions at the west end of the structure. A projecting canopy which, from its appearance, was also a Great Eastern addition, was attached to the platform-facing facade of the building.

The layout was large enough to justify the provision of two signal boxes, which were sited at the north and south ends of the station and known as Wymondham North and Wymondham South Junction boxes respectively. They were both erected in 1877 in connection with the major reconstruction that was carried out at Wymondham at that time. Subsequent remodellings in 1880-82, 1903, 1913 and 1917 meant that the boxes, and certainly their frames, were renewed on several occasions. The North box contained a 30-lever McKenzie & Holland frame when it was inspected in connection with signalling alterations carried out in May 1917.

Wymondham South Junction box was situated on the down side near the convergence of the Ely and Wells lines. In had a 40-lever McKenzie & Holland frame when listed in the post-Grouping LNER survey of Great Eastern section lever frames. In British Railways days Wymondham North box was replaced by ground frames, and the station was then signalled from the surviving South box, which had acquired a 42-lever frame by 1938. Wymondham's two signal boxes were both variants of the usual GER 'Type Two' timber-framed gable roof

A general view of the west end of Wymondham station in 1964, looking towards Wymondham South Junction. The Wells route diverges to the right.   *Mowat Collection*

Wymondham South Junction signal box had a 42-lever McKenzie & Holland frame. The Wells line passes behind the box, while the Norwich to Cambridge main line is visible in the foreground.   *Douglas Thompson*

design, albeit with much shallower windows, which may have resulted from later rebuilding operations.

The facilities provided at Wymondham included a locomotive siding and a 45 ft diameter locomotive turntable, which was sited at the south end of the station in the 'V' of the junction between the diverging Ely and Dereham lines. The turntable was useful when tender engines were employed on the Forncett branch service, but Wymondham was not regarded as an engine shed in the normal sense of the term. Although in the early days it is conceivable that some form of shed building had been provided, in later years Wymondham might more accurately be described as a stabling point, with no covered accommodation.

In the 1950s, Wymondham's usual locomotive allocation was a 'J69' 0-6-0T or a 'J15' 0-6-0, engines noted at the station around 1950-56 being 'J69' class 0-6-0Ts Nos. 68602, 68603 and 68616. These locomotives were used for local shunting duties, for which purpose an 0-6-0T or 0-6-0 would be sent out from Norwich and stabled overnight in the engine siding. Other classes may also have appeared, while during the diesel era shunting duties at Wymondham were normally carried out by a class '03' 0-6-0 diesel shunting locomotive.

Wymondham was the site of various private sidings, although not all of these were in use at the same time. The 1938 *Railway Clearing House Handbook of Stations* reveals that four such sidings were then in use, including the Ayton Asphalte Company Siding, King & Son's Siding, Standley & Son's Siding and S.D. Page & Son's Siding. These sidings were used for agricultural traffic, timber and aggregates, and they ensured that Wymondham dealt with considerable quantities of freight traffic until the British Railways period. The Asphalte Company's siding was entered via a trailing connection from the down main line, and it remained in use until January 1968.

In staffing terms, Wymondham provided employment for a number of signalmen, booking clerks, porters and other grades. The station was important enough to justify the provision of a class one station master. In GER days, around 1910, the station master here had been Mr F.G. Randall, who afterwards moved to Ely.

Wymondham's importance stemmed from its role as a junction, not only for the Kings Lynn and Wells lines, but also for the Forncett branch. The latter route diverged south-eastwards from the main line at Wymondham South Junction. This line, opened in 1881, formed a useful link between the Ely, Dereham and Ipswich lines, and although there were very few through trains to or from Forncett, there was at one time a useful local service from Wymondham. The junction between the main line and the Forncett branch was of interest, in that it was at one time formed of interlaced trackwork which extended towards the station from the point of convergence. This unusual feature was abolished in May 1917, and the junction then became a conventional double track intersection.

It is interesting to note that Wymondham station has occasionally featured in films and television programmes, notably a particularly funny episode of the Home Guard comedy *Dad's Army*, in which the 'Wilmington-on-Sea' heroes take part in a carnival procession that starts in the station yard.

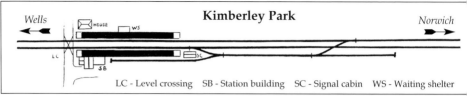

Kimberley Park

Wells ←   → *Norwich*

LC - Level crossing   SB - Station building   SC - Signal cabin   WS - Waiting shelter

A view along the platform towards Wells at Kimberley Park. Note the miniature 'repeater' at the rear of the up home signal. This enabled the signalman to see the position of the signal arm, which would otherwise have been obscured by the sighting screen.   *Douglas Thompson*

A rear view of Kimberley Park station in 1969, showing characteristic brick-and-flint walling on the original Norfolk Railway building. The canopy visible here was probably a Great Eastern addition.   *G.R. Mortimer*

Kimberley Park

From Wymondham, trains diverged north-westwards onto the double track Dereham route at Wymondham South Junction. Curving north-westwards, the route passed through a cutting, beyond which the line passed over Church Lane level crossing. To the left, an ornate Tudor-style gatekeeper's cottage was a reminder of the early days of the line, while to the right the lofty towers of Wymondham Abbey Church rose impressively above the railway.

In 1920, a private siding was installed at Church Lane to serve a nearby brush factory. This new facility was sited on the up side of the line, and it was controlled by a new signal cabin known as Church Lane box.

Falling slightly from Wymondham South Junction, the double track route dipped into a shallow valley, after which trains climbed through cuttings on a modest 1 in 280 rising gradient. Curving westwards, the line passed through further cuttings as it neared the village of Crownthorpe. It is interesting to reflect that, having departed from Norwich Thorpe as 'up' workings, Wells branch trains became 'down' services as soon as they entered the branch. Now running on the down line, branch trains traversed a length of embankment, before cuttings resumed on the approaches to Kimberley Park (13 miles 77 chains), the first intermediate station *en route* to Dereham and Wells-next-the-Sea.

It appears that the promoters of the Norwich & Brandon Railway had always intended to provide a station at Kimberley Park, and as we have seen, when giving evidence before the House of Lords Committee appointed to consider the 1845 Bill they stated that Kimberley would be 'a first class station at which all trains would stop'. The reasons for this were clearly connected, at least in part, with the presence of Kimberley Park, the home of the influential Wodehouse family, which was situated immediately to the north of the railway. (To some extent, therefore, Kimberley was intended as a 'private station', serving the needs of the park as well as the nearby village.)

The facilities provided at Kimberley were transformed during the 1880s, when the Great Eastern decided to double the Wymondham to Dereham cross-country line. This work was put in hand towards the end of 1881, and completed in the following year; the newly doubled line was inspected in November 1882 and brought into use shortly afterwards. In connection with this scheme, the station was extensively rebuilt, with raised platforms and new or extended buildings, of standard GER design, on both sides. Kimberley thereby reached its final form as a double track station with up and down platforms and buildings on both sides in 1882; there were no major changes between that date and the down-grading in the 1960s of the station.

Although Kimberley may well have been considered to be a 'first class station' when it was first opened to traffic, this elevated status was not reflected in its architecture. Like many wayside stations in East Anglia, Kimberley appears to have started life as a small, halt-like stopping place beside a convenient level crossing. A Tudor-style lodge was built for the resident crossing keeper, who also sold the tickets, this distinctive structure being sited beside the level crossing on the down side of the line. Contemporary Ordnance

A view looking towards Wells showing Kimberley Park signal box, with the station building visible beyond. A 'D16/3' 4-4-0 No 62564 heads a passenger train at the up platform.

Stephenson Locomotive Society

A view looking south towards Wymondham and Norwich after rationalization with the main station building to the right.

Lens of Sutton Collection

Survey maps suggest that a low platform was sited on the up side - travellers having to cross an intervening loop siding in order to join their trains.

In its fully-developed form, Kimberley Park was a two-platform station with its main building on the down, or northbound platform, and a level crossing immediately to the south. Two distinct periods of construction were clearly visible - the original Norfolk Railway building being a two-storey structure with a steeply-pitched gable roof placed at right angles to the running lines, while the Great Eastern additions of *circa* 1882 were constructed on an alignment that was parallel to the platform. The resulting structure was, therefore, an L-plan building with a two-storey house portion to the north and a single-storey booking office and waiting room block to the south.

The original Norfolk Railway building was constructed of traditional Norfolk brick-and-flint walling, while the later Great Eastern additions were built of brick with a wood and glass frontage. The enlarged building contained booking office and waiting room facilities, together with a lamp room, toilets and the station master's private quarters. The down side building was equipped with a typical Great Eastern type canopy supported on decorative iron spandrels displaying the company's entwined initials, while the wooden valancing was enlivened by the provision of saw tooth decoration and trefoil holes.

The up platform was equipped with its own waiting room block in a similar architectural style to the new buildings on the down side. This subsidiary building was also equipped with a projecting canopy with 'GER' spandrels and trifoliated fretwork, which obviously dated from the time of the 1882 doubling. These new structures were constructed by the local builder W.R. Skipper, who had been awarded a contract for the rebuilding of Kimberley, Hardingham, Thuxton and Yaxham stations at a cost of £4,129 in August 1881.

The track layout at Kimberley Park consisted of a single goods siding on the down side that was linked to the down running line by a trailing connection and to the up line by a similar connection that crossed the down line by means of a 'diamond' crossing; the 1919 Great Eastern System Map suggests that this was a fixed crossing without the usual single slip connection.

Minor details at this attractive country station included the usual Great Eastern type glass lanterns, which contained simple oil lamps, together with at least two platform seats, one of which sported GER initials in its end ironwork. There was no cattle dock, yard crane or end-loading dock, the amount of goods traffic handled here being comparatively small.

The signal box was a standard Great Eastern 'Type Two' structure with an 18-lever McKenzie & Holland frame controlling up and down distant, home and starting signals. The box, which was situated on the down side of the line to the south of the down platform, was inspected in November 1882 in connection with the doubling of the line. It should, perhaps, be mentioned that there were two main GER signal cabin designs during the late Victorian period, the so-called 'Type Two' design being widely employed during the 1870s and early 1880s, whereas the visually-similar 'Type Seven' design was introduced around 1886 and remained in favour for several years.

Both types were normally built of timber, with low-pitched gable roofs and horizontal weather boarding. 'Type Two' cabins such as that at Kimberley Park

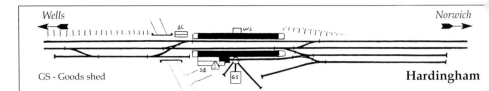

An Edwardian view of Hardingham station looking north-west. Unfortunately this photograph does not show the wagon turntable which is hidden from view by the platform.

Lens of Sutton Collection

A rear view of the attractive Tudor-style station buildings at Hardingham.

Lens of Sutton Collection

featured overhanging roofs, and most examples had six-paned window frames. The slightly later 'Type Seven' boxes were neat, and well-proportioned structures, with narrower eaves and nine-paned window frames. Most of the signal boxes between Wymondham and Wells were of fairly uniform dimensions, being approximately 24 ft long and 12 ft wide - the 'Type Two' cabins being formed of four six-foot bays. (It should be noted that these classifications have been devised by modern railway enthusiasts, and were unknown in GER days.)

The station master at Kimberley in the 1870s and 1880s was James Raney, who remained in office for many years. By 1905, Mr Raney had been replaced by W.J. Hood, who was subsequently replaced by Gabriel Paynter. Later station masters included Walter Tallent, who later served at Hardingham, and Francis Belton, who was in charge of the station at the time of the 1923 Grouping. In the British Railways period, Kimberley Park was placed under the control of the Hardingham station master, the staffing establishment at that time being two signalmen and one porter.

Hardingham

Departing from Kimberley Park, down trains crossed the B1108 road on the level, and reaching a short section of embankment, passed over an occupation bridge. Climbing at 1 in 168, the double track route turned imperceptibly north-westwards before trains entered a series of cuttings that extended almost as far as Hardingham, the next stopping place. Situated some 15 miles 60 chains from Norwich, Hardingham was similar in many ways to neighbouring Kimberley, being another two-platform station, with extensive Tudor-style buildings on the down side and a simple waiting room on the up platform.

The main station building was another 'Elizabethan' style structure, with a two-storey domestic block and a single-storey booking office and waiting room wing. Like neighbouring Kimberley Park, it featured prominent gables, ornate chimneys and distinctive cottage-style windows. The platform frontage was protected by a projecting canopy which, on closer examination, was really two canopies placed side-by-side; the southernmost section was of Great Eastern vintage, but the northern half, with its plain, saw-tooth decoration, was possibly of Norfolk Railway origin.

Facilities on the up side were more modest, the southbound platform being equipped with another *circa* 1880s Great Eastern style waiting room, with a flat roof that projected over the platform to create a small canopy; as usual on buildings of this type, the platform frontage was formed by a glazed screen. The up and down sides of the station were linked by a barrow crossing at the Dereham end of the platforms.

The nearby signal box was situated to the north of the platforms on the up side. It was a typical Great Eastern 'Type Two' gable roofed structure with a 21-lever McKenzie & Holland frame. It was inspected in November 1882, in connection with the doubling of the line.

The goods yard was sited on the down side, and although only two sidings were available, each of these had its own headshunt, the resulting configuration

A close up of the rear entrance of the brick-and-flint station building at Hardingham in 1969.
Note the Victorian letter box.   *G.R. Mortimer*

A Cravens class '105' two-car dmu leaves Hardingham station with the 15.50 service Norwich Thorpe to Dereham on 27th September, 1969. *G.R. Mortimer*

A detailed view of Hardingham signal box. The standard GER 'Type Two' signal box had a 21-lever McKenzie & Holland frame. *Douglas Thompson*

These two views show Hardingham station in BR days *circa* 1968 after singling of the line. The view above is looking north-westwards, and the lower one to the south-east.

(Both) Lens of Sutton Collection

being more complicated than would otherwise have been the case. A wagon turntable gave access to three short spurs, and the yard layout was made more complex by the presence of a double slip. An additional siding was sited to the north of the down platform, and this siding was linked to both the up and down running lines.

Other facilities at Hardingham included the usual cattle pens, loading dock, and a rail-connected granary belonging to J. Baly & Sons. Hardingham village was over a mile to the south of the railway, but as there was no competing bus service the station was quite well used. Like other rural stations, Hardingham functioned as a convenient railhead not for one, but for a group of dispersed villages. Moreover, the presence of a station often became a focus for Victorian development, and something of this nature took place at Hardingham, where an inn, chapel and several houses grew up around the station during the 19th century.

Hardingham's longest-serving station master was probably Charles Howard Smith, who entered GER service in 1867, and retired in 1917 after a career spanning 50 years. Mr Smith's first appointment was as a clerk at Yarmouth Vauxhall, and he became a station master in 1878, serving first at Buckenham before moving on to Ashwellthorpe, Brundall and finally Hardingham. He arrived at Hardingham around 1887, and remained for no less than three decades; after his retirement, Mr Smith lived for several years at 'Venetian House', Wymondham. One of Charles Smith's immediate successors was Walter Tallent, who had served at Kimberley Park and other local stations before transferring to Hardingham.

The station was staffed by around seven or eight people during the pre-Grouping era, including one station master, one chief clerk, two booking clerks, two signalmen and two porters. Later, however, the staffing establishment was reduced to just two porter-signalmen under a class three station master, who was also responsible for Kimberley Park. Hardingham was reduced to unstaffed halt status in August 1966, but the signal box remained in commission until September 1968.

Thuxton

Leaving Hardingham, Wells trains headed north-westwards, with the River Yare to the right, and the B1135 road running parallel to the left of the railway. Thuxton, the next stop (17 miles 10 chains), was an attractive country station with a level crossing to the south of its two platforms, and a small goods yard on the down side.

The main station building was on the down platform, and like its counterparts elsewhere on the line, this L-shaped structure exhibited an interesting mixture of architectural styles, reflecting two distinct periods of construction. The main block, with its two-storey station master's house and quaint 'Tudor-gothic' details was of Norfolk Railway origin, whereas the detached brick-and-timber waiting room was of typical Great Eastern appearance, and displayed the initials 'GER' in its iron canopy supports. A matching waiting room block was situated on the up platform.

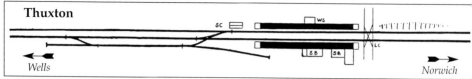

Thuxton

Wells   Norwich

Thuxton station looking north towards Wells on 15th February, 1955. The original Norfolk Railway station buildings were much altered during the Great Eastern period to give increased passenger accommodation.   *Douglas Thompson*

A platform view at Thuxton after the singling of the line. The Great Eastern waiting room can be clearly seen to the right.   *Lens of Sutton Collection*

Goods facilities here were, in later years at least, suitable only for occasional loads of coal, fertilizer or other wagon load consignments. There were no cattle pens or end-loading docks, and no goods shed or yard crane was provided. The single siding goods yard was situated to the north of the platforms on the down side, and linked to the down main line by the usual trailing connection, while a crossover and single slip arrangement allowed access from the up main line. Sundries traffic was dealt with by road vehicles based at nearby Dereham.

An 18-lever signal box was constructed at Thuxton when the line was doubled in the 1880s, this standard GER cabin being inspected in November 1882. The signal box was sited to the north of the platforms on the up side. Changes ensued during the LNER period, the signal box being closed in 1933. In BR days, Thuxton was worked from two ground frames, one of which released the siding connections, while the other locked the level crossing gates and worked the protecting stop and distant signals. As part of this rationalization of facilities, the connection between the up and down lines was removed, and freight trains then called in the down direction only.

The key to the goods yard ground frame was kept in Hardingham signal box, and when wagons were collected or set down at Thuxton the key was obtained by the guards of the trains concerned. When the necessary shunting operations were completed, the key was taken to Yaxham and handed over to the station master, who then ensured that it was taken back to Hardingham by the next available passenger train.

Many country stations had several different station masters in a short space of time, while others enjoyed the services of a single, long-serving incumbent. This was certainly the case at Thuxton in that station master William Barker remained in office for a period of at least 30 years from the early 1890s until the 1920s. In British Railways days, there was a staff of just two, a single porter being supervised by a class four station master. These two individuals normally worked a two shift system, so that one man was always on duty to work the level crossing gates during the period when the line was open; in the 1950s the station was open from 6.45 am until 10.15 pm.

In contrast to many other country stations, Thuxton was well-sited in relation to the small settlement that it purported to serve and Thuxton village was within easy walking distance of the railway. The parish church, with its Perpendicular nave and Decorated tower, was on the south side of the line.

Yaxham

Continuing north-westwards on a 1 in 213 rising gradient, the double track railway passed within a quarter of a mile of the village of Garveston, beyond which the route ran first on embankments and then through cuttings before eventually reaching the next stopping place at Yaxham.

This small station, some 19 miles 59 chains from Norwich Thorpe, was very similar to neighbouring Thuxton; it was another two-platform stopping place, with picturesque Tudor-style buildings on the down side, and a level crossing to the north of the platforms. The main station building, of Norfolk Railway design,

Ex-GER 'J15' 0-6-0 No 65469 passing through Yaxham station with the North Elmham milk train

Dr G R Siriour

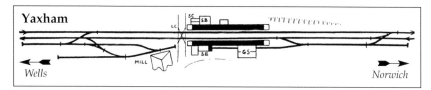

Yaxham

Wells

Norwich

incorporated a two-storey station master's dwelling, while an adjacent glass-fronted waiting room was an obvious Great Eastern addition to the original fabric.

When first opened in 1846, Yaxham station had consisted of little more than a low platform beside a level crossing, with a small gatekeeper's lodge on the down side of the line. The original cottage building was extended during the 1880s, this work being carried out under the contract awarded to W.R. Skipper in August 1881. By analogy with the other wayside stations between Wymondham and Dereham, the original platform was probably situated on the up side of the line, the station building being a physically-detached structure on the opposite side. In 1881-82, however, two full-height platforms were constructed, and the station then reached its fully-developed form.

There was an accretion of structures on the up platform, including an unusually-tall GER 'Type Two' gable-roofed signal cabin with a 26-lever McKenzie & Holland frame. The signal box was situated alongside another standard Great Eastern style glass-fronted waiting room block, which dated from the substantial rebuilding carried out in the 1880s. Examination of this building suggested that the left-hand side (when viewed from the platform) had been modified at some stage in its life, to provide additional accommodation for parcels or similar traffic.

The goods yard, containing one long siding, was situated on the down side. The siding was linked to the up and down running lines by the usual arrangement of trailing crossovers, while the goods yard contained a large brick goods shed, together with a cattle-loading dock and a coal wharf. Other sidings diverged from the down side of the line in order to serve a neighbouring granary, and it was possible, by means of a connection between the up main line and the granary headshunt, for southbound goods trains to reverse across the down main line in order to work traffic into the private siding.

Yaxham station looking towards Wells. The goods shed is to the left and the signal box and crossing gates are at the northern end of the station.   *Douglas Thompson*

Yaxham station and signal box viewed from the level crossing.   *Provenance Unknown*

Yaxham station after rationalization looking north towards Wells.   *Lens of Sutton Collection*

The station master in 1888, and indeed for many years thereafter, was Harry Stokes, but by 1912 Mr Stokes had been replaced by Robert Simpson, who came to Yaxham from Middleton and remained for 11 years before moving to Wroxham in 1922. In British Railways days, Yaxham was under the control of a class three station master, who supervised two class four signalmen and one porter. Yaxham signal box was closed in June 1965, an open gate frame being installed at the north end of the down platform. The station was reduced to unstaffed halt status with effect from 15th August, 1966.

From Yaxham, the route fell at 1 in 185 as it dropped into the Tudd Valley and crossed the River Tudd on a small bridge before burrowing into the opposite hillside by means of another cutting. The line was virtually level at this point, although as trains neared Dereham they faced a stretch of 1 in 165. Nearing Dereham, trains passed the quaintly-named hamlet of Dumpling Green where, in 1803, the writer George Borrow had been born; cuttings prevented a clear view, but a few houses could be glimpsed in the distance as trains crossed the B1135 road on the level.

Nearing Dereham, the line forked; to the left, a south-to-west curve provided a direct route to Kings Lynn for freight and excursion traffic, but passenger trains continued straight on past the west-to-north curve which converged from the left, and immediately entered the down platform at Dereham, the principal intermediate station on the Norwich to Wells-next-the-Sea route.

A post-rationalization photograph at Yaxham, looking south towards Wymondham.
Lens of Sutton Collection

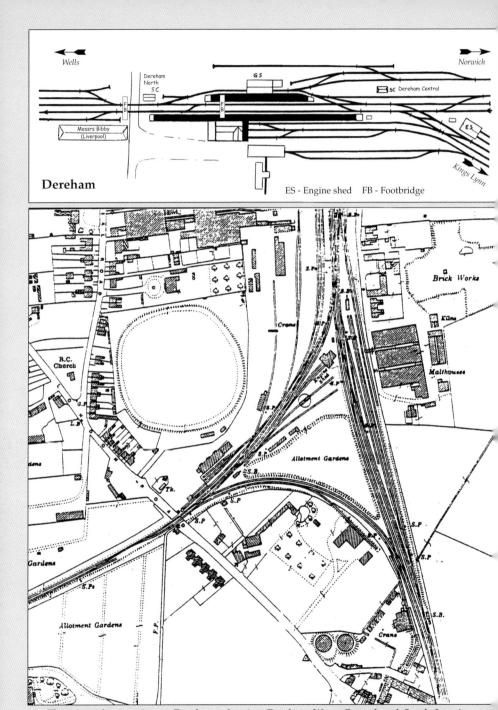

The triangular junction at Dereham, showing Dereham West, Central and South Junctions. Dereham station is immediately to the north of this map. The line to the left is the Lynn & Dereham Railway route to Swaffham and Kings Lynn.

Reproduced from the 1906, 25" Ordnance Survey Map

Chapter Six

The Route from Dereham to Wells

Situated some 21 miles 51 chains from Norwich Thorpe, Dereham station was a place of some importance, being shared by trains from Norwich, Wroxham, Kings Lynn and Wells-next-the-Sea. Long up and down platforms were available, the down platform being much longer than its counterpart on the up side. There was an additional, dead-end bay on the down side, and this bay had run-round facilities for the benefit of trains which terminated their journeys here.

Dereham

The main station building was on the down side. In common with the other stations en route from Wymondham, its flamboyant architecture exhibited a pronounced 'Tudor-gothic' atmosphere, the most striking feature, to casual observers, being a profusion of tall, cylindrical chimney stacks, with ornate helical mouldings. In 1846, the *Norfolk Chronicle* described the station building as a 'very handsome' structure, 'built of red bricks, with an elegant frontage to the road'. The station's long platforms were partially covered by extensive awnings, and a refreshment room on the down platform catered for the needs of hungry and thirsty travellers. There was, in addition, a small bookstall.

The up and down platforms were linked by a lattice girder footbridge, and a similar bridge was available to the north of the passenger station for the benefit of pedestrians using Norfolk Street. Other details at the north end of the station included a substantial brick water tower, beyond which a water column was sited for use by engines heading north towards Wells-next-the-Sea. Locomotives needing water were normally detached from their trains and run 'light' for the short distance to the watering point, this movement being controlled by a raised disc signal near the water tower.

Dereham's goods facilities were lavish, and in addition to the main goods yard on the up side, there were several loops and various private sidings, which branched out to serve Dereham gasworks, Whitbread's maltings, Fison & Son, Stammer's mill, and the East Dereham Foundry. Two agricultural stores on the down side of the line near Dereham North signal box received van loads of bagged cattle feed, which was unloaded by British Railways staff on behalf of Messrs Bibbys.

The goods shed was sited behind the up platform, in which position it formed a convenient support for a length of platform canopy. The goods shed was built of brick, and it incorporated an internal loading platform, so that small freight and sundries traffic could be unloaded undercover. An office extended from the south gable as a sort of lean-to addition, and photographs confirm that it dated from a rebuilding of the goods shed that had been carried out under LNER auspices around 1939. The interior of the lean-to goods office contained sloping

Dereham South Junction in GER days, looking towards Norwich. Dereham South box stands on the up side of the main line, while the gas works siding can be seen the opposite side of the railway.   *National Railway Museum*

A panoramic view of Dereham station, looking north towards Wells, with the main passenger buildings to the left and the large gabled good shed on the right.   *National Railway Museum*

Dereham South Junction looking north towards Dereham station. The direct line to Kings Lynn veers off sharply to the left. The engine shed is visible in the distance.

National Railway Museum

The original wooden engine shed at Dereham. This ramshackle structure was demolished *circa* 1926, and a new shed, of brick construction, was erected in its place. The Norwich line can be seen to the left while the north-to-west curve is visible to the right. *National Railway Museum*

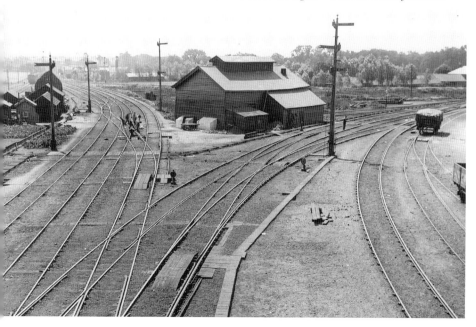

The main station buildings at Dereham, seen from Station Road. Note the fine chimneys in this *circa* 1910 view. *Lens of Sutton Collection*

'E4' class 2-4-0 No. 62782 pauses at Dereham station on 13th September, 1952, with a train from Wroxham via County School. Messrs Hobbies Ltd engineering works and saw mills can be seen on the extreme left. *H.B. Priestley*

Trains occupy both platforms at Dereham in this view of the north end of Dereham station on 19th July, 1958. Notice the substantial water tower to the right. *John Langford*

'B12' class 4-6-0 No. 61572 leaves Dereham with the mid-afternoon Norwich to March vans train in the early 1960s. *Dr G.R. Siviour*

The LNER brick-built shed at Dereham *circa* 1948. The two locomotives on the shed roads, 'E4' class 2-4-0 No. 2782 and 'D15' class 4-4-0 No. 2502, still carry their LNER identities. The unidentifiable 'F5' class 2-4-2T in the background has already been rebranded and is in British Railways livery.   *N.E. Stead Collection*

'E4' class 2-4-0 No. 62793 on shed at Dereham in British Railways days.

N.E. Stead Collection

'J17' class No. 65567 with a pick-up goods train at Dereham in March 1962. As the last working steam locomotive allocated to Norwich shed, this engine was kept in immaculate condition.

Dr G.R. Siviour

A busy scene at Dereham during the early 1960s. Up and down Wells trains wait in the main platforms while a Metro-Cammell class '101' dmu waits in the Kings Lynn bay. A Brush type '2' A1A-A1A locomotive (later class '31') stands in the goods yard. Note the swan-necked water crane on the up platform.

N.E. Stead

A two-car class '105' dmu waits with a Norwich train on 4th October, 1969. This view looks along the platform towards the footbridge at the northern end of the station. A buffer stop can be seen beyond the train, passenger services having ceased between Dereham and Wells in October 1964.   *E. Wilmshurst*

Another view of the same train, this time as it departs for Norwich. The goods shed can be seen to the right.   *E. Wilmshurst*

desks for the goods clerks, while an additional goods office was located in a small brick building at the north end of the up platform.

Minor structures in and around Dereham station included the usual diverse collection of sheds, huts and permanent way stores - a number of platelayer's huts and storage sheds being scattered around the passenger station and goods yard area. A diminutive brick structure at the south end of the up platform served as a gentlemen's urinal and, a few feet away, an elegant swan-necked water crane provided watering facilities for southbound trains.

The station was liberally supplied with signal boxes, the station proper being controlled from a large 50-lever cabin containing a McKenzie & Holland frame. This cabin, known as Dereham Central Box, was built in 1880 and inspected in April 1880. Another box, known as Dereham South box, controlled the southern extremity of the station layout, including the western end of the south-to-west curve. When the LNER carried out its survey of GER section signal boxes shortly after the Grouping, Dereham South box had a 27-lever McKenzie & Holland frame, though as a result of alterations carried out under LNER auspices the box was reconstructed with a 32-lever frame.

Dereham West box, controlling the western end of the triangular junction, was inspected in April 1880; at that time it was known as 'Dereham D' box, and like most of the other signal cabins in the Dereham area it was a standard Great Eastern timber-framed structure, with a glazed upper floor and a slated, gable roof. In 1932 the LNER moved Dereham West box to a new site to the west of the junction points, although the 36-lever McKenzie & Holland frame was apparently retained.

A fourth signal cabin, originally designated 'Dereham C' box, later Dereham North, was situated at the north end of the platforms beside a busy level crossing. This standard GER 'Type Two' cabin was also inspected in April 1880, but like the other boxes at Dereham it was subjected to many alterations. At the time of the Grouping it had a 25-lever McKenzie & Holland frame.

Many trains were divided at Dereham - the usual practice, around 1930, being for the front portions of northbound workings to continue on to Wells, while the rearmost vehicles were worked through to Kings Lynn behind another locomotive. In the opposite direction, a few trains from Kings Lynn were combined with those from Wells-next-the-Sea, and the two portions would then go forward to Wymondham and Norwich as one working. These operations gave Dereham an atmosphere of bustle and activity which was perhaps unusual at such a rural station. Underlining its importance as a traffic centre, Dereham had a small engine shed, which usually housed an interesting assortment of ex-Great Eastern locomotive types.

Dereham's two-road engine shed was situated in the 'V' of the junction formed by the main line and the west-to-north curve. The original shed building was a wooden structure with a prominent clerestory along the apex of its roof, but the shed was later rebuilt in more durable brick. The new brick shed was slightly longer than its timber predecessor, with a total length of around 52 ft. The usual allocation in steam days included ex-GER 'E4' class 2-4-0s, 'F3' class 2-4-2Ts, 'J15' class 0-6-0s and other typical Great Eastern classes, and these locomotives could often be seen in the shed or alongside the primitive coaling stage.

Dereham station in 1964, looking south-west with Dereham Central signal box and the engine shed in the distance. The line to Wymondham and Norwich is on the left, and the line to Kings Lynn on the right. By this date the signalling incorporates an interesting mixture of GER, LNER and BR components. *Mowat Collection*

A Cravens class '105' dmu leaves Dereham with the 14.35 for Norwich on 6th September, 1969. Dereham Central signal box is in the background. *G.R. Mortimer*

Dereham Central signal box was a relatively large structure, with a 50-lever McKenzie & Holland frame. It was built around 1880.   *Douglas Thompson*

Dereham was, even more than Wymondham, an important rural junction, and in its heyday it required a large staffing establishment including a large number of passenger clerks, goods clerks, porters, passenger shunters, goods shunters, foremen, checkers, signalmen, permanent way men, engine crews and guards. The station was supervised by a class one station master who was, needless to say, an important figure in the local community.

In 1862, Dereham's station master was John Playford, while in the later Victorian period the station was supervised by Charles Eastaugh. Francis Arthur Easton had taken over by 1904, and he remained in office for several years thereafter. Later station masters included Frederick Young, who was in charge of the station at the time of the Grouping, Frank Stone, who was in control towards the end of the LNER era, and Albert Cussons, who succeeded him around 1950. In 1955, the station master's grading was changed to 'Special Class A'.

2nd-SINGLE   SINGLE-2nd

North Elmham to

North Elmham   North Elmham

Dereham   Dereham

DEREHAM

(E)   1/3   Fare   1/3   (E)

For conditions see over   For conditions see over

3 6 8 5   3 6 8 5

The northern extremity of Dereham's down platform, with maltings and other lineside industries visible in the distance. Next to the level crossing on the right is Dereham North signal box. *Lens of Sutton Collection*

A detailed view of Dereham North signal box, which was a standard GER 'Type Two' cabin. *Robert Humm Collection*

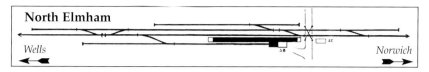

North Elmham

Continuing northwards, Wells trains ran through the eastern environs of Dereham, passing over three closely-spaced level crossings in quick succession. The double track ended at Dereham North signal box, and drivers had to be in possession of a single line tablet before proceeding. Climbing slightly, the railway entered a cutting which was spanned by five overbridges - one of which carried a minor road leading from Dereham to the outlying hamlet of Northall Green. Emerging from the cutting, down trains passed over Hoe level crossing (26 miles 14 chains), where the gates were worked by a resident female crossing keeper.

Surmounting a miniature summit, the route then descended on gradients of 1 in 151 and 1 in 135, and with a minor road running parallel to the left, trains entered the Wensum Valley. About four miles from Dereham, the minor road turned to the right, and having crossed the railway on the level at Worthing level crossing (26 miles 54 chains), it then diverged north-eastwards. North Elmham, the next station, was slightly less than a mile further on.

This small station was 26 miles 14 chains from Norwich Thorpe, and its facilities consisted of a single platform on the down side, with a level crossing immediately to the south. The running line was flanked by a long goods loop, and sidings were available on both sides. The neat, brick-built station building, with its angular platform canopy, dated from a rebuilding that had been carried out during the LNER period around 1936. Internally, it contained the usual booking office and waiting room facilities, the waiting room being entered via double doors that faced the platform, while the booking office was sited immediately to the right. A separate station master's office was situated at the right-hand end of the building (when viewed from the platform), while the ladies toilets and gentlemen's urinal was sited to the left of the waiting room.

Photographs suggests that the original station building, which had probably been of timber-framed construction, was a simple, two-storey, cottage with a low-pitched hipped roof. This earlier building appears to have been a somewhat insubstantial structure - the likelihood being that, over the years, it became so dilapidated that an entirely new station building was erected on more or less the same site.

North Elmham station in July 1964, showing the austere, modern-style building, with the goods loop to the right. *D. Thompson*

A general view of North Elmham station, looking north, with R.J. Seaman's granary visible beyond the level crossing. *Lens of Sutton Collection*

A view from the train at North Elmham on 19th July, 1958, looking towards Wells.

John Langford

A United Dairies milk depot was sited behind the platform, and this was served by a single siding which formed a trailing connection with the running line. Empty milk tanks could be backed into the siding by northbound trains, but this arrangement was inconvenient when loaded vehicles were picked up by southbound trains, and full milk tanks were therefore collected from a separate siding on the up side of the line; a shunting horse was employed to transfer these vehicles from one side of the line to the other. Further traffic, in the form of grain and agricultural fertilizer, was generated by another private siding on the down side, which served the premises of Messrs R.J. Seaman & Sons.

North Elmham was a comparatively busy station, which was able to deal with a full range of goods traffic including coal, livestock, furniture, vehicles and general merchandise. Up to half a dozen milk tanks were sent each day to a bottling plant at Ilford, this traffic being conveyed by passenger trains until the introduction of diesel multiple units in 1955. Thereafter, a separate milk and parcels train left Norwich at 2.40 pm each day, the usual formation being five or six empty tank wagons and a passenger brake van. On arrival at North Elmham the locomotive ran-round its train, and then returned southwards with the loaded milk tanks.

Two passenger trains were not allowed to cross here, but the passing loop could, if necessary, be used to cross two freight trains, or one passenger train and one goods working. The station was signalled from a standard Great Eastern signal box with a 20-lever McKenzie & Holland frame, this structure being sited to the south of the level crossing on the down side. A 15-lever ground frame was sited on the down side of the line at the north end of the station.

In British Railways days, the staffing establishment at North Elmham included one class three station master, two signalmen, one porter, and the female crossing keepers at Hoe and Worthing level crossings who, for administrative purposes, were controlled by the North Elmham station master. There were, in addition, a number of locally-based permanent way men, although these employees were not regarded as part of the station staff. One of North Elmham's longest-serving station masters was Albert Kingsbury, who was in charge of the station from 1931 until his retirement in 1956. He was succeeded by Stanley Lincoln, who had previously served at Narborough & Pentney.

Originally called simply Elmham, the station served both North Elmham and nearby Worthing villages - though the passenger platform, being on the down side, was more convenient for North Elmham residents. In situations where station served two or more villages, Victorian railway companies invariably named their stations after the senior (though not necessarily the largest) village; thus North Elmham - the seat of an important Saxon bishopric - inevitably took precedence over humble Worthing.

The single line sections beyond North Elmham were all operated by the train staff and ticket system, which allowed successive trains to enter a single line, provided that their respective drivers possessed written authorization (a 'ticket') in lieu of a train staff; the staff itself would be carried by the last train in an up or down series. This method of single line control was particularly useful between County School and North Elmham, as this short section of line was used by Wroxham to Dereham services as well as Norwich to Wells workings.

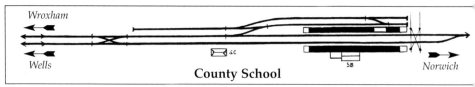

An Edwardian scene at County School station, looking north towards Wells, with the Wroxham platform visible on the extreme right. *Lens of Sutton Collection*

A general view of County School station *circa* 1963. A British Thomson-Houston Bo-Bo (later class '15') approaches with a goods train on the up line. *Mowat Collection*

County School

Following the River Wensum, the line continued northwards along more or less level alignments. Passing within half a mile of North Elmham's famous Anglo-Saxon ruins (later incorporated into a 14th century Bishop's Palace), trains soon reached County School, the next stopping place, which was only 1 mile 43 chains further on. County School was not one of the original stations, having been opened on 1st March, 1884 to serve as the junction for branch services from Wroxham.

County School was an isolated rural station, with up and down lines for Norwich to Wells traffic and an additional bay on the up side for Wroxham workings - some of which started or terminated their journeys here. Perhaps surprisingly, the distance from Norwich to County School via Wroxham (32 miles 31 chains) compared quite favourably with that via Wymondham and the Dereham line (27 miles 57 chains), though the latter was regarded as the principal route. There was a level crossing immediately to the south of the station, and the up and down platforms were equipped with substantial, GER style station buildings, both of these structures having projecting platform canopies.

The Norfolk County School, which gave the station its name, was sited just a few hundred yards to the east of the railway, and approached by a leafy carriage drive. The school was founded in 1874 and closed in 1895, but in the Edwardian period it was re-opened as 'The Watts Naval Training School' - a branch of Dr Barnardo's Homes. Apart from the school, County School station served only scattered farms and cottages, the nearest village being North Elmham, around one mile to the south.

The layout at County School was confined to the main up and down lines, and the Wroxham branch bay. The bay was equipped with its own run-round loop, and a short siding or headshunt extended northwards from the bay line. There was also a scissors crossover at the Wroxham end of the station, at the point where the crossing loop merged into the independent single lines to Broom Green. This modest track layout was sufficient for County School to be used as a junction station and passing place, while as the only two-platform stopping place between Dereham and Wells, County School became the usual crossing place for passenger workings on the northern part of the Wells-next-the-Sea branch.

The main station building, containing booking office and waiting room facilities, was on the down side. It was solidly and substantially-constructed of brick, with a hipped roof and a projecting platform canopy edged with typical 'V-and-double-hole' fretwork valancing. The window and door apertures were slightly arched, and the canopy was supported by decorative iron brackets bearing the initials 'GER' in their spandrels. The up side building was a smaller structure, in a matching architectural style, with an all-round canopy of generous proportions. Other buildings included a station master's house, which stood beside the level crossing on the down side of the line.

Although the station was essentially a passenger interchange point, the *Railway Clearing House Handbook of Stations* reveals that it could also deal with goods traffic. In practice, this related mainly to small parcels and packages that could be carried in the guards' compartments of passenger or freight workings.

On the other hand, Great Eastern working timetables indicate quite clearly that goods trains were booked to call at the station to load or unload what was described as 'brake goods' traffic. There was a small goods yard on the up side, and this was able to deal with small amounts of coal or other wagon load traffic if required.

County School was signalled from a typical Great Eastern gable-roofed signal cabin, which was sited to the north of the platforms on the down side. The post-Grouping survey of GER section signal cabins reveals that the box was equipped with a 44-lever Saxby frame, and the station was signalled with an impressive array of Great Eastern semaphore signals including two tall bracketed starting signals and two similar assemblies which controlled entry to the station from the Wells and Wroxham directions.

The position of the signal cabin, about eight chains to the north of the station, was dictated by the presence of the above-mentioned scissors crossover, which was in effect the point of bifurcation between the Wells and Wroxham routes. As the signal cabin was sited at some distance from the level crossing, a two-lever gate frame was provided at the south end of the up platform. The gates were normally operated by porters or other station staff, who were also responsible for exchanging the single line train staff or tickets.

Amusingly, the station master here during World War I had rejoiced in the vaguely-Biblical name of Gabriel Paynter, while (in continuation of the religious theme) one of his subordinates was called Mr Herod! Until 1912 the station master had been Walter Tallent, who enjoyed a long association with the Wells branch and worked at several of its stations. In later years, County School was staffed by two signalmen and two porters.

County School was the setting for an unusual accident that took place on 14th March, 1918, when a train collided with a milk float, the incident being described as follows in *The Times* on 15th March, 1918:

RUNAWAY HORSE ON RAILWAY LINE - While driving through County School, near Dereham, Norfolk, in a milk float yesterday, Eva Wicks, who delivers milk for Mr Charles Roberts of the Old Hall, North Elmham, and Mr Robert's daughter Alice, aged 14, had an exciting experience. The horse took fright, bolted, and attempted to leap the railway gates, which were closed. The gate was smashed, and Miss Wicks was thrown from the float. The horse ran along the railway with the milk float still intact, Alice Roberts pluckily tugging at the reins. At this moment the train from Norwich was coming in, but the driver, Alfred Swann, saw the danger and stopped the train just before the milk float crashed into it near the signal box. The float struck the buffers of the engine and was smashed and overturned, and the liberated horse dashed up the line, dragging after it the girl, who still gripped the reins. Miss Roberts, who was drawn 20 yards along the line, was badly injured.

Accelerating past an impressive array of characteristically-tall Great Eastern semaphore signals, trains headed north on what appeared to be a conventional double track section, but was in reality two parallel single lines - the left-hand track being the 'main line' while the right-hand line was the Wroxham branch. The two lines ran side by side for the next mile until the Wroxham route diverged eastwards near the village of Broom Green.

Occasionally, a late-running Dereham to Wroxham branch train might be shunted into the bay platform at County School in order to provide connections for people travelling north to Wells. Having made their connection, the two trains would then depart from County School more or less simultaneously, resulting in what appeared to be a neck-and-neck 'race' along the parallel single lines. On these occasions schoolboy travellers would urge on their respective trains - knowing, however, that the Wells-bound 'Claud Hamilton' would always 'win' when the Wroxham-bound 'E4' 2-4-0 slowed for the sharp curve at Broom Green!

In later years there was no physical connection between the two lines at Broom Green, although Board of Trade records show that a signal box and associated signals were inspected in April 1882. The original layout had consisted of a crossing loop, with a double track junction for the Wroxham line. The loop was soon extended southwards to County School, and the junction at Broom Green was then abolished, the former up line becoming the Wroxham branch, while the down line became the Wells-next-the-Sea line. These modifications seem to have taken place as early as 1884, the likeliest explanation being that Broom Green box was used during the construction of the Wroxham line and then abandoned.

It is interesting to recall that a triangular junction had also been planned at Broom Green, and this would have enabled Wroxham trains to run northwards to Fakenham or Wells. Indeed, the earthworks which might have carried an east-to-north curve were actually constructed but, as far as can be ascertained, these never carried any track, except perhaps temporary contractor's lines for use during the construction of the Wroxham branch during the 1880s.

Ryburgh

Climbing on gradients of 1 in 148 and 1 in 151, the railway headed north-westwards beside the sparkling River Wensum, running first in cuttings and then on an embankment. With attractively-wooded hillsides visible to the right, trains rumbled beneath a road overbridge and then entered a further cutting. Nearing Ryburgh, the line emerged onto another embankment which was pierced, at one point, by a small road underbridge. Although the surrounding countryside was unspectacular, the rolling hills and ample woodlands ensured that it was never dull, and discerning travellers were treated to a continually changing panorama of rural English scenery at its best.

Continuing northwards along the embankment, down workings arrived at Ryburgh station (31 miles 21 chains), where the somewhat basic facilities consisted of a single platform, some 291 ft in length, on the down side of the line, with a gated level crossing immediately to the south. The station served the villages of Great Ryburgh (near the station) and Little Ryburgh (visible on higher ground to the north of the railway), while Messrs F.G. Smith's huge, rail-connected maltings, which could be seen on the west side of the line, provided a useful source of originating traffic for the railway.

A view of Ryburgh station looking south towards Norwich. This interesting photograph shows the original station building which was subsequently demolished after sustaining damage as a result of enemy action.   *R.M. Casserley Collection*

By the time this photograph was taken in 1958 there was little trace of the station building at Ryburgh.   *John Langford*

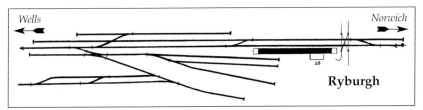

The track layout at Ryburgh provided goods sidings on both sides of the running line. There was a loop siding on the up side, together with a second, much shorter dead-end siding which was entered via a connection that was facing to up trains. Further goods sidings fanned out on the down side to serve the adjacent maltings. Although Ryburgh was not a block post or crossing station, it was equipped with a standard Great Eastern 'Type Seven' signal cabin, this characteristic structure being sited to the south of the platform on the down side, in convenient proximity to the level crossing. The box contained a 25-lever Saxby frame.

Ryburgh's station buildings were peculiar. The main block was a two-storey, timber-framed structure clad in horizontal weather boarding, while toilets and other facilities were contained in a single-storey shed to the right of the main building (when viewed from the platform). The two-storey block featured a low-pitched hipped roof and a projecting platform canopy, while the single-storey building featured a pitched roof that sloped towards the platform - suggesting that, when first erected, this small structure may have abutted a goods shed which is clearly marked on the 25 inch Ordnance Survey map. There was, in addition, a large brick-built station master's house. The latter structure, which was obviously a later addition, was sited to the rear of the wooden station building. It was authorized in 1889 at an estimated cost of £40.

As mentioned in Chapter Four, Ryburgh station suffered severe damage as a result of an air raid that took place on 25th August, 1942, in the middle of World War II. Ironically, the destruction wrought on that fateful night was caused, not by high-explosive bombs, but by comparatively innocuous incendiary bombs - which may have been dropped by Luftwaffe 'pathfinder' aircraft in an attempt

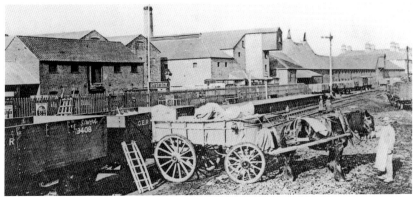

The extensive maltings at Ryburgh, seen here in the Great Eastern period.
Lens of Sutton Collection

to guide the main bomber force towards more important targets such as the nearby RAF airfields. One or more of these small 'fire bombs' remained undiscovered on the adjacent maltings, with the result that a major fire broke out several hours after the 'All Clear' had been called. The ensuing conflagration was so severe that the glow in the sky could be seen from Norwich, while the extensive maltings continued to burn for around seven weeks.

The flames quickly spread to the vulnerable wooden station buildings, and although the single-storey shed and the brick-built station master's house escaped destruction, the main station building could not be saved. The surviving station building were pressed into use as a makeshift booking office and waiting room while, in an attempt to hide the scars of war, the station staff planted an attractive flower garden on the site of the bombed-out two-storey block. The resulting floral displays ensured that Ryburgh won many awards in the annual station gardens competition.

In Victorian days, Ryburgh had a staff of around half a dozen. The station master here in 1881 was Joseph Butters, who later moved to Wells-next-the-Sea. Later station masters included Frank Henry Stone, who supervised the station around 1908, and Reg Dunnett, who was in charge during the 1950s. In its final years of operation the station was staffed by one class three station master and two porter-signalmen.

Ryburgh station in dilapidated condition *circa* 1964 The left foreground (fenced off) was the site of the wooden station building. The rebuilt maltings can be seen in the distance.
Lens of Sutton Collection

Fakenham

Beyond Ryburgh the line - still rising gently - curved onto a more westerly heading as it followed the south bank of the River Wensum. A glance to the right revealed the Midland & Great Northern line running parallel on the opposite bank of the river, and for the next mile the two lines ran side by side. Eventually, the Great Eastern route curved north-westwards crossing the river and then the M&GN line before trains reached the Great Eastern station at Fakenham.

The principal intermediate station between Dereham and Wells, Fakenham was 33 miles 62 chains from Norwich and 23 miles 44 chains from Wymondham. Its track layout was relatively complex, although (perhaps surprisingly) there was only one long platform and a short bay on the down side. The main crossing loop was situated to the north of the platform, and separated from it by an intervening level crossing. This unorthodox arrangement was necessary because of the position of the goods yard, which had prevented the installation of a normal crossing loop with up and down platforms on each side.

When first opened on Tuesday 20th March, 1849, Fakenham had been little more than a single-platform branch line terminus at the end of the Norfolk Railway's line from Dereham. The opening of the Wells & Fakenham Railway on 1st December, 1857 produced few immediate changes, though a turntable that had hitherto been situated at the end of the line was removed (possibly to Wells). In its new guise as a through station, Fakenham retained its single platform on the down side, the track layout being adequate in relation to local traffic demands. In the late 1880s, however, the GER company decided that various modifications were necessary, and a programme of improvements was put into effect.

It was agreed that the station would be fully interlocked, and two standard Great Eastern 'Type Seven' signal cabins, which were designated 'Fakenham North' and 'Fakenham South', were erected. The new signal boxes were probably built in 1889, in which years their frames were ordered from Messrs Saxby & Farmer. In connection with this scheme, a crossing loop and a new bay platform were installed, the new works being inspected in November 1889 and re-inspected in the following May.

The post-1880s layout at Fakenham incorporated a longish section of double track that commenced near the site of Fakenham South signal box and extended northwards through the passenger station before converging into a single line at Fakenham North box. A 'scissors' crossover was sited on the north side of the level crossing, and this marked the start of the actual crossing loop. The two lines on the south side of the level crossing were not signalled for double track working - the westernmost line being the running line for up and down traffic, whereas the eastern line was a merely a goods loop. The crossing gates were worked from a 4-lever ground frame on the down side of the line.

In later years, Fakenham South box was abolished, this work being carried out during the LNER period between 1927 and 1928. Thereafter, all signals were controlled from the former North box, the points at the south end of the station being worked from ground frames, or by electric point motors. The surviving

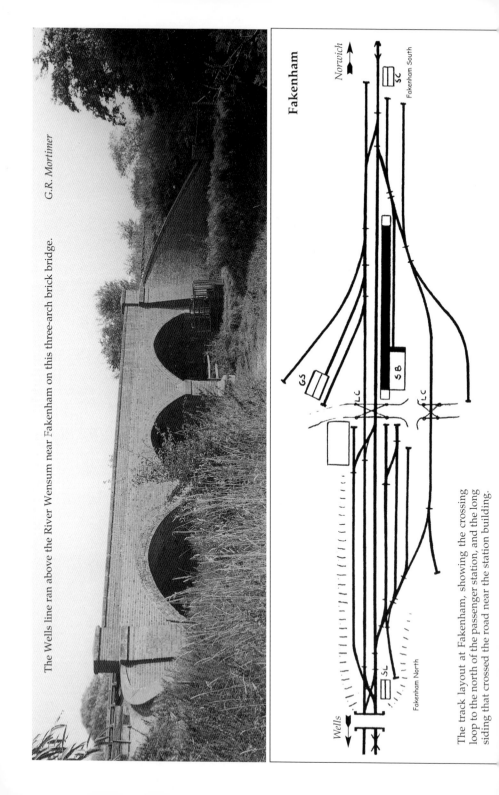

The Wells line ran above the River Wensum near Fakenham on this three-arch brick bridge.　　G.R. Mortimer

Fakenham

Norwich

Fakenham South

GS

SB

LC

LC

SL

Fakenham North

Wells

The track layout at Fakenham, showing the crossing loop to the north of the passenger station, and the long siding that crossed the road near the station building.

Fakenham station in the early years of the 20th century. The timber-framed station building was, in effect, a larger version of the original wooden buildings at Ryburgh and North Elmham.

Lens of Sutton Collection

This 1958 view shows the subtle changes to Fakenham's station building over time, along with the rather more significant changes to road transport. Note the good siding which crosses the road in the foreground by means of an ungated level crossing. *John Langford*

A view along the platform at Fakenham on 1st September, 1955, looking towards Wells. In the distance Fakenham North signal box is just visible, as are the two road overbridges.

H.C. Casserley

This photograph was taken from almost the same position on the same day. The station comes to life as 'Claud Hamilton' 4-4-0 No. 62577 arrives from Wells with a train for Norwich. To the right is the goods yard.

H.C. Casserley

North box had originally contained a 37-lever frame, but the number of levers was later increased to 39; the box was sited to the north of the platform, on the down side of the crossing loop. The South box was situated to the south of the platform, and it had contained a 25-lever Saxby & Farmer frame, with seven spare levers.

The station building here was a two-storey, hipped-roof design, incorporating a station master's dwelling. As at Ryburgh, the building was of timber-framed construction, although by the BR period the weather-boarded walls had been clad in plywood sheets. The projecting platform canopy, with its large spandrels, was a later Great Eastern addition. The canopy was attached to a brick extension that was sited to the left of the wooden station master's house (when viewed from the platform). To the left of this was a small, hipped roof brick building which served as a porters' room and lamp room.

The main goods yard, with three dead-end sidings, was sited opposite the passenger station on the up side. One of the yard sidings passed through a goods shed, while another was used for coal traffic. Other goods facilities included the usual cattle pens, loading docks, and a 7 ton yard crane. A curious feature of the track layout at Fakenham concerned the presence of a lengthy goods siding on the down side that passed behind the station building and crossed the A1065 road in order to reach granaries and other facilities to the north of the passenger station. This goods crossing was protected by ground discs, although (in later years at least) there were no gates.

In operational terms, Fakenham was especially important in so far as it was sited roughly halfway between Dereham and Wells. Moreover, the station possessed the only passenger crossing loop between County School and the end of the line at Wells-next-the-Sea. As mentioned above, the loop was installed in November 1889, but there must have been some means of crossing up and down workings before that date. The 1882 timetable shows that trains regularly passed each other at Fakenham at that time; the 1.12 pm passenger service from Wymondham, for instance, crossed the 1.50 pm up service from Wells at 2.14 pm, while the 3.10 pm from Norwich crossed the 4.50 pm (Thursdays Only) market train from Fakenham.

It must be assumed that these trains made use of some form of loop or refuge siding at Fakenham, though the loop or siding involved may not have been signalled in accordance with modern practice and Board of Trade regulations (hence the programme of new works carried out at the station in the late 1880s). After 1889, there were two methods whereby up and down trains were able to pass each other at Fakenham - either in the crossing loop, or by shunting into the bay platform at the passenger station. When the loop was used for crossing purposes, southbound trains were held on the up line until the down working had left the platform, this being the usual mode of operation during the British Railways period.

In earlier years, many passenger trains had crossed in the passenger station with the aid of the bay platform line. In 1938, for instance, the 9.07 am up service from Wells arrived at Fakenham at 9.28 am, and then reversed into the bay platform to await the arrival of the 8.17 am down train from Norwich Thorpe. The latter working arrived at around 9.35 am, and at 9.37 am the up and down services resumed their respective journeys. This procedure went tragically

A Metro-Cammell class '101' dmu stands at Fakenham with a Norwich to Wells train on 11th September, 1963. Notice the station nameboard now reads 'Fakenham East'. *S. Creer*

Fakenham station in 1964, showing the single platform with its unusual canopy (the substantial brick wall possibly supported an overall roof when the station was first opened). Fakenham station marked the northernmost limit of Norfolk Railway ownership – the Wells & Fakenham Railway commenced several chains beyond the level crossing. *E. Wilmshurst*

wrong on the morning of Wednesday 27th May, 1932, when the 8.17 am down service overran its signals and ran into the bay platform, where it collided head-on with the up train, killing Mrs Marjorie Foster of the Black Lion, Walsingham.

The station was, throughout most of its life, known as 'Fakenham', but after nationalization British Railways renamed it 'Fakenham East' to distinguish it from the Midland & Great Northern establishment ('West') at the other end of the town. Fakenham town centre was about half a mile to the west of the railway, and the tall tower of its parish church was a conspicuous local landmark.

Alfred Wootton is listed as Fakenham's station master in the 1881 census, while in the early 1930s the station was supervised by Stanley Smith. The Midland & Great Northern line had, by that time, been placed under LNER control, and as a staff economy measure Mr Smith controlled both the GER and M&GN stations. He was succeeded by Tom Rattee in the early BR period. Later station masters included A. Harvey, Joe Bayliss and Leslie Seal. Until 1959, the station master's office was located at Fakenham West, but following the closure of the M&GN in that year, Mr Seal, the then station master, moved his office to Fakenham East.

Class '31' A1A-A1A No. 31161 at Fakenham waits to return to Norwich with the daily freight train on 5th September, 1979. *G.R. Mortimer*

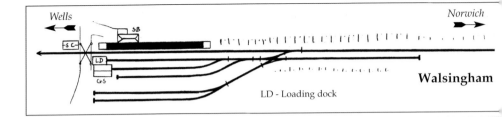

Wells ◄◄— Norwich ►►

SB
SC
LD
GS

LD - Loading dock

Walsingham

A general view of Walsingham station, looking north towards Wells on 18th September, 1959.
R.M. Casserley

A Derby lightweight two-car dmu arrives at Walsingham with a train bound for Wells in 1960. 'J17' class 0-6-0 No. 65586 waits in the goods yard with the Wells to Norwich (Trowse) pick-up goods train.
Dr G.R. Siviour

Walsingham

Leaving Fakenham, northbound trains entered a substantial cutting, and passing beneath four road overbridges in rapid succession, commenced their 1 in 81 climb out of the Wensum Valley. With the staccato beat of the labouring engine leaving no doubt that the general direction was now upwards, the branch continued towards its summit. About 1½ miles beyond Fakenham, trains crossed a minor road on the level and then passed a rail-connected granary on the up side; access to the single siding was controlled from a 5-lever ground frame which was released by an Annett's Key carried on the Fakenham-Walsingham train staff.

The siding, known as Coleman's Siding, was facing to down trains, and for this reason it was shunted only by up workings; the 1917 working timetable reveals, however that 'down road traffic for Coleman's Siding' could be detached at Walsingham and worked back by up freight workings. The siding was installed in 1915 for Messrs Coleman, though by 1938 it was known as 'Parker's Siding', and served Messrs E.J. Parker, Isaac Fisher and J.A. Keith.

Continuing northwards, the branch crossed the B1105 road on the level at Barsham level crossing; it is interesting to record that the B1105 level crossing was protected an ancient 'crossbar' signal which indicated danger when the gates were closed across the railway. (This presumably dated from the Wells & Fakenham era.)

Reaching its modest summit elevation of approximately 175 ft above mean sea level, the line then curved gradually north-east towards the Stiffkey (pronounced 'Stewkey') Valley. As their train crossed the valley, travellers could, by glancing to the right, see the picturesque village of East Barsham with its archetypal Tudor manor house where, in 1511, King Henry VIII had lodged prior to walking (it is said) barefoot to the shrine of Our Lady of Walsingham.

As we have seen, the railway originally crossed the Stiffkey on a timber viaduct, but this had been replaced by an embankment in the late 19th century. It is interesting to recall a local legend which suggests that the old viaduct was actually buried rather than replaced; this would have been a sensible course of action, and the operation could have been carried out without serious disruption to traffic. Contemporary photographs show that the wooden viaduct was a six-span structure, with five principal trestles supported by a system of subsidiary struts and secondary trestles. The replacement embankment was pierced by a single-arched brick bridge, with a cattle creep above it.

Falling steeply, the line entered a deep cutting with concrete retaining walls (36 miles 68 chains); this marked the site of Barsham tunnel, which according to the *Great Eastern Railway Magazine*, had been opened-out 'a few years' before 1912. When built in the 1850s the tunnel had been the only one in Norfolk. It was 176 yards long and 14 ft wide, the single-track bore being about 60 ft below local ground level. It is likely that when the tunnel was removed around 1898, the resulting spoil would have been used to bury the nearby viaduct - surplus material being tipped to form the new embankment.

Beyond Barsham, trains crossed the River Stiffkey for a second time, and approached Walsingham with the little river flowing parallel to the right. For many travellers, this was perhaps the highlight of their journey; to the right, the so-called 'Slipper Chapel' recalled the days when Medieval pilgrims would remove their shoes prior to walking barefoot for the final mile north to Walsingham. Walsingham station was only a short distance further on, and here, some 38 miles 58 chains from Norwich, the 'Claud Hamilton' 4-4-0s brought their trains of veteran panelled coaches to a stand beside a single platform on the up side of the line.

In Medieval times, Walsingham had been the most famous shrine in England, owing no doubt to a popular superstition (carefully fostered by the local monks) that when Nazareth had fallen to the Moslems the Holy Virgin had abandoned the Sancta Casa there and taken up her abode at Walsingham. By the time of the Reformation, commercialism had become rampant, and the reformer Desiderious Erasmus (who visited the shrine in 1511) recorded that he had been shown the 'milk of the Virgin' still in pristine condition!

The shrine itself, he noted, was like 'the seat of the gods, so bright and shining … with jewels, gold and silver'. A few years later, Henry VIII ordered the destruction of the monasteries, and Walsingham sank back into a picturesque obscurity which lasted until 1931, when an Italian-style shrine was built as a centre of Anglican pilgrimage. Incongruous in Puritan East Anglia, the new shrine soon attracted large numbers of visitors, and with the revival of the Slipper Chapel as a Roman Catholic shrine, Walsingham once again became a major centre of religious pilgrimage.

This sudden revival caught the LNER somewhat by surprise, for (unlike certain stations in the Catholic part of Ireland) Walsingham was by no means well-equipped to handle even occasional excursion traffic, and it lacked even a run-round loop. The facilities provided consisted of a single platform on the up side, and five parallel goods sidings on the down side. The station was, however, a block post, and it was theoretically possible (with the aid of some manoeuvring) for two goods trains, or one goods and one passenger train to pass.

When excursions were run, the usual practice was for the 'Pilgrimage Specials' to set down at Walsingham, and then run empty to Wells for turning and watering. The pilgrims, meanwhile, would visit either the Anglican or the Roman Catholic shrine (perhaps both!) together with other places of historic or religious interest such as the Parish Church or the Priory ruins. In the late afternoon or early evening the excursion trains would return empty from Wells and pick-up at Walsingham station or at the so-called 'Slipper Chapel Halt'. This last-named stopping place was in fact an occupation crossing near the Roman Catholic shrine; no platform was ever provided, and passengers boarded their trains with the aid of portable wooden steps. The name 'Slipper Chapel Halt' did not appear in public timetables, although it was referred to as such in special train notices.

Walsingham station building was a single-storey, L-plan structure with one wing at right angles to the track, and another wing arranged on a parallel alignment to the platform. Both parts of the building were of brick construction, with low-pitched slate-covered roofs and disproportionately tall brick chimney stacks. The platform frontage was recessed to form a small loggia or covered waiting area for local travellers. The station building was built on the side of a gently-sloping hill, for this reason the road-side entrance was at a slightly lower level than the platform.

The neighbouring goods shed was a brick structure with a gable roof and an internal loading platform; it contained a 1 ton 10 cwt hand crane, while a loading gauge was affixed to the rail entrance. An end-loading dock abutted the east side of the shed, while the cattle loading pens were situated on the west side of the goods yard, with a separate entrance from Sandy Lane. The 1906 25-inch Ordnance Survey maps shows five dead-end sidings comprising (from east to west): two short spurs which terminated at the end-loading dock; the goods shed road; a coal and mineral siding and the cattle dock siding.

The track layout was altered slightly around the time of the Great War, and by 1919 one of the loading dock sidings had been removed, while an additional coal siding had appeared on the western side of the goods yard. At the same time, a somewhat complex double slip system had been introduced to facilitate entry to the headshunt. A third and final alteration was carried out around 1959, when the remaining end-loading dock spur was abolished, leaving just four sidings *in situ*. The main sources of freight traffic, by that time, were domestic coal, sugar beet and fuel oil - the latter being conveyed in oil tank wagons and discharged into road vehicles for final delivery to a grass drying plant.

A road known as Market Lane crossed the line on the level at the north end of the platform, and a second public level crossing was needed at Egmere Road, which was barely a quarter of a mile beyond the station. Walsingham station was signalled from another standard Great Eastern 'Type Seven' gable-roofed signal cabin, with a 19-lever McKenzie & Holland frame. The box, dating from around 1888, was sited beside the level crossing gates on the up side of the line. Its upper storey was of conventional appearance, with the usual nine-pane window frames, but the ground floor locking room was encased in brickwork -

A general view along the single platform station at Walsingham, looking south towards Norwich in the early 1960s. A British Thomson-Houston Bo-Bo (later class '15') can be seen in the goods yard.   *Mowat Collection*

'D16/3' class 4-4-0 No. 62608 arrives at Wighton Halt in August 1953 with a train bound for Norwich.   *Dr Ian C. Allen*

This later, 1964, view of Wighton Halt shows that a bicycle shed had been provided in the station's twilight years.   *D. Thompson*

presumably as a result of modifications carried out during World War II as an Air Raid Precaution measure.

The absence of any form of run-round facilities at Walsingham meant that when goods trains called in the down (northbound) direction, vehicles were picked-up or deposited in the lengthy headshunt. One assumes that, in Victorian days, horses would have been employed to move these incoming vehicles to and from the yard sidings, though during the British Railways period incoming freight traffic in the down direction was either fly-shunted out of the headshunt or moved manually with the aid of a pinch bar.

The station master here in 1881 was Thomas Wild, who perhaps unusually for a Great Eastern employee, had been born in Birmingham. In British Railways days the staff establishment at Walsingham consisted of one class four station master, two signalmen, one porter, and the resident female crossing keeper at Egmere Road level crossing. There was also a gang of around half a dozen locally-based permanent way men, who were controlled by the permanent way inspector at Dereham. The position of station master at Walsingham was abolished as an economy measure during the mid-1950s, the last post-holder being Mr Ken Green. In its final years, the station was under the control of the station master at Wells-next-the-Sea.

Wighton Halt

Departing from Walsingham, northbound trains immediately glided across the two level crossings and entered a cutting. Falling steadily, the railway emerged onto an embankment, from which travellers could glimpse the River Stiffkey, away to the east. Wighton Halt (40 miles 38 chains), the last stop before Wells, was a simple halt with a single platform on the up side of the running line. With a length of around 50 ft, the platform was able to accommodate just one coach and, in steam days, any passengers wishing to travel to or from Wighton were requested to ride in 'the compartment next to the guard's van'.

Wighton Halt was opened by the LNER shortly after the Grouping on 1st February, 1924. It appeared in the timetables in the summer of 1924, and its modest facilities consisted of a tiny, wood-and-corrugated iron waiting shelter. An open-sided extension was added at the south end of the shelter during the early BR period to form a covered storage area for bicycles, while the name 'Wighton Halt' was displayed on a single nameboard. The only other building here was a two-storey, brick-built gatekeeper's cottage, which stood on the side of a shallow cutting and pre-dated the halt by many years. At night, this simple stopping place was lit by oil lamps placed in two GER-type glass lanterns. The halt was staffed by a female ticket-collector who issued and collected tickets.

A minor road known as 'Clipper Lane' provided a means of access to nearby Wighton village, which was situated about a quarter of a mile to the east of the railway. It earlier days, Wighton had been the site of a little-used private siding known as 'Everitt's Siding', but this facility was lifted as far back as the 1860s, having seen little (if any) use; it was presumably controlled from the adjacent gatehouse.

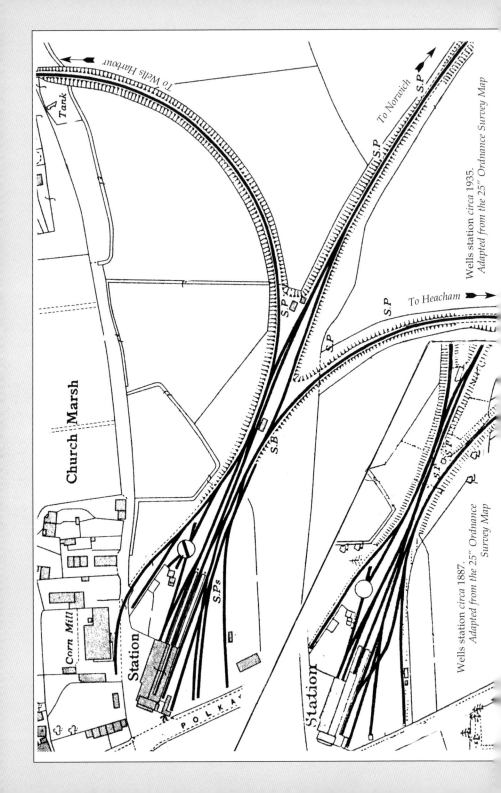

To Wells Harbour

Tank

To Norwich

S.P

S.P

S.P

Church Marsh

To Heacham

S.P

S.P

S.B

S.Ps

Corn Mill

Station

POLKA

Wells station circa 1935.
Adapted from the 25" Ordnance Survey Map

Station

Wells station circa 1887.
Adapted from the 25" Ordnance
Survey Map

Wells-next-the-Sea

Approaching its destination, the railway followed the River Stiffkey down towards the sea. A short distance beyond Wighton, the line passed within half a mile of a Celtic hill fort which was known erroneously as the 'Danish Camp'. About one mile beyond Wighton Halt, down trains crossed another minor road at Warham level crossing; the resident female crossing keeper in BR days was Mrs Staines, the wife of Wally Staines the Walsingham porter.

Turning north-westwards, down trains clattered beneath a road overbridge that carried B1106 road above the line, beyond which they passed a private siding known as the Leicester Lime Company Siding (42 miles 58 chains). This facility was installed by the LNER during the early 1920s, following a proposal from the Leicester Lime Company, which produced carbonate of lime from locally-excavated chalk.

Falling at 1 in 85, the route then curved north-westwards for its final entry to Wells. An overbridge carried the B1105 road across the railway for the last time, and after a further half mile the A149 coast road crossed the line on the level at Stiffkey level crossing. As usual on the Wells-next-the-Sea route, the crossing was worked by a female crossing keeper. The approach to the crossing was protected by an unusual signal with two semaphore arms, the upper arm being the Wells fixed distant while the lower arm, also of the fish-tailed 'distant' type, was a workable 'gate distant' that gave drivers a visual warning when the Stiffkey level crossing gates were closed across the railway.

As their trains passed over the level crossing, observant travellers may have discerned an abandoned line on the left. This marked the site of a south-to-west spur linking the West Norfolk branch and the Wymondham to Wells 'main line', which was completed in the 1880s but never opened for passenger traffic.

With Wells now visible on the horizon, trains ran through a final short cutting, beyond which the harbour branch and the West Norfolk branch converged from the right and left respectively. Slowing to walking pace, the 'Clauds' entered their terminus, and with the Heacham line running parallel to the left, finally came to a stand beneath the station's miniature overall roof. Here, 43 miles 21 chains from Norwich Thorpe, journeys came to an end. (There had, at one time, been a small ticket platform outside the station, and when this facility was in use, trains would pause briefly before drawing forward into the station proper.)

Wells-next-the-Sea station was a curious, old-fashioned place which, throughout its life had two distinct parts. When first opened in 1857 the original line from Dereham had terminated in a single platform station, with a wooden overall roof and a combined engine shed-cum-goods shed to the north. Nine years later the opening of the West Norfolk branch from Heacham necessitated a modest enlargement, but instead of rebuilding the station in its entirety, the Great Eastern authorities allowed the West Norfolk company to erect a makeshift wooden platform beside the existing terminus.

This second platform was an island, its outer face being used by Heacham branch services, while the inner face flanked the Fakenham 'main line' - giving travellers from Fakenham the option of alighting from either side of their train.

A general view of the approaches to Wells. The loop line seen disappearing behind the GER-style signal box was added in LNER days.   *Mowat Collection*

Class 'D13' 4-4-0 enters Wells on 29th June, 1936. Note the assorted coaching stock and the line to Heacham on to the right. The harbour branch veers off to the left.   *H.C. Casserley*

Although unusual, the resulting platform layout was not unique, and similar arrangements could be found at Ventnor on the Isle of Wight Railway and at Ulverston, on the Furness Railway main line.

Another unusual feature of Wells-next-the-Sea station concerned its run-round facilities - which were far too short for most passenger trains! There were, it is true, loops available beyond the limits of the passenger station, but in order to make use of them trains had to reverse out of the platforms and up the rising gradient towards Fakenham.

Having backed their trains uphill, it seemed sensible for train crews to let them return to the platforms with the aid of gravity, and what may have started as an unofficial operating expedient soon became the accepted mode of operation. When passengers had alighted, trains were reversed out of the station and brought to a stand on the nearby gradient. The engine was then detached, and proceeded 'light' to the engine shed for turning and servicing. Meanwhile, the passenger vehicles were allowed to roll down into the platforms under the control of the guard's hand brake. (As a safety measure, trains were always marshalled with a guard's compartment at the Wells end of the train.) In the 1930s, the LNER decided to improve the layout at Wells; a new connection was therefore installed between the Fakenham and Heacham halves of the terminus, and this at last gave the station an adequate run-round facility.

The two platforms at Wells could accommodate only four bogie coaches, and when longer formations had to be turned round, complicated manoeuvres were necessary - sometimes involving two engines, if a spare one happened to be 'on shed' at the appropriate time. Long trains did not appear with any regularity until the development of pilgrimage traffic in the 1930s - by which time the new loop was available. However the new loop was of little use when long excursions arrived from the West Norfolk line, and on such occasions the trains had to be divided, reversed (in two operations) and then re-united before proceeding to Walsingham.

The main station buildings at Wells were 'L' shaped, with one wing parallel to the platforms and the other extending at right angles behind the buffer stops. Of typical Great Eastern appearance, they were built of red brick with low-pitched 'Georgian' style hipped roofs and large-paned sliding sash windows. Internally, they contained domestic quarters for the station master and his family, in addition to the usual booking office, waiting rooms, toilets and staff accommodation. Two-storey buildings of similar design were constructed elsewhere in East Anglia during the 1850s, notably at Aldeburgh, Framlingham, and other stations on the East Suffolk Railway.

Until the 1930s, the adjoining train shed had covered only the Fakenham platform - Heacham passengers being left very much 'out in the cold'. A programme of improvements was belatedly carried out during the LNER period, and in its later years the station was provided with a modernized roof which extended horizontally across both platforms; an uncovered area was left directly above the track to facilitate smoke emission.

Goods facilities consisted of a small goods yard to the north of the passenger station, with four additional sidings to the south. One of the goods sidings gave access to Dewing & Kersley's nearby granary, while others served coal wharves

Wells station in the 1930s, after the station had lost its original overall roof. The combined engine/goods shed can be seen to the right. Class 'E4' 2-4-0 No. 7415 is waiting to depart to Heacham. *H.C. Casserley*

The station terminal buildings at Wells viewed from Polka Road in 2009. Although built by the Wells & Fakenham Railway, these buildings were not unlike the Great Eastern's 1860s-style stations. This building now houses a pottery and bookshop. *John Hendy*

and a cattle dock. The goods shed, which adjoined the main terminal buildings, was most unusually sited in relation to the engine shed; in fact it occupied one end of the same building! The goods loading bay was situated behind the locomotive department, which meant that it could not be shunted when the loco shed was occupied - though as the latter was usually empty during the day, this was perhaps no real problem.

Nearby a small turntable could accommodate 'E4' class 2-4-0s, but it was unable to turn 'D16' or other 4-4-0 classes until the LNER period, when the old 42 ft diameter turntable was replaced by a slightly larger example with a nominal diameter of 45 ft. In practice, there was an overhang of around 2 ft 6 in. at the edges, and this meant that the actual diameter of the new turntable was roughly 50 ft overall. The new turntable could officially accommodate 'Claud Hamilton' 4-4-0s, but not 'B12' class 4-6-0s or other larger engines. On the rare occasions when such locomotives appeared at Wells they sometimes had to leave the terminus running tender-first.

It was possible, albeit with considerable difficulty, for 'B12' class 4-6-0s or Ivatt class '4MT' 2-6-0s to use the turntable, although the drivers concerned had to position their engines as precisely as possible. It was impossible for two men to turn the engines without help from station staff, passengers, youthful train spotters - or indeed anyone else who happened to be around at the time! There was, moreover, a very real possibility that a large engine might become stuck on the turntable, and this happened on at least one occasion; in the end, enough helpers were assembled to complete a full revolution, and the trapped 'B12' was eventually released from its embarrassing predicament.

In the late 1940s and early 1950s the Wells shed normally housed two 'Claud Hamilton' 4-4-0s, which were shedded overnight at the station in order to work the first up trains on the following morning. Until 1952, the branch sub-shed also housed an 'E4' class 2-4-0 which worked on the West Norfolk line, while in addition there would sometimes be a 'J15' or 'J17' class 0-6-0 for local goods work. The 0-6-0s were used for shunting duties on busy weekends, and they were also be pressed into service on Saturday football specials from Wells to Norwich.

Other facilities at Wells-next-the-Sea included a cattle loading dock, water tower (with well beneath) and a standard Great Eastern 'Type Seven' gable-roofed signal cabin, which was sited at the convergence of the Fakenham and West Norfolk lines. The box, which dated from around 1888, contained a 45-lever McKenzie & Holland frame. The frame was modified in 1938 in connection with the installation of the run-round loop. Changes effected at that time included the provision of two new connections, both of which were fitted with facing point locks.

The water column, which stood just a few feet away from the brick-built water tower, was a simple 'fixed' type, without a rotating horizontal arm. The flexible hose was attached to a simple, swan-necked pillar and the water flow was controlled by a raised wheel which projected vertically from the ground about five feet from the base of the column. A 'fire devil' was provided for winter use, and in true Great Eastern fashion this useful accessory was clipped upright beside the column.

Wells station on 31st May, 1952. An ex-GER 0-6-0 stands in the West Norfolk platform, while a 'Claud Hamilton' 4-4-0 simmers outside the engine shed.   *H.B. Priestley*

Three 'D16/3' 4-4-0s at Wells on 17th May, 1948. Nearest the camera, No. 2599 waits to depart for Norwich Thorpe on the 10.05 am service; in the centre No. 2582 is ready with the 10.07 to Kings Lynn; and on to the right No. 2570 is on shed.   *Stephenson Locomotive Society*

Wells was the scene of an accident that took place on the evening of 29th May, 1879 when a train ran through the buffer stops and crashed into the station building. The mishap was reported as follows in the *Bury & Norwich Post & Suffolk Herald* on Tuesday 3rd June, 1879:

SINGULAR & FATAL RAILWAY ACCIDENT - An accident of a singular character has occurred on the Great Eastern Railway at Wells. The Wells station is situated at the lower end of a rather steep incline, and on Thursday evening the 7.50 pm train from Norwich, which was a heavier one than usual, gathering impetus in its descent, rushed into the station with such force as to carry away the buffer stoppers, breaking down that portion of the platform at that end and it then dashed into the porters' room and the closets, amongst the debris of which it came to a standstill. No passenger was injured, but on examination of the fallen brickwork, etc., the officials found the body of a young man named George Cooke, employed by Dr Foote. He had come to the station to meet some persons arriving by the train, and gone into one of the closets, where he was killed.

In its heyday, Wells station gave employment to a considerable number of porters, clerks and signalmen, together with various other grades in the locomotive and permanent way departments. The station master, around 1904, was Joseph Butters, and one of his immediate predecessors was Gabriel Paynter, who subsequently served at County School. Later, in the years following World War I, the station master at Wells-next-the-Sea was Edward P. Friend.

Wells itself was an attractive coastal town, redolent of ships and the sea. Famous sailors associated with the area included Captain Marryat, who lived at nearby Langham, together with Sir Cloudsley Shovel and Sir John Narborough - both of whom were born at Cockthorpe, some four miles to the west of Wells. The area was also very closely associated with Horatio Nelson, who was born in the parsonage at nearby Burnham Thorpe in 1758.

The 5.54 pm for Norwich at Wells on 29th June, 1936. The first carriage is a 48 ft 3 in. x 8 ft 6 in. lavatory composite with luggage compartment at the far end, 120 of these were built between 1900 and 1906 and most lasted to BR days (the last one was withdrawn in 1955).

H.C. Casserley

A 'full house' at Wells on 15th June, 1952 with 'Claud Hamilton' 4-4-0s Nos. 62570 and 626212 in front of the shed and 'J15' class 0-6-0 No. 65460 beside the water column.   *L.R. Peters*

Ex- GER 'E4' class No. 62797 stands outside the goods shed at Wells on 17th June, 1951.
L.R. Peters

'J17' class 0-6-0 No. 65586 carries out shunting operations at Wells in March 1961.   *Dr G.R. Siviour*

A later view (*circa* 1964) of Wells after the lifting of one of the engine shed tracks (the surviving line ran through the abandoned engine shed to reach the goods shed). A Metro-Cammell dmu stands in the station platform.   *Mowat Collection*

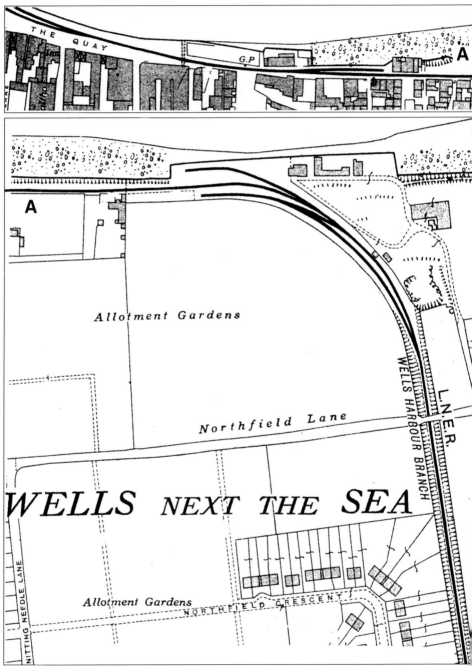

Wells harbour branch *circa* 1935.   *Adapted from the 25" Ordnance Survey Map*

Later, during a long period of unemployment, Captain and Mrs Nelson returned to Norfolk, and during that bitter and frustrating period England's greatest naval hero is likely to have been a frequent visitor to Wells. (Later still, while Nelson was living with Lord and Lady Hamilton, Lady Nelson lived more or less alone in the old vicarage at Burnham Thorpe, with only the ageing Reverend Nelson for company.)

The Wells harbour branch

The Wells harbour branch, which diverged northwards near the station throat, was 69 chains in length, and it served as a useful link between Wells station and the busy quays on the opposite side of the town. Leaving the main line, this short, goods-only spur curved first north and then westwards in a great arc as it followed the approximate course of the original harbour channel. Reaching the quay it ran past a large grain mill, and then terminated at the bottom end of Staithe Street.

The harbour branch was, technically, in two parts, and in their reports to the shareholders the Wells & Fakenham Directors usually distinguished between the 'tramway' which actually ran along the quay, and the goods branch which connected it to the main line. The Harbour branch proper was about 30 chains in length, and it ended near a small wharf belonging to the Wells & Fakenham Railway; a short loop allowed locomotives to run-round their trains, and there were two short sidings, one of which ended on the aforementioned Wells & Fakenham Wharf.

Wells & Fakenham Railway minutes indicate that construction of the Harbour Branch was well advanced by 1857, but the opening of the tramway section was delayed by legal problems. The line was finally completed under an Act obtained on 13th August, 1859 (22 & 23 Vict. cap. 139), but there is reason to believe that parts of the goods branch had been in operation before this Act was passed. The tramway ran westwards along Wells Quay, and finally ended in another loop; a short siding diverged from the terminal loop, and a similar siding was available roughly mid-way between the Wells & Fakenham Wharf and the end of the tramway.

The harbour line was worked on the 'one-engine-in-steam' system though, in later years at least, no train staff was needed. In GER days, there were normally two daily trips along the harbour branch. A note in the 1913 working timetable, for instance, reveals that on weekdays 'the engine of the 4.30 am goods train from Norwich, and the engine of the 4.50 pm goods train from Wymondham' would each make a trip between Wells station and Wells harbour. Locomotives proceeded only as far as the first loop, the quayside tramway being worked by shunting horses or (in later years) by one of the station lorries.

From the holidaymaker's point of view, the presence of busy sidings on an otherwise picturesque quayside may have been an unwelcome intrusion, but in the days when all freight was moved by rail these harbour sidings gave Wells a useful transport facility. In any case, Wells was not a seaside resort in the conventional sense - rather it was a working port and, as such, the harbour branch was an important part of what today might be termed the 'local infrastructure'.

Vessels seen in Wells harbour were, typically, small coasters of up to 150 gross registered tons carrying corn, cattle cake or grain. Spritsail barges and other small sailing vessels were a feature of the local scene until comparatively recent times - a regular visitor being the big 150 ton 'Thames' spritsail barge *Will Everard*.

Other barges seen at Wells included the *Zenobia*, *Scone*, *Cabby* and *Kindly Light*, while in earlier days, around 1900, the schooners *Cymric*, *Peggy*, *Patrician*, *Edith Crossfield* or *Mary Armstead* might have been seen tied-up alongside the quay. Methods of loading and unloading were primitive in the extreme, and Captain Jim Unglow recalled unloading bags of cattle cake with the aid of the ship's own rigging and anchor winch. Once the 16 or 18 stone bags were on the quayside they would be carried by gangs of labourers for a distance of some 50 yards - it could take three days to unload the entire hold of an East Coast sailing barge!

At one point on its circuitous course between Wells harbour and Wells station, the harbour branch skirted a field used by local cricketers. One amusing anecdote suggests that the 'home' team would sometimes arrange for noisy shunting operations to take place at critical moments throughout important matches in the hope that sudden whistling and the crashing of buffers would distract opposing batsmen! (This view was of course held by visiting players, but denied by the Wells team.)

The harbour tramway was little used after World War II, and it was officially closed in October 1952. The quayside lines were soon lifted or covered over with tarmac, though a truncated remnant of the harbour branch remained *in situ* at the Wells station end. The latter line was used as a siding, and in this capacity it was particularly useful when 'pilgrimage specials' or other excursions arrived at the station.

The increasing popularity of Walsingham as a religious centre during the 1950s meant that Wells was sometimes inundated with incoming excursion stock. In therefore became the practice, on busy weekends, for the yard to be emptied as much as possible, the displaced goods vehicles being stored either on the Harbour line or the closed West Norfolk branch. Alternatively, excursion trains might be reversed onto the harbour branch, where they could remain out of the way until the late afternoon, when the empty coaching stock was worked back to Walsingham.

Chapter Seven

The British Railways Era and Beyond

The immediate post-war era was a time of hope, in which the British people could look ahead to a brighter future with no poverty and no mass unemployment. Railwaymen in particular, anticipated that their newly-nationalized industry would receive long-overdue investment to replace worn-out locomotives and rolling stock - much of which dated from the pre-Grouping period.

Evidence of public ownership was provided by the application of bright new liveries - the red and cream colours applied to main line coaching stock being particularly attractive. Non-corridor vehicles received an overall LMS-type crimson lake livery (which was in effect a reversion to the final GER livery) while locomotives classified as 'mixed traffic' engines were given LNWR type lined black livery. When freshly applied, these new colour schemes looked much brighter than the dreary black and brown of the LNER period - though in practice it took months, even years, before the older liveries were replaced.

Locomotives and rolling stock in the BR era

Apart from these new liveries, the British Railways era produced few immediate changes, and the Wells branch still looked much the same as it had done in Great Eastern days. Although Norwich retained some 'E4' 2-4-0s, 'Claud Hamilton' 4-4-0s had virtually assumed command of branch passenger services by the 1950s. Large numbers of these ex-main line locomotives were still active in the north Norfolk area, some typical examples being Nos. 62510, 62512, 62513, 62522, 62540, 62556, 62559, 62561, 62564, 62570, 62577, 62581, 62584 and 62585.

A handful of 'E4' class 2-4-0s remained in use, and in the late 1940s and early 1950s these could still be seen at work on the West Norfolk line and other local routes. Freight workings were handled by a variety of ex-Great Eastern six-coupled locomotives, including 'J15' class 0-6-0s such as Nos. 65373, 65390, 65404, 65422, 65426, 65469 and 65471, and 'J17' class 0-6-0s including Nos. 65537, 65553, 65567, 65568, 65574 and 65586. On a less regular basis, 'J19' class 0-6-0s also appeared, together with 'N7' class 0-6-2Ts.

Other types occasionally appeared, including 'B12' 4-6-0s and ex-LMS Ivatt '4MT' 2-6-0s, which worked through to Walsingham with 'Pilgrim Specials' - sometimes taking the West Norfolk route via Heacham and Burnham Market. Excursion trains were sometimes double-headed on the hilly Wells branch, and local enthusiast Mr W.J. Sutton remembered one such train that ran from Wells to London at the time of the 1953 Coronation. On that occasion, two 'Claud Hamilton' 4-4-0s were needed to haul the lengthy train up the steep inclines between Wells and Dereham, although on arrival at Wymondham the 4-4-0s were replaced by a 'B17' 4-6-0, which took over for the remainder of the trip to London.

'E4' class 2-4-0 No. 62796 departs from County School station with the 2.15 pm from Dereham on 15th March, 1952, bound for Norwich the long way around, via Wroxham.   *E. Tuddenham*

'D16/3' 4-4-0 No. 62577 stands besides the turntable at Wells on 15th June, 1952.   *L.R. Peters*

Some of the locomotives employed on the Wymondham to Wells route were out-stationed in the sub-sheds at Dereham or Wells. Wells shed normally housed two 'Claud Hamilton' 4-4-0s for use on the Norwich route, together with an 'E4' 2-4-0 for use on the West Norfolk branch. Mr Sutton, who knew the Wells line during the late 1940s and early 1950s, recalled that the regular Wells-based engines were 'D16' class 4-4-0s Nos. 62540, 62561, 62570 and 62577. No. 62561 was kept in immaculate condition, but its less fortunate companions were seldom cleaned.

Coaching stock also retained a predominantly pre-Grouping flavour, and Norwich-Wells services were invariably composed of antiquated, gas-lit vehicles from the former Great Eastern, Great Northern, Great Central or North Eastern companies. More modern LNER vehicles also appeared, but as these Gresley-designed coaches were of Great Northern design their comparative modernity was by no means apparent to ordinary travellers! A summary of locomotive classes seen on the Wells branch is given below.

Principal locomotives classes used on the Wells branch 1900-1969

GER class	Type	LNER/BR class	Notes
No. 1	2-4-0	–	Worked most services until about 1912.
T26	2-4-0	E4	Became standard motive power on both Wells-Norwich and Wells-Heacham lines from 1912 until late 1930s.
Y14	0-6-0	J15	Worked on goods services during the 20th century.
T19	4-4-0	D13	Built as 2-4-0s, many of these engines were later given a leading bogie in which form they were designated 'D13s' by the LNER; while not as characteristic as the 'E4s', they occasionally worked on the branch in the 1920s and 1930s.
Claud Hamilton	4-4-0	D15 D16/2 D16/3	Gradually assumed command of branch passenger services in the late 1930s, supplementing and then finally superseding the 'E4s'. Thereafter these ex-main line engines remained standard motive power until dieselisation in 1955.
	0-6-0	J17	Worked freight traffic from the 1930s until replaced by diesels.
	0-6-0	J19	Less common than the earlier 0-6-0s, these Gresley rebuilds first appeared in the 1930 and lasted until the BR era.
	2-4-2T	F3	Often worked the Tuesdays-only through coaches from Liverpool Street to Wells via Forncett and Wymondham.
1000	0-6-2T	N7	These former suburban tanks appeared in East Anglia in the 1950s, and worked freight (possibly some passenger) services on the Wells branch.
1500	4-6-0	B12	Worked some excursion traffic to Walsingham, but were hardly ideal types for use on the branch as they were too big for the turntable at Wells!
	2-6-0	4MT	Ex-LMS Ivatt 2-6-0s occasionally worked on 'Pilgrimage Specials'.
	4-4-0	D2	These former GNR engines worked some services before and during World War II.
	A1A-A1A	31	Worked excursion traffic to Walsingham and also freight services, eventually became the usual motive power on surviving freight workings to Ryburgh and Fakenham.
	Bo-Bo	15	Occasionally worked on Walsingham excursions, coupled in pairs, and they also appeared on local freight services.

'D16/3' class 4-4-0 No. 62577 with the 3.45 pm Wells to Norwich service near Ryburgh on 24th July, 1955. Notice the fish van immediately behind the engine.   *E. Tuddenham*

The platform indicator at Wells in 1959 still showed information for passengers to Burnham Market, Docking, Heacham and Kings Lynn even though passenger services over the West Norfolk line had ceased in September 1952. The East Coast Floods of 1953 severed the, by now frieght-only, line between Burnham Market and Wells, and this section of railway never re-opened to traffic.   *H.B. Priestley*

Post-war train services on the Wells-next-the-Sea route were, in effect, merely a continuation of the basic pattern established in the GER period. In 1950, for example, there were six trains each way daily, taking around two hours for the 43¼ mile journey. Extra services ran on Saturdays, including a short-distance Wells to Dereham working. The Sunday service provided two trains each way, with additional workings in the summer months.

There were still, in the early 1950s, two freight workings each way, but the freight service was later reduced to just one (except during the busy sugar beet season). The West Norfolk branch had a slightly improved passenger service with five trains each way, rising to six on Mondays, Wednesdays and Saturdays. Fares were in the 1950s remarkably cheap and a single ticket from Liverpool Street to Wells cost the prospective traveller only 22s. 9d.!

With petrol rationing in force, and private road hauliers restricted by government legislation, the Wells to Norwich line remained relatively busy throughout the late 1940s and early 1950s. The neighbouring Hunstanton and Cromer lines, on the other hand, were enjoying a massive revival as holidaymakers - eager to experience the freedom of civilian life after six years of total war - flocked to the seaside in increasing numbers. Sadly, the West Norfolk branch failed to experience a comparable post-war boom, and on Saturday 31st May, 1952 the Wells to Heacham passenger service was withdrawn.

Freight and excursion traffic continued to run via Heacham; on 29th June 'B12' 4-6-0 No. 61533 traversed the route with a Kettering to Walsingham 'Pilgrimage Special'. At Wells the long train was divided and the 'B12' continued into the station with the front portion; there, a 'Claud' 4-4-0 backed on to the rear of the divided train, bringing it out of the terminus and onto the Dereham line. The operation was then repeated with the rear half of the excursion, and in this way the train was transferred from the West Norfolk branch to the Dereham 'main line'.

These complicated manoeuvres were repeated in the evening and, having regained the West Norfolk line, No. 61533 set off for Heacham - running tender first as it was too big to fit on the Wells turntable! In the event, this was the last passenger train to run through from Wells to Heacham. Sadly, The West Norfolk branch was not the only line to be closed at this relatively early date, for on Saturday 13th September, 1952 all passenger services were withdrawn from the 'round the world' route between Wroxham and County School.

The East Coast Floods

A few months later, the local railways became involved in one of the worst flood disasters to take place in Britain in modern times. The late summer of 1952 had been unusually wet, and on the night of 15th-16th August the Devon village of Lynmouth was wrecked by a devastating flash flood. This major disaster was fresh in the public mind, when, on the night of 31st January, 1953, the low-lying eastern counties suffered an immeasurably greater catastrophe. On that day, a deep depression moved south from Iceland producing gale force winds which coincided with a high flood tide - the result being a tidal surge that breached

A Metro-Cammell class '101' dmu arrives at Walsingham with an up passenger train on 31st July, 1956. Note the goods shed and adjacent loading dock to the left.   *H.B. Priestley*

Dereham station looking north with the Wymondham-Wells line on the right and the Swaffham and Kings Lynn bay on the left on 19th July, 1958. The 3.29 pm Wells-Norwich has just left, having crossed the 3.25 pm Norwich-Wells, which will soon depart. The 4.17 pm to Kings Lynn is on the left.   *John Langford*

protective coastal defences all around the east coast from Lincolnshire to Kent. Inevitably, the low-lying parts of East Anglia suffered severe flood damage.

Coastal villages were flooded to a depth of up to six feet, while at Wells the inundating waters swept along the harbour branch, and (following the course of the original harbour channel) poured into the station, flooding its platforms and sidings. Between Wells and Burnham Market, the angry seas scattered sleepers and ballast in all directions and effectively severed the West Norfolk branch. At Blakeney, the famous nature reserve on Blakeney Point was submerged, and the sea flowed inland for two miles. At Hunstanton, meanwhile, a train had attempted to reach Kings Lynn - but came to a stand near Heacham when the locomotive was struck by a floating bungalow and the rising waters extinguished its fire.

Dawn, on the 1st February, 1953, revealed a picture of utter devastation, and it seemed that centuries of land reclamation work had been undone in a matter of hours. Dykes were broken, dunes partially dispersed, and thousands of specially-planted pine trees had been destroyed. Over 30 people had been drowned north of Heacham, and there had been several more local fatalities at Salthouse (a few miles along the coast from Wells). A curious feature of the flood damage was the way in which, for mile after mile, telegraph poles were left leaning at the same drunken angle.

Wells station was re-opened on 4th February, but damage to the West Norfolk branch was so severe that British Railways did not consider that the Wells to Burnham Market section was worth reinstating. The line was therefore closed to through traffic (though a few goods trains later traversed parts of the damaged line in connection with flood repair work on the surrounding farmland). At Holkham, a marker was placed on the former station building to show how high the waters had risen.

Dieselization

In September 1955 British Railways introduced a fleet of brand new diesel multiple units (dmus) in the Norwich area, and at the same time the entire pattern of local passenger services was radically altered. Taking full advantage of the flexibility inherent in multiple unit operation, BR introduced what was perhaps the best passenger services ever provided on the Norwich to Wells line, with 10 trains each way between Norwich and Wells-next-the-Sea, and 12 in each direction between Kings Lynn and Dereham. Some of the latter services ran through from Dereham to Norwich, while at other times good connections were available at Dereham.

The new trains were popular with travellers who liked their companionable 'open plan' interiors and novel 'all round' windows (which gave people travelling in the front saloons a superb forward view of the line ahead). Although trains still stopped at all stations, the rapid acceleration after each intermediate stop enabled overall times to be cut to an average of about 90 minutes for the 43½ mile journey between Norwich and Wells-next-the-Sea.

The trains themselves were of two distinct types, some units being two-car Derby sets, while the remainder were Metro-Cammell units (later class '101'). In

Table 45 NORWICH, DEREHAM, KING'S LYNN and WELLS-ON-SEA

Second class only between Norwich and King's Lynn and Wells-on-Sea except where otherwise shown

Week Days

Miles		am	am	am	am		am	am	am	am	am	am	am	am		pm	pm	pm	pm ¶	pm	pm	pm
—	**Norwich(Thorpe)...... dep**	..	..	6 35	..	..	7 48	..	..	9 21	1030	..	1039	..	..	12 5	12 11	..	..	1 8	..	2 10
6¼	Hethersett	....	....	....	....	....	....	....	....	....	....	....	1050	....	....	....	....	....	....	1 19	....	2 21
10¾	**Wymondham ...... arr**	..	..	6 50	..	..	8 6	..	..	9 36	1048	..	1056	..	..	1219	12 25	..	..	1 25	..	2 27
—	**6 London(L'pool St)5 dep**	....	....	....	....	....	....	4 24	....	4A35	....	6 51	6e54	....	....	9A30	9B47	....	Saturdays only	10P30	....	10V30
—	**Wymondham .. .. dep**	..	..	6 51	..	..	..	8 13	..	9 37	..	1057	1057	..	..	1220	12 28	..		1 28	..	2 28
14	Kimberley Park	....	....	6 57	....	....	....	8 19	....	9 43	....	11 3	11 3	....	....	1226	12 34	....		1 34	....	2 34
15½	Hardingham	..	..	7 1	..	..	..	8 24	..	9 48	..	11 8	11 8	..	..	1231	12 39	..		1 39	..	2 39
17¼	Thuxton	....	....	7 5	....	....	....	8 28	....	9 52	....	1112	1112	....	....	1235	12 43	....		1 43	....	2 43
19½	Yaxham	..	..	7 11	..	..	..	8 34	..	9 58	..	1118	1118	..	..	1241	12 49	..		1 49	..	2 49
21½	**Dereham .... arr**	....	....	7 15	....	....	....	8 38	....	10 2	....	1122	1122	....	....	1245	12 53	....		1 53	....	2 53
—	**Dereham .. .. dep**	..	6 47	..	8 6	..	..	..	8 46	..	..	Saturdays only	Except Saturdays	1127	..	Except Saturdays	Saturdays only	1 1	..	..	2 12	3 2
25¼	Wendling	....	6 55	....	8 14	....	....	....	8 53	....	....			1135	....			1 9	....	....	2 20	3 10
28¼	Fransham	..	7 1	..	8 20	..	..	..	8 59	..	..			1141	..			1 15	..	..	2 26	3 16
29¾	Dunham	....	7 5	....	8 24	....	....	....	9 3	....	....			1145	....			1 19	....	....	2 30	3 20
33¼	**Swaffham**	..	7U17	..	8 31	..	..	..	9 10	..	..			1152	..			1 25	1 35	..	2 38	3 28
39¼	Narborough & Pentney	....	7 26	....	8 40	....	....	....	9 22	....	....			12 5	....			....	1 47	....	2 47	3 37
43	East Winch	..	7 33	..	8 47	..	..	..	9 29	..	..			1212	..			..	1 55	..	2 54	3 44
45	Middleton Towers	....	7 38	....	8 52	....	....	....	9 34	....	....			1217	....			....	2 0	....	2 59	3 49
48½	**King's Lynn .. arr**	..	7 43	..	8 58	..	..	..	9 41	..	..	..	..	1224	..	..	..	..	2 8	..	3 6	3 58
89½	43 Cambridge ...... arr	....	9 56	....	10C 7	....	....	....	12H7	....	....	....	....	2 45	....	....	....	....	3J50	....	4L39	6D50
145¼	**43 London (L'pool St) „**	..	1121	..	11C28	..	..	..	1Y37	..	..	..	..	4 52	..	..	..	..	5J12	..	6L 2	..
—	**Dereham .... dep**	6 4	....	7 17	....	....	....	8 54	....	10 6	....	1123	1124	....	....	1254	12 54	....	....	2 3	....	....
26¼	North Elmham	6 13	..	7 26	..	..	..	9 3	..	1015	..	1131	1132	..	..	1 3	1 3	..	..	2 11	..	..
27¾	County School	6 17	....	7 30	....	....	....	9 7	....	1022	....	1136	1136	....	....	1 7	1 7	....	....	2 18	....	....
31¼	Ryburgh	6 24	..	7 37	..	..	..	9 14	..	1029	..	1141	1142	..	..	1 14	1 14	..	..	2 25	..	..
33¾	**Fakenham (East)**	6 29	....	7 43	....	....	....	9 19	....	1034	....	1146	1147	....	....	1 19	1 19	....	....	2 30	....	....
38¾	Walsingham	6 38	..	7 52	..	..	..	9 28	..	1043	..	1154	1155	..	..	1 28	1 28	..	..	2 39	..	..
40¼	Wighton Halt	....	....	7 57	....	....	....	9 33	....	1048	....	1158	1159	....	....	1 33	1 33	....	....	2 44	....	....
43¼	**Wells-on-Sea .. .. arr**	6 47	..	8 3	..	..	..	9 39	..	1054	..	12 4	12 5	..	..	1 39	1 39	..	..	2 50	..	..

Week Days—*continued* / **Sundays**

	pm	pm	pm	pm	pm	pm	pm	pm	pm	pm	pm		pm	pm	pm		Sun am	Sun am	Sun pm	Sun pm	Sun pm	
Norwich(Thorpe)...... dep	3 5	3 22	..	..	4 56	5 35	..	6 10	6 20	..	..	..	8 56	9 32	..	..	9 51	..	..	5 45	8 15	..
Hethersett	3 16	3 33	....	....	5 8	....	....	6 21	6 31	....	....	....	....	9 42	....	....	10 2	....	....	....	8 26	....
Wymondham ...... arr	3 23	3 40	..	..	5 15	5 50	..	6 28	6 38	..	..	..	9 11	9 48	..	..	10 9	..	..	6 0	8 33	..
6 London(L'pool St)5 dep	12A30	12A30	....	....	1A30	3G30	....	3A30	....	....	....	....	6K30	6K30	Saturdays only	....	....	....	....	2 24	....	....
Wymondham .. .. dep	3 26	3 41	..	..	5 16	5 51	..	6 29	6 39	..	..	..	9 12	9 49		..	1010	..	..	6 1	8 34	..
Kimberley Park	3 32	3 47	....	....	5 22	5 57	....	6 35	6 45	....	....	....	9 18	9 55		....	1016	....	....	6 7	8 40	....
Hardingham	3 37	3 52	..	..	5 27	6 2	..	6 40	6 50	..	..	..	9 23	10 0		..	1021	..	..	6 12	8 45	..
Thuxton	3 41	3 56	....	....	5 31	6 6	....	6 44	6 54	....	....	....	9 27	10 4		....	1025	....	....	6 16	8 49	....
Yaxham	3 47	4 2	..	..	5 37	6 12	..	6 50	7 0	..	..	..	9 33	1010		..	1031	..	..	6 22	8 55	..
Dereham .... arr	3 51	4 6	....	....	5 41	6 16	....	6 54	7 4	....	....	....	9 37	1014		....	1035	....	....	6 26	8 59	....
Dereham .. .. dep	Except Saturdays	Saturdays only	4 17	5 14	..	..	6 18	Saturdays only	Except Saturdays	7 18	8 19	..	9 43	Saturdays only	1018	..	..	..	..	..	From Yarmouth (Vauxhall) dep 7 33 pm (Table 48)	..
Wendling			4 25	5 22	....	....	6 26			7 26	8 27	....	9 51		1026	....	....	....	....	....		....
Fransham			4 31	5 28	..	..	6 32			7 32	8 33	..	9 57		1032	..	..	..	..	..		..
Dunham			4 35	5 32	....	....	6 36			7 36	8 37	....	10 1		1036	....	....	....	....	....		....
Swaffham			4 42	5d43	..	..	6 44			7d47	8d48	..	10 9		1044	..	..	..	..	..		..
Narborough & Pentney			4 52	5 52	....	....	6 54			7 56	8 57	....	1019		1054	....	....	....	....	....		....
East Winch			4 59	5 59	..	..	7 2			8 3	9 4	..	1026		11 1	..	..	..	..	..		..
Middleton Towers			5 4	6 4	....	....	7 7			8 8	9 9	....	1031		11 6	....	....	....	....	....		....
King's Lynn .. arr			5 10	6 10	..	..	7 14			8 14	9 15	..	1038		1113	..	..	..	..	..		..
43 Cambridge ...... arr	....	....	7 7	7H32	....	....	8R36	....	....	....	12F46	....		....	....	....	....	....	....	....		....
43 London (L'pool St) „	..	..	8 40	11Q23	..	..	9T58	..	..	..	a2F23	..		..	..	..	..	..	..	..		..
Dereham .... dep	4 15	4 15	....	....	5 42	....	....	7 12	7 12	....	....	....	Except Saturdays	1016	....	....	1037	1047	1 20	6 30		....
North Elmham	4 24	4 24	..	..	5 50	..	..	7 21	7 21	..	..	..		1025	..	..	..	1056	1 29	6 39		..
County School	4 28	4 28	....	....	5 57	....	....	7 25	7 25	....	....	....		1029	....	....	....	11 1	1 33	6 46		....
Ryburgh	4 35	4 35	..	..	6 4	..	..	7 32	7 32	..	..	..		1036	..	..	..	11 8	1 40	6 53		..
Fakenham (East)	4 40	4 40	....	....	6 9	....	....	7 37	7 37	....	....	....		1041	....	....	....	1113	1 46	6 58		....
Walsingham	4 49	4 49	..	..	6 18	..	..	7 49	7 49	..	..	..		1050	..	..	11 7	1122	1 55	7 7		..
Wighton Halt	4 54	4 54	....	....	6 23	....	....	7 54	7 54	....	....	....		1055	....	....	....	1127	2 0	7 12		....
Wells-on-Sea .. .. arr	5 0	5 0	..	..	6 29	..	..	9 0	8 0	..	..	..		11 1	..	..	1116	1133	2 6	7 18	..	..

¶ First and Second class
A Via Norwich (Thorpe)
a am
B On 16th June, 8th and 15th September departs Liverpool Street 9 30 am via Norwich
C Fridays and Saturdays only. Runs 30th June to 8th September inclusive
D Via March and St. Ives
d Arrives 4 minutes *earlier*
E Except Saturdays
e Via Norwich (Thorpe). Second class only Ipswich to Norwich
F Via March. On Saturday nights via Downham
G Via Norwich. On Saturdays departs Liverpool Street 2 24 pm via Ely
H On Fridays and Saturdays 29th June to 8th September inclusive arrives Cambridge 12 18 pm
J Saturdays only. Runs 14th July to 1st September inclusive
K Via Norwich (Thorpe). The East Anglian. Limited accommodation
L On Fridays and Saturdays 7th July to 1st September inclusive arrives Cambridge 4 48 pm and Liverpool Street 6 10 (6 13 pm on Saturdays)
N Not after 8th September. On Saturdays arrives Cambridge 7 40 pm. Also runs on Wednesday 12th and Saturday 15th September Cambridge arrive 9 16 pm via St. Ives
P Saturdays only. Via Norwich (Thorpe)
Q Runs Mondays to Fridays until 6th July and from 3rd to 7th September. Also runs every Saturday until 8th September Liverpool St. arr 9 53 pm
R Mondays to Fridays. Runs 9th July to 31st August inclusive. Also runs on Saturdays 28th July to 1st September inclusive Cambridge arrive 9 18 pm
S Saturdays only
T Except Saturdays. Runs 9th July to 31st August inclusive
U Arrives 5 minutes *earlier*
V Except Sats. Via Norwich (Thorpe)
Y On Fridays and Saturdays 29th June to 8th September inclusive arrives Liverpool St. 1 42 pm and on Saturdays 16th, 23rd June & 15th Sept. 1 33 pm

For OTHER TRAINS between Wymondham and Norwich, see Table 6

Passenger timetable for down trains, 1956.

Table 45—*continued* **WELLS-ON-SEA, KING'S LYNN, DEREHAM, and NORWICH**

Second class only between Wells-on-Sea and King's Lynn and Norwich except where otherwise shown

Week Days

Miles	Mls	Station	am		am	am		am	am		am		am	am		am	am	am ¶	pm	pm	pm	pm	pm
–		**Wells-on-Sea** .. .. dep				6 55			8 8					9 49		11 2	11 2	Saturdays only	From Thetford dep 11E31 am 11S38 am (Table 37)	1210	1234		1 44
2¾		Wighton Halt				7 1			8 14					9 55		11 8	11 8			1216	1240		1 50
4¼		Walsingham				7 6			8 19					10 0		11 13	11 13			1221	1245		1 55
9½		**Fakenham** (East)				7 16			8 29					1010		11 23	11 23			1230	1254		2 5
12		Ryburgh				7 21			8 34					1015		11 28	11 28			1235	1259		2 10
15½		County School				7 32			8 40					1021		11 37	11 37			1241	1 8		2 17
17		North Elmham				7 36			8 44					1025		11 41	11 41			1245	1 12		2 21
21½		**Dereham** arr				7 44			8 52					1033		11 49	11 49			1252	1 19		2 28
—	Mls	**43 London** (L St) dep											5 54					8C27				8R24	
—		43 Cambridge ... „											8H 2					10C 3				10T15	
—	-	**King's Lynn** .. dep			6 48			7 48			9 3		9 52			Except Saturdays	Saturdays only	11 42		Except Saturdays	Saturdays only	1 5	
—	3½	Middleton Towers			6 54			7 54			9 9		9 58					11 49				1 12	
—	5¼	East Winch			6 59			7 59			9 14		10 3					11 55				1 17	
—	8¾	Narborough & Pentney			7 6			8 6			9 21		1010					12 3				1 24	
—	14¼	**Swaffham**			7h20			8 15			9 30		1019					12 15	1225			1 34	
—	18¼	Dunham			7 28			8 25			9 37		1026						1233			1 42	
—	19¾	Fransham			7 32			8 29					1030						1237			1 46	
—	22½	Wendling			7 38			8 35			9 45		1036						1243			1 52	
—	26½	**Dereham** .. .. arr			7 45			8 41			9 51		1043						1250			1 59	
—		**Dereham** dep	6 50			7 50			8 58		9 56			1047		11 50	11 54			1253	1 20		2 29
23½		Yaxham	6 54			7 55			9 3					1051		11 54	11 58			1257	1 24		2 33
26		Thuxton	7 0			8 1			9 9					1057		12 0	12 4			1 3	1 30		2 39
27½		Hardingham	7 4			8 5			9 13					11 1		12 4	12 8			1 7	1 34		2 43
29¼		Kimberley Park	7 8			8 9			9 17					11 5		12 9	12 12			1 11	1 38		2 47
33		**Wymondham** .. .. arr	7 13			8 14			9 22		1014			1110		12 13	12 17			1 16	1 43		2 52
146¾		**6 London** (L'pool St) 5 arr	10A0			1121			12J35		1V37			1K55		3A30	3A30			4A34	5 0		6A39
—		**Wymondham** dep	7 14			8 16			9 24		1015			1112		12 15	12 19			1 17	1 44		2 53
37		Hethersett				8 24								1120							1 52		3 1
43½		**Norwich** (Thorpe) .... arr	7 31			8 34			9 39		1028			1130		12 29	12 37			1 31	2 3		3 10

Week Days—*continued* / **Sundays**

Station	pm	pm	pm	pm	pm		pm	pm	pm	pm	pm	pm	pm	pm			Sun am	Sun am	Sun pm	Sun pm	Sun pm	
Wells-on-Sea .. .. dep		3 15			5 24				7 18		8 18	Saturdays only	Except Saturdays	11 6				1145	4 0	6 12	7 26	
Wighton Halt		3 21			5 30				7 24		8 24			1112				1151	4 6	6 18		
Walsingham		3 26			5 35				7 29		8 29			1117				1156	4 11	6 23	7 36	
Fakenham (East)		3 36			5 45				7d42		8 39			1127				12 7	4 21	6 34		
Ryburgh		3 41			5 50				7 47		8 45			1132				1212	4 26	6 39		
County School		3 47			5 56				7 53		8 51			1138				1218	4 33	6 45		
North Elmham		3 51			6 0				7 57		8 55			1142				1222	4 37	6 49		
Dereham arr		3 59			6 8				8 5		9 3			1150				1230	4 45	6 57	8 4	
43 London (L St.) dep	12B24			12S27			2U24	4G30				5 54	5 54	Saturdays only			To Yarmouth (Vauxhall) arr 11 2 am (Table 48)					
43 Cambridge ... „	1B49		1D53	2 35			3U56	5G46				7 22	7 27									
King's Lynn .. dep	3 14		4 8	5 15			6 15	7 19		8 19		9 20	9 20									
Middleton Towers	3 21		4 15	5 21			6 21	7 25		8 26		9 26	9 26									
East Winch	3 26		4 20	5 26			6 26	7 30		8 31		9 31	9 31									
Narborough & Pentney	3 38		4 31	5 33			6 33	7 37		8 38		9 38	9 38									
Swaffham	3 48		4d43	5 42			6d45	7 46		8 47		9k51	9k51									
Dunham	3 56		4 51	5 49			6 52	7 53		8 54		9 58	10d2									
Fransham	4 0		4 55	5 53			6 56	7 56		8 58		10 1	10 6									
Wendling	4 6		5 1	5 59			7 2	8 2		9 4		10 7	1012									
Dereham .. .. arr	4 12		5 8	6 6			7 9	8 9		9 11		1013	1019									
Dereham dep		4 16			6 10				8 12		9 15						9 38		4 47	6 59	8 6	
Yaxham		4 20			6 14				8 16		9 19						9 42		4 51	7 3	8 10	
Thuxton		4 26			6 20				8 22		9 25						9 48		4 57	7 9	8 16	
Hardingham		4 30			6 24				8 26		9 29						9 52		5 1	7 13	8 20	
Kimberley Park		4 34			6 28				8 30		9 33						9 56		5 5	7 17	8 24	
Wymondham .. .. arr		4 39			6 33				8 35		9 38						10 1		5 10	7 22	8 29	
6 London (L'pool St) 5 arr		7N55			11Q56						2a23						1A 4		8 19	12A14	2a18	
Wymondham dep		4 44			6 35				8 36		9 39						10 3		5 12	7 24	8 31	
Hethersett		4 52			6 43												1011			7 32	8 39	
Norwich (Thorpe) .... arr		5 4			6 56				8 49		9 52						1020		5 27	7 41	8 48	

¶ First and Second class
A Via Norwich (Thorpe)
a am
B On Saturdays departs Liverpool Street 12 14 and Cambridge 1 47 pm (12 10 and 1 35 pm respectively on 16th, 23rd June and 15th September)
C On 8th and 15th September departs Liverpool Street 8 24 and Cambridge 9 53 am
D Via St. Ives and March
d Arrives 4 minutes *earlier*
E Except Saturdays
G On Saturdays departs Liverpool Street 4 27 and Cambridge 5 56 pm
H From 23rd July to 1st September inclusive departs Cambridge 8 37 pm
h Arrives 6 minutes *earlier*
J Via Norwich (Thorpe) On Saturdays arrives Liverpool St. 12 45 pm
K Via Norwich (Thorpe). The East Anglian. Limited accommodation On Fridays and Saturdays arrives Liverpool Street 2 6 pm
k Arr 5 minutes *earlier*
N Via Norwich (Thorpe). On Saturdays arrives Liverpool Street 8 6 pm
Q Via Norwich (Thorpe). On Saturdays arrives Liverpool St. 9 53 pm via Ely
R Mondays to Fridays. Also Runs Saturdays 14th July to 25th August Liverpool Street departs 9 50 am
S Saturdays only
T Via St. Ives and March. On Saturdays 14th July to 25th August departs Cambridge 11 14 am via Ely
U On Fridays and Saturdays 29th June to 8th September departs Liverpool Street 2 27 and Cambridge 4 9 pm
V On Saturdays arrives Liverpool Street 1 33 pm (1 21 pm via Norwich (Thorpe))

For OTHER TRAINS between Wymondham and Norwich, see Table 6

Passenger timetable for up trains, 1956.

April 1956, Norwich's allocation included 13 Derby units and 11 Metro-Cammell sets. The Metro-Cammell units included motor brake seconds Nos. 79047, 79048, 79054, 79065, 79066 and 79075, together with driving trailer seconds Nos. 79263, 79281, 79282 and 79291, while the Derby twin units included motor brake seconds Nos. 79034 and 79046 and driving trailer composite No. 79250.

Evidence of the improvements resulting from the introduction of modern rolling stock is provided by an examination of the June 1956 timetable. The day's train service began with the departure of the first down working which left Dereham at 6.04 am and arrived in Wells at 6.47 am. The flexibility of multiple unit operation allowed a turn round to take place in a matter of minutes, thus at 6.55 am the first up working of the day set off for Norwich, arriving in the county town by 8.34 am and allowing sufficient time for office workers to be at their desks by 9.00 am.

Meanwhile, a second dmu had left Norwich at 6.35 am and, having passed the first up train at County School, it reached Wells at 8.03 am. A similar pattern of services was maintained throughout the day, with further return trips from Wells at 8.08, 9.49, 11.02 am, 12.10, 1.44, 3.15, 5.24, 7.18 and 8.18 pm. In all, there were 10 up services between Wells and Norwich, balanced by nine down workings between Norwich and Wells and one short distance service between Dereham and Wells-next-the-Sea.

The apparently unbalanced distribution of up and down services was a result of the closure of Wells engine shed, which meant that stock was stationed overnight at Dereham; the short distance trips from Dereham to Wells were balanced by various other workings between Norwich, Dereham and Kings Lynn.

By 1958, when the dieselization of Norfolk branch services had been extended to other local lines, Dereham had become a stabling point for six dmu sets which jointly worked a complex series of diagrams covering services to Wells, Hunstanton, Ely, Thetford, Norwich and Kings Lynn.

It is perhaps worth pointing out that 'dieselization' was not necessarily synonymous with rationalization of facilities, and the Wells branch did not become the kind of run-down 'basic railway' associated with the later, post-Beeching era. Indeed, apart from the closure of Wells engine shed and the shortening of one or two platforms at some of the intermediate stations, the Wells-next-the-Sea branch retained most of its Victorian infrastructure.

The line remained fully signalled with traditional semaphores, many of which were of Great Eastern origin, while its expensive, fully-manned level crossings remained *in situ*. Freight traffic was still an important feature of branch operation, and the profitable full load, private siding traffic which emanated from Ryburgh mill and other rail-connected installations was the kind of bulk traffic that BR hoped to encourage in the years ahead.

In retrospect, there was still, by the 1960s, every reason to hope that the Wells branch would continue as a permanent part of BR's freight and passenger network. Wells was at last beginning to develop as a popular holiday centre, with a large caravan park and other facilities concentrated near the beaches to the north of the town. With the decline of commercial traffic in and out of Wells harbour the port was growing in favour as a yacht haven - while nearby

Walsingham continued to attract growing numbers of pilgrims and summer visitors.

Another encouraging sign was the growth in population at Fakenham, Dereham and Wymondham. The three towns had, for many years remained relatively small, with populations ranging from about 3,000 at Fakenham to over 5,000 at East Dereham and Wymondham. These figures increased significantly in the years following World War II, when Wymondham and Dereham virtually doubled in size. With freight traffic, particularly to Ryburgh (where the mill had been rebuilt following wartime damage) running at a healthy level, the Wells branch appeared to be one of East Anglia's more profitable rural branch lines.

Closure between Dereham and Wells

The years immediately following World War II were a time of rigid austerity in which petrol and other commodities were strictly rationed, and this ensured that the railway system remained busy. Moreover, the post-war Labour government was openly pro-rail in its transport policies, and this factor seemed to guarantee that the railway system would have secure future as part of a fully co-ordinated transport policy. In 1951, however, an incoming Conservative administration initiated reversal of policy, and the railways were soon being portrayed as obsolete relics of the industrial revolution that would have to be replaced by private road transport wherever possible.

There was, furthermore, an inevitable desire to eliminate competing routes - after all, the railway system was now under unified management, and in this context it made sense for scarce investment resources to be concentrated on the most viable lines. Viewed in this light the Midland & Great Northern system became an obvious candidate for rationalization. Built to challenge the GER monopoly, this sinuous cross-country route was duplicated by other lines between Leicester, Kings Lynn and Norwich, and in practice the M&GN system could be closed without causing undue hardship. Accordingly, on Saturday 28th February, 1959 the M&GN was deleted from the BR network, leaving only a few truncated stubs for local passenger and freight traffic.

The pace of closure and rationalization increased after the October 1959 general election, when Ernest Marples was appointed Minister of Transport by Prime Minister Harold Macmillan. The new Transport Minister was the founder of a road-building firm known as Marples, Ridgway & Partners, and he was known to be in favour of a programme of grandiose motorway construction schemes as the answer to Britain's transport problems.

It was, by this time, abundantly clear that the government of the day was simply no longer interested in maintaining the national railway system in anything like its entirety, and in 1963 the publication of a report by Dr Richard Beeching entitled 'The Reshaping of British Railways' sounded the death knell for vast swathes of the railway network. The report recommended the withdrawal of passenger services from around 5,000 miles of line and the closure of 2,363 stations out of a total of 4,709.

'B12/3' class 4-6-0 No. 61572 at Dereham with the Yarmouth-Dereham-Kings Lynn-Whitemoor parcels train in 1960. No. 61572 is now preserved and currently resides on the North Norfolk Railway at Sheringham. 'J15' class 0-6-0 No. 65469 with the North Elmham milk train takes water from the water crane on the adjacent platform.   *Dr Ian C. Allen*

'J17' class 0-6-0 No. 65586 near Walsingham with a Wells-next-the-Sea to Norwich goods train in 1960.   *Dr G.R. Siviour*

'J17' class 0-6-0 No. 65583 approaches Wymondham with a train of sugar beet in autumn 1960.
Dr G.R. Siviour

The North Elmham milk train saw a variety of motive power. On this occasion Ivatt '4MT' class 2-6-0 No. 43161 works northbound empties at the site of what is now the Mid-Norfolk Railway's Wymondham Abbey terminus.
Dr G.R. Siviour

'B12/3' 4-6-0 No. 61572 marshals the milk train at North Elmham prior to departing for Norwich in the winter of 1960.   *Dr G.R. Siviour*

'J15' class 0-6-0 No. 65471 climbs towards Dereham with the Norwich-bound milk train in May 1960.   *M.J. Esau*

Basing his findings on an extremely narrow financial model, Dr Beeching concluded that rural lines carrying less than 17,000 passengers a week were 'uneconomic' in cases where there was no other traffic. When freight traffic absorbed a proportion of the costs, the minimum acceptable passenger figure came down to 10,000 a week. The report took little cognisance of future population trends, but worse than this it seemed to apply its tests of viability in a highly selective way, taking sections of line in isolation from the main system and ignoring the fact that otherwise 'unprofitable' branch lines might feed lucrative passenger and freight traffic onto the main line system.

As far as East Anglia was concerned, the Beeching proposals envisaged the deletion of several branch lines, but a substantial network of main line and cross-country routes would remain, albeit with a modified pattern of services. In general, these proposals would entail the elimination of local passenger and freight services, leaving the railways to concentrate on profitable activities such as Inter-City passenger traffic and the carriage of coal, aggregates and other forms of bulk freight traffic which could be conveyed in whole train loads.

Inevitably, the Wells-next-the-Sea branch came under scrutiny, and the northern extremity of the line between Dereham and Wells was marked down for closure under the Beeching proposals leaving, however, a full passenger service between Norwich, Dereham and Kings Lynn. Freight traffic would continue as far as Fakenham, but the Wells to Dereham passenger service would be replaced by buses.

The closure took effect from Monday 5th October, 1964, and the last trains ran on Saturday 3rd October. Wells retained its goods services for a further month, but by 31st October the line had been closed for good beyond Fakenham. The last out-going goods wagons were collected on 1st November. Goods facilities had, meanwhile, been withdrawn from Kimberley Park, Thuxton, Yaxham and County School stations.

Closure between Wymondham and Dereham

On the face of it, north Norfolk had escaped the worst of the Beeching axe, and the election of a new, less anti-railway government in 1964 seemed to guarantee the survival of lines that had escaped the initial pruning. The railway trade unions were confident that no Labour government would implement a large-scale closure programme, but in retrospect the new Labour administration was not as sympathetic as some commentators had predicted and in 1968 Barbara Castle's Transport Act (which allowed socially-necessary routes to be subsidized by local authorities) did little to help rural lines.

Plans published at the time showed a 'basic system' of about 11,000 route miles, but on closer scrutiny, the revised railway network excluded many lines that had escaped the 1963 closure programme, and in Norfolk the basic system did not include the Lynn-Hunstanton, Lynn-Norwich, and Norwich-Sheringham lines. In effect, the 'Castle Plan' had sentenced the southern end of the Wells line to death - unless of course local councils wished to provide some form of grant aid.

In the meantime, the Norwich-Dereham-Kings Lynn cross-country route had not prospered and, faced with the prospect of a slow bus journey to Dereham station, most travellers from Wells or Fakenham to Norwich went direct to their destination by bus or private car, thereby depriving the Dereham to Norwich line of valuable through traffic. All stations became unstaffed halts in August 1966, but these economies did little to restore profitability, and the Dereham to Kings Lynn line was closed to passenger traffic on Saturday 7th September, 1968; the last day was marked by the running of an M&GN Society 'East Anglian Branch Line Farewell' special.

Elimination of this further section of line contributed to another reduction of through traffic on the surviving 11¼ miles of line between Wymondham and Dereham. Although the basic costs of the line were surely covered by its freight revenues, BR claimed that this last remnant of the Wells branch was still unprofitable, and proposed to axe the remaining diesel multiple unit services.

The Wymondham to Dereham line was, by this time, merely a shadow of its former self. Once the busiest section of the Wells to Wymondham branch, it had been reduced to a single line branch with rationalized passenger facilities. At Yaxham, for example, all loops and sidings had been lifted and trains used the former down platform; the level crossing gates were manually-operated from an outside lever frame. At Dereham, passenger trains terminated in the former down platform, and the down main line was severed just short of the level crossing.

On the other hand, with significant quantities of freight traffic still being handled at Ryburgh, Dereham, Fakenham and North Elmham, the line retained much of its trackwork and signalling. Services in these last months were handled by several multiple unit types, including Metro-Cammell, Cravens, and Gloucester RC&W sets. Branch freight services were usually hauled by English Electric class '31' A1A-A1A diesel locomotives.

On 15th September, 1968 the doomed line was involved in another flood drama, comparable to that of 1912. It had rained continuously for several days, and the rain persisted for a full 24 hours on 14th-15th September, creating chaos in the Norwich area. Norwich was cut off by earth slips on the Ely, Ipswich and Yarmouth lines, and until these lines could be brought back into service, the only available permanent way materials were on the recently-singled Wymondham to Dereham branch. Two engineer's trains were therefore sent onto the branch to recover ballast and other materials for use on the damaged main lines, and branch passenger services were suspended while these operations took place.

The Dereham branch remained popular locally, but in September 1969 the Eastern Region finally announced that the surviving passenger services between Wymondham and Dereham would be withdrawn with effect from 6th October, 1969, and as this was a Monday, the final trains would be run on Saturday 4th October. The stations at Kimberley Park, Hardingham, Thuxton, Yaxham and Dereham would be closed, but goods services would continue to run between Wymondham, Dereham and Fakenham.

The last day was, as usual, marked by the appearance of numerous extra travellers - among them many railway enthusiasts who turned up to photograph the final hours of operation. The closure of the line was, however, conducted with decorum, and the few regular travellers were not swamped by hordes of 'last day' revellers. Only towards the end of the day did that final Saturday assume an especial historical significance, and as the very last up and down trains proceeded along the line little knots of people gathered to pay their last respects. This was indeed the end of an era, and those who had participated in the finalities sensed that an old and much-loved institution had passed away.

A freight-only branch

The withdrawal of regular passenger services allowed BR to implement further economies and the line was soon reduced to a long siding, worked on the 'one engine in steam' system. Most level crossings were worked by train crews, resulting in extended journey times for the surviving freight workings.

Continuing rationalization obviously resulted in reduced facilities, though much of interest remained. At Wymondham, the junction layout was simplified in June 1977, and the branch was then entered via a single turnout from the down main line. Freight trains from the Norwich direction were, in consequence, no longer able to proceed directly onto the Dereham line, a reversal onto the down main line being necessary before the northwards journey to Dereham could resume.

From Wymondham, the route continued as a single line to Dereham, where facilities were surprisingly complex. The former goods shed was trackless, although much of the track layout remained *in situ* to serve adjacent maltings and granaries. The station buildings continued to serve the public as a bus depot. Similarly, at North Elmham a loop and sidings were retained to serve R.J. Seaman & Sons' grain silos, while at Ryburgh the extensive private sidings remained intact. The two-storey station buildings at Fakenham were occupied by BR and the National Bus Company and they remained in good repair. Elsewhere on the line, the station buildings at Kimberley Park, Hardingham, Thuxton, Yaxham and County School were occupied as private dwellings, as such they remained intact.

The rear of a Fakenham to Norwich goods train, hauled by Brush type '2' A1A-A1A (later class '31') No. D5682 at Hoe, north of Dereham, on 3rd October, 1969.   *G.R. Mortimer*

Class '31' No. 5633 departs from Fakenham with the 13.00 goods train on 6th September, 1971.
G.R. Mortimer

No. 5633 arrives at Dereham with a Fakenham to Norwich goods train on 6th September, 1971.
G.R. Mortimer

Public goods traffic was handled at North Elmham and Ryburgh until July 1971, the two stations remaining open thereafter for private siding traffic. Coal class traffic was accepted at both Dereham and Fakenham, but the main sources of bulk freight were grain and fertilisers. There was, by the late 1970s, just one freight working each way daily, taking up to five hours for the 23¼ mile journey between Wymondham and Ryburgh. The daily train normally left Norwich at 5.45 am, and having left Wymondham at 6.43 am, it arrived in Fakenham at 11.30. After carrying out any shunting duties that might be required, the train left Fakenham at 1.00 pm, and arrived back in Norwich by 6.34 pm.

In 1978, the branch from Wymondham was continuing to deal with about 55,000 tons of freight a year, but BR claimed that the line was unable to cover its operating costs, and in a further contraction the route was cut back from Fakenham to Ryburgh in 1980. The Ryburgh to North Elmham section lingered on until 1981, but in that year the line was closed beyond North Elmham (although the redundant track from Ryburgh to North Elmham was not immediately lifted). North Elmham remained the end of the line for several years, the main forms of traffic during the 1980s being grain and fertilizers.

First steps towards re-opening

Although the Dereham branch had lost its passenger services, there were persistent attempts to secure a restoration of dmu services between Wymondham and Fakenham. These attempts were intensified after the 1974 oil crisis increased the cost of private motoring. In 1975 the 'Wymondham, Dereham & Fakenham Railway Action Committee' was formed as a result of a meeting called by the East Anglian branch of the Railway Invigoration Society, and these two related organizations commenced a vigorous campaign for a reinstatement of passenger services over the Dereham branch. Pointing out that the line remained in being as a freight route, the campaigners argued that some form of railbus or diesel multiple unit service could have been provided at comparatively little cost, while the population growth in Dereham and the surrounding area would, they suggested, ensure the longer term future of the Wymondham to Dereham route.

It was suggested that, if re-opened, the Wymondham to Fakenham line could provide useful public transport facilities for the growing towns of Dereham (pop. around 10,000), Wymondham (pop. 10,000) and Fakenham (pop. 4,500). One problem concerned the large number of level crossings which would require modest investment if they were to be replaced by automatic lifting barriers; the need to accommodate freight traffic in addition to railcar-worked passenger services would also require investment in some form of new signalling. In spite of these potential problems, the case for reinstatement seemed to be sound - though much depended on the attitude of local authorities vis-à-vis grant aid.

On 8th April, 1978 the campaigners organized a special train service between Norwich and Dereham, and over 600 people took the opportunity to travel on the otherwise freight-only branch. A six-car multiple unit formation made two return trips over the line, and large numbers of well-wishers turned out to welcome the train at intermediate stations such as Yaxham and Hardingham.

Fakenham station on 21st April, 1979 after the arrival of a four-car dmu set with the 'Fakenham Flyer'. This train was about to make a trip to Dereham and back. It finally left Fakenham for Norwich at 17.10, becoming the last passenger train to do so. The section of line from Ryburgh to Fakenham was closed on 3rd April, 1980.   *C.A. Allenby*

The Great Ryburgh Charter train at North Elmham station on 11th October, 1980. The train was organized by the Fakenham & Dereham Railway Society. Cars Nos. 56413+50383 and 56186+50376 made up the dmu set, all of these being Cravens vehicles except for odd-man-out Birmingham RC&W driving trailer No. 56186. The charter train's route was Cambridge-Ely-Wymondham-Ryburgh-Wymondham-Norwich Thorpe-Norwich Victoria-Norwich Thorpe-Cambridge.   *Ray King*

The journey to and from Norwich took about 80 minutes each way, inclusive of five stops at unmanned level crossings. In all, the two special trips were regarded as an overwhelming success, and local travellers were encouraged in their belief that the line could one day be revived as a commuter route.

Growing interest in rural lines such as the Dereham branch brought a series of further special trains to the route during the ensuing years. On 21st April, 1979 the Wymondham, Dereham & Fakenham Rail Action Committee repeated its earlier success by providing a shuttle dmu service between Norwich, Dereham and Fakenham. On that occasion, the Action Committee joined forces with the Railway Development Society and the newly-formed Fakenham & Dereham Railway Society to organize the aptly-named 'Fakenham Flyer'; again, the chartered train was an instant success and plans were made for similar trips in the years ahead.

On Sunday, 23rd April, 1981 the Fakenham & Dereham Railway Society arranged a seaside special from Ryburgh, North Elmham, Dereham, Yaxham, Thuxton, Kimberley Park and Wymondham to Clacton, Frinton and Walton-on-the-Naze, the return fare for this attractive excursion being just £6.50. A few months later, on Saturday 19th September, 1981, the Wymondham, Dereham & Fakenham Rail Action Committee arranged another chartered dmu service between Norwich and Dereham. Four up and four down trains were provided and, with stops at Yaxham, Hardingham and the other intermediate stations, the Action Committee effectively brought the Wymondham to Dereham line back to life - albeit for only a day!

A Metro-Cammell class '101' dmu was used for the Wymondham, Dereham & Fakenham Rail Action Committee's charter the 'Seaside Special' on 23rd April, 1981. It is seen here at Ryburgh, the last passenger train to work from there.   *Ray King*

Two foot gauge quarry Hunslet *Cackler* (Works No. 671) in steam on the Yaxham Park Light Railway (YPLR) on 24th September, 1971. D.C. Potter had taken over the tenancy of Yaxham station in 1967 and he laid narrow gauge track in the old goods yard for his locomotive. In 1969 this engine was moved to the opposite side of the standard gauge line on the newly-established YPLR, this line ran for just over half a mile into meadows. The YPLR evolved into today's Yaxham Light Railway which runs parallel with the Mid-Norfolk Railway.   *A.R. Taylor*

Two foot gauge rolling stock in the old goods yard in Yaxham on 19th July, 1986. The locomotive is Ruston & Hornsby-built No. 6 *Colonel*. Notice Yaxham signal box in the background.
      R.E. Ruffell

These special excursions became something of an institution on the Dereham line. On 28th September, 1985, for instance, the branch was brought back to life for another day's passenger operation, while on 25th May, 1986 the Railway Development Association joined forces with the Wymondham, Dereham & Fakenham Action Committee to run a seaside excursion from Dereham to Sheringham. The fare, for this dmu trip, was £5 per head.

At the end of 1988 rumours began to circulate in the Dereham area to the effect that the whole line would soon be closed and, following enquiries made by the transport pressure group Transport 2000, BR admitted that the 4½ mile section between Dereham and North Elmham would be closed to all traffic with effect from 25th January, 1989. The future of the Wymondham to Dereham line was, by this time, also in considerable doubt, and in announcing the impending demise of the North Elmham service, BR added that the Dereham line was scheduled to close in June 1989 - thereby forcing the last regular rail users onto the already-crowded local roads.

The news that the Dereham branch would be closed completely in June 1989 led to renewed pressure for a reinstatement of the line for passenger services. Public attitudes towards railway closure had changed dramatically since the 1960s, and whereas in the 'Beeching era' the general public had repeatedly been told that railways were 'old fashioned' and 'Victorian', the oil crisis of 1974 had effectively tipped the balance back towards energy-efficient forms of transport and away from road transport.

Class '31' No. 31113 at North Elmham on 9th January, 1989.   *Ray King*

The Ruston diesel-hydraulic shunter stands at County School station platform with a brake van in June 1990.
Ray King

Class '20' Bo-Bo No. 20069 at the southern end of County School station on 19th June, 1992.
Ray King

There was, moreover, much greater interest in the whole concept of privately owned and operated branch lines, and against this background a new company known as the Great Eastern Railway Company (1989) Holdings Ltd was formed with the aim of purchasing 16 miles of line between Wymondham, Dereham and North Elmham.

It was suggested that one and a quarter million pounds would be enough to purchase and re-open the branch, and the company planned to raise this sum by a mixture of share issues, EEC and local grants, and public donations. Further cash could be generated by development of the 13 acre station site at Dereham, the intention being that, in addition to a fully-revived GER-style station, there might also be shops, a hotel and a museum or heritage centre. Feasibility studies indicated that 500 Dereham residents worked in Norwich, while 700 Norwich residents commuted to work in Dereham, and it seemed that a regular commuter service would be welcomed by increasingly frustrated road users.

The line would be worked mainly by dmus, though it was envisaged that tourist traffic would be catered for by the provision of steam-operated services. The Mid-Norfolk Railway Society - which had already established an operating base in the goods yard at County School - supported the re-opening scheme, and it was hoped that other railway societies would provide steam locomotives or vintage rolling stock for use on the proposed tourist services. In the early months of 1991, the *Railway Magazine* stated that the work required to bring the line up to passenger-carrying standards would 'take around two years'.

Meanwhile, the remaining portion of the Dereham to Wymondham line remained intact but out of use, though the activities of the Mid-Norfolk Railway Society ensured that the railway saw sporadic activities. New rolling stock was delivered from time to time, one of the first arrivals being a Ruston diesel-hydraulic shunter from the British Sugar factory at Bury St Edmunds, which was delivered by road to Hardingham on 15th October, 1983. In the summer of 1992, it was announced that class '20' Bo-Bo No. 20069 would be sent to the Dereham line as soon as it had been stripped of asbestos. The engine would, on arrival in Norfolk, be restored to its original green livery as No. D8069.

In 1994, the Mid-Norfolk Railway Society was granted access to the line between Wymondham and North Elmham, and a programme of low-level maintenance and vegetation clearance was then put into effect. Two years later, in 1996, the British Rail Property Board accepted an offer of £100,000 for the freehold of the trackbed between Wymondham and Dereham on condition that the land and buildings were not sold for non-railway purposes. The Mid-Norfolk Railway Preservation Trust completed its purchase of 11½ miles of line in April 1998, and the BR Property Board also accepted an offer of £25,000 for the track and trackbed between Dereham and North Elmham.

The Mid-Norfolk Railway

The railway was re-opened for freight traffic on 8th July, 1998, when the English Welsh & Scottish (EWS) train operating company ran a revenue-earning service on behalf of the Ministry of Defence. On that day, class '37' Co-Co No.

The first preserved steam locomotive to arrive at County School station was Manning, Wardle 0-6-0 *Sir Berkeley* (Works No. 1210 of 1890) which was loaned by the Vintage Carriage Trust. It is seen here on its first day in service, 17th July, 1993. Ray King leans out of the cab and looks back along the train.
Melvyn Hopwood

A pair of class '20' Bo-Bos, Nos. 20069 (leading) and 20209, at Yaxham on 24th December, 1994. These engines had only recently been moved from County School and this was the first locomotive movement after the transfer to Dereham. On the left, Quarry Hunslet 0-4-0ST *Elin* (Works No. 705 of 1899) is in steam on the part of the Yaxham Light Railway that runs parallel with the Mid-Norfolk Railway.
Ray King

37263 worked a train of 20 'VGA' vans over the line conveying 850 tons of simulated ammunition for the Royal Logistical Corps at RAF Sculthorpe. The locomotive returned to Bicester Central Ordnance Depot on the following day, hauling a mixed formation of 'Warflat' and 'Warwell' bogie vehicles.

A similar train ran from Didcot to Dereham on 17th July, 1998, when class '37' No. 37707 worked a train of empty wagons over the branch in order to collect a consignment of armoured fighting vehicles. On 24th July the same train returned to Dereham behind class '47' Co-Co No. 47053, while further military trains ran over the Dereham line in the following months. On 26th May, 1999, class '66' Co-Co No. 66061 worked through to Dereham with a representative selection of EWS goods vehicles as part of a one-day event held in Dereham to promote rail freight in the Norfolk area.

Meanwhile, passenger trains had commenced operations on the two miles of line between Dereham and Yaxham. The railway was formally re-opened for passenger traffic on the weekend of 1st-3rd May, 1999, and since that time the Mid-Norfolk line has gone from strength to strength. County School station, which had been taken over by another preservation group, has been adapted for use as a tea room and visitor centre, while elsewhere on the line, some of the other stations - notably Yaxham and Hardingham - have been attractively restored by private owners.

The privatization of Britain's railway system during the 1990s has inevitably resulted in a blurring of the distinctions that once existed between private lines and what was once the BR network. There are, as a result, many new opportunities for preserved railways such as the Mid-Norfolk line. As we have seen, freight traffic has returned to the route in connection with military transport requirements, but at the same time Anglia Railways has made use of Dereham station as a convenient road-rail interchange point - its own depot at Norwich Crown Point having poor road links.

Members of the Mid-Norfolk Railway Preservation Trust at work on 15th February, 1997 when two panels of track were connected to the existing railhead to the south of Dereham station, 150 years to the day after commencement of passenger services between Wymondham and Dereham. A Metro-Cammell dmu set is visible in the distance.

Roland Hummerston

An MOD test train at Hardingham top and tailed by class '20' Bo-Bo No. 20069 and class '47' Co-Co No. 47241 on 29th June, 1998. In the right foreground are two shunters, furthest from the camera is Bagnall 0-4-0 diesel-hydraulic No. 2 (Works No. WB 3213/RSH8368), with Drewry 0-4-0 diesel-mechanical No. 3 (Works No. DC2589/RSH7922). *Ray King*

Andrew Barclay 0-4-0ST (Works No. 2069 of 1939) *Little Barford* on its first day in steam at Dereham on the Mid-Norfolk Railway, 7th April, 2000. This engine was the first steam locomotive to work through to Wymondham. *Little Barford* is now at the Mid-Suffolk Railway. *Ray King*

Rail access charges over the national network has meant that many train operating companies now send their locomotives and rolling stock to and from various engineering centre by road transport. Thus, in 1999, Anglia Railways dispatched class '08' 0-6-0 shunter No. 08810 by rail to Dereham for onwards road transport to RMS Locotec at Derby, while sister locomotive No. 08870 was delivered by road to Dereham on a return journey to Norwich. Similarly, on 1st December, 2001, class '86' electric locomotive No. 86252 - formerly No. E3101, the pioneer class '86 locomotive - was hauled 'dead' from Norwich to Dereham following fire damage at Ardleigh behind class '47' No. 47786 *Roy Castle OBE*. On arrival at Dereham, the 86 ton locomotive was winched aboard a low-loader for the remainder of its journey to Alstom Glasgow.

Over the years a number of railtours have used the Mid-Norfolk Railway. The first to do so was a Kings Cross-Dereham train organized by Hertfordshire Railtours on 8th May, 1999. Most of the subsequent railtours have been operated by Nenta Railtours, with motive power provided by class '47' and class '67' diesel locomotives. On 5th May, 2007 the Railway Touring Co. organized a Norwich to Dereham excursion using class '47' No. 47812 and ex-Southern Railway 'West Country' class 4-6-2 No. 34067 *Tangmere.*

Steam-operated passenger trains had returned to the line on the 30th April, 2006. Motive power for the inaugural service was Great Western 0-6-0PT No. 9466, on loan from the Buckinghamshire Railway Centre. In 2009 'N7' class 0-6-2T No. 69621 arrived from the North Norfolk Railway and BR Standard 'Britannia' class 4-6-2 No. 70013 *Oliver Cromwell* also visited.

Dereham yard was used by Direct Rail Services as a servicing depot in 2007 and 2008, and since 2008 Network Rail has used the yard for track plant. On

'West Country' class Bulleid Pacific No. 34067 *Tangmere* is seen at the head of the Railway Touring Co.'s Norwich-Dereham excursion at Kimberley Park on 5th May, 2007.

Ray King

Great Western Railway '94XX' class 0-6-0PT No. 9466 passes through Hardingham station with
a train comprising a goods van and brake van in 2009.   *Ray King*

LNER 'N7' class 0-6-2T No. 69621 at the northern end of Dereham station in 2009.   *Ray King*

26th September, 2008 EWS class '66' Co-Co No. 66105 was used on a Ministry of Defence (MOD) trial train over the line and on 8th January, 2009 class '66' No. 66157 worked an MOD train made up of 'VGA', 'Warwell' and 'Warflat' wagons. Another MOD train ran on 28th November, 2009.

The autumn diesel gala of 2010 used the newly-installed loop at Thuxton. The new loop enabled hourly departures from both Wymondham and Dereham. The diesel locomotives now based at Dereham are:

Class '08' 0-6-0 diesel shunter No. 08361 *Eagle*
Class '20' Bo-Bo No. D8069
Class '31' A1A-A1A No. 5662, 31438, 31530 *Sister Dora*
Class '37' Co-Co No. 37219 *Shirley Ann Smith*, 37360
Class '47' Co-Co No. 47580 *County of Essex*, 47596 *Aldeburgh Festival*
Class '50' Co-Co No. 50019 *Ramillies*
Class '56' Co-Co No. 56101
Electro-diesel class '73' Bo-Bo No. 73210 *Selhurst*

The numbers and names shown are those currently carried by the locomotives. There are also some diesel-multiple-units, predominantly Metro-Cammell class '101', but also Gloucester RC&W driving trailer composite No. 56301 and Gloucester RC&W single car unit 'Bubble Car' No. 55009. Rather unlikely residents at the Mid-Norfolk Railway are three cars from Southern Region 'CIG' (class '421') electric-multiple-unit sets.

The Mid-Norfolk Railway's current extent from Wymondham to Dereham is 11½ miles. The railway owns a further six miles of track towards County School station, although there is a short section between North Elmham and County School where the track has been lifted. Beyond County School the trackbed to Fakenham is largely intact and has been reserved for railway use by the council. The route mileage from Wymondham to Fakenham is 23 miles and re-opening throughout to Fakenham is the Mid-Norfolk Railway's ultimate aim.

A line up of class '37' locomotives at Dereham on Diesel Gala day, 25th September, 2010. *Left to right*, Nos. 37709, 37906, and 37109.   *Ray King*

The former Wells & Fakenham Railway station building at Walsingham viewed from the road in 2010, with the former goods shed visible at the rear. In 1967 the old station found a new lease of life as St Seraphim's Russian Orthodox church. The building is sited at the highest point in the village and the dome and cross which were mounted on the roof at that time give the old station a distinctive look. The Wells & Walsingham Railway's terminus is sited a little to the north of the former Wells branch station. *John Hendy*

Wells Harbour Railway on 26th August, 1979. The locomotive is 0-4-2T *Edmund Hannay* which was built by David King in 1972. *John C. Baker*

Chapter Eight

Revival at Wells -
The Wells & Walsingham Railway

The abandoned Fakenham to Wells section of the branch was dismantled after the cessation of freight services, but the former trackbed remained substantially intact throughout its 9½ mile length. At Wells, the redundant terminal buildings eventually found a new lease of life as a pottery, while (even more unusually), Walsingham station was adapted for use as a place of worship by the Russian Orthodox church.

In the meantime, Wells had blossomed as a holiday resort in its own right, attracting considerable numbers of caravaners, boating enthusiasts and other self-catering holidaymakers. Aware that the area had potential for further development, the newly-created North Norfolk District Council actively promoted the little town, advertising it (along with the established resorts of Mundesley, Cromer and Sheringham) in guides prepared mainly for tourists and holidaymakers. With the quays cleared of railway lines, the Wells 'water front' at last began to look like a real promenade, and with its quaint old streets and houses, Wells-next-the-Sea could stand comparison with any other seaside town.

The first steps

In 1975 the District Council asked Lieutenant-Commander Roy Francis, a retired naval officer, to build a miniature railway between Wells harbour and the beaches and caravan parks at 'Abraham's Bosom'; this would provide a further attraction for holidaymakers while at the same time fulfilling a need for transport between Wells and its beaches. The result was the mile-long Wells Harbour Railway, a 10¼ inch gauge miniature railway which provided a timetable service at 40 minute intervals throughout the summer.

0-4-0 *Weasel* departs from the northern terminus of the Harbour Railway, Pinewood. The locomotive was built by David King in 1980 and it is powered by an Alfa Romeo petrol engine. Notice the Alfa badge on the locomotive's front grille.   *John C. Baker*

The harbour line was highly successful, but once it was complete and in operation, Lt-Commander Francis felt that there would be scope for a much longer 10¼ inch gauge line, which would allow this unusually-narrow gauge to be exploited to its full potential as a means of transport. Driving past the abandoned Wells branch every evening, he realised that the formation - which connected the holiday centres of Wells and Walsingham - was sufficiently intact to provide a foundation for his projected narrow gauge line.

Of equal significance was the thought that people staying in Wells (or touring the area by car) would welcome the chance to travel to Walsingham by steam railway and there would thus be a market for the new railway. Although the purchase of four miles of disused railway would be an immensely costly exercise, further research suggested that the project was viable, and once committed, Lt-Commander Francis soon put his scheme into effect, acquiring the necessary land and obtaining a light railway order for the proposed line.

Once these obstacles were overcome, the rest was, in a sense, easy, and construction proceeded with commendable speed. Most of the heavy works were already in existence, but there was a major problem at the place known locally as 'Barnard's Cutting', where thousands of tons of refuse had been tipped by the local council. Around 3,000 tons were removed, but in the end it was decided to lay the rails over the remaining infill - the result being a gradient which would test the miniature locomotives to their limit!

Unlike many other light and narrow gauge lines, the 'Wells & Walsingham Railway' was designed and built as an efficient means of transport, using as many modern ideas and materials as possible - the object being to run the line cheaply and efficiently with the minimum of staff and no unnecessary frills. The choice of gauge was an important aspect of Lt-Commander Francis's scheme for, although much narrower than usual, it could be maintained by a two-man permanent way crew without the need for cranes or other heavy lift equipment.

Much of the line was laid with channel or 'U'-shaped steel rail, which had already proved itself in operation on the Wells Harbour line. At stations, conventional 20 lb. per yard flat-bottomed rail was employed, this being more convenient for the construction of pointwork.

Some details of the line

The Wells & Walsingham Railway (W&W) was opened for the carriage of passengers on 6th April, 1982, from which date a basic train service of six trains each way connected Wells, Walsingham and Wighton Halt; an additional stopping place was also established at Warham St Mary. Journey time, for the four mile journey, was 25 minutes in each direction. At Wells, the railway starts and terminates near the former A149 level crossing, where facilities originally consisted of a simple run-round loop, with a turntable and a short dead-end siding.

From Wells, the line continues southwards along the trackbed of the Wells & Fakenham Railway, with excellent views of the sand dunes, nature reserve and sea, together with many tantalizing glimpses of picturesque Norfolk villages and churches. The steady climb up to Barnard's Cutting ensures that locomotives must work flat out to lift their 6 ton trains over the summit, and lineside photographers and recording enthusiasts are rewarded with the unique sights and sounds of a steam locomotive achieving an optimum performance under everyday conditions. At Walsingham, the line terminates in a leafy cutting, a short distance to the north of the original station. The facilities provided here at the time of opening included another turntable and run-round loop.

The line, which is worked as efficiently as possible on the 'one engine in steam' system, has no need for expensive signalling installations, but under the terms of its Light Railway Order the Wells & Walsingham Railway is responsible for the provision of fixed warning boards at Warham St Mary level crossing, and these must be illuminated whenever the railway is used during the hours of darkness.

Narrow gauge locomotives and rolling stock

The design of locomotives and rolling stock was another important aspect of the railway and, as with the trackwork, Lt-Commander Francis incorporated many innovations in his initial locomotive and passenger vehicles. The first locomotive was built by D.H. King of Suffield Norfolk in 1981/82, and displaying considerable historical prescience, the Lt-Commander decided to call it *Pilgrim*. The new locomotive was an 0-6-0T with 4 inch by 6 inch outside cylinders and a boiler diameter of 14 in. Suspension was achieved by a combination of springs on the centre axle and hard rubber blocks on the leading and trailing axles; total weight, in working order, was one ton.

Despite its small dimensions, *Pilgrim* was designed as a narrow gauge engine rather than a miniature locomotive - in other words it was a full size engine running on 10¼ in. gauge track; the cab for instance was designed to accommodate a fully grown man in reasonable comfort. All bearing surfaces were fabricated from standard parts, with generous surfaces to ensure free running. Externally, the engine was finished in a mid-green livery, with polished brass boiler bands, dome, whistle and safety valves.

By 1985, it was becoming obvious that longer trains were needed, together with a more powerful locomotive. For this reason, the railway ordered a large Beyer-Garratt 2-6-0+0-6-2 locomotive, which was built by Neil Simkins of Ashby-de-la-Zouch in 1986. The new locomotive was named *Norfolk Hero* - presumably in an oblique reference to Horatio Nelson, who was born just a few miles away in the parsonage at Burnham Thorpe.

With a length of 20 ft 6 in., *Norfolk Hero* must be the largest and most powerful 10¼ in. gauge engine in the world, with a generously-proportioned boiler suspended between two powered bogies. Benefiting from the lessons learned with *Pilgrim*, the new locomotive has roller bearings, a large footplate and cab, and ample provision for coal and water fuel. There are four 4 inch by 5½ inch cylinders, and the boiler pressure is 140 lb. per square inch.

Rolling stock at the time of opening consisted of an air-braked, articulated set, running on rubber block suspension and seating 38 passengers. Special refinements included a wheel-driven compressor to ensure a supply of air for

Pilgrim waits to depart from Wells with the 12.40 pm train to Walsingham on 4th July, 1982.
John C. Baker

Norfolk Hero hauls 100 passengers at 8 mph up the 1 in 29 gradient at Wighton on 11th October, 1986.
Adrian Vaughan

the main braking system, and electric bell communication between guard and driver. Designed to run as an integral unit with *Pilgrim*, the coach at the Wells end of the train had a built-in water tank to supplement the engine's small capacity side tanks. An electric compressor ensured an additional source of air, and there were also two hand pumps; the whole braking system was twin-line and failsafe, with emergency valves in the covered guard's compartments at each end of the articulated set.

The Wells & Walsingham Railway is primarily a passenger line, but in common with other railways it needs a small number of 'goods' vehicles for permanent way work and the carriage of locomotive coal, and there are at present two such vehicles on the line - both transferred from the original Wells Harbour line. One of these service wagons is a large bogie coal vehicle, while the other is a Hudson tipper wagon, which has been regauged from 2 ft to 10¼ inch gauge.

As with permanent way vehicles, there was an inter-change of locomotives between the Wells & Walsingham and Wells Harbour lines, and in the interests of completeness these 'visitors' should be mentioned. As *Pilgrim* was not delivered until 1982, the W&W line was built with the aid of *Weasel* - an 0-4-0 petrol-engined shunter built by D.H. King of Suffield which, with its full size cab and green livery, looked very much like an internal combustion-engined version of *Pilgrim*. A later acquisition was an unnamed 0-6-0 petrol-mechanical engine, which was built by Alan Keef Ltd of Cote, near Bampton (Oxfordshire) in 1985; this locomotive, with its fully-roofed central cab, was a typical industrial shunter.

A complete list of locomotives and rolling stock used on the Wells & Walsingham line at the end of the 1990s is given in the following table.

Wells & Walsingham locomotives and rolling stock

Locomotives

Name	Type	Notes
Weasel	0-4-0 petrol-engined shunter	Built by D.H. King of Suffield
Pilgrim	0-6-0T steam locomotive	Built by D.H. King of Suffield, 1981
	0-6-0 petrol-engined shunter	Built by Alan Keef of Bampton, 1985
Norfolk Hero	2-6-0+0-6-2 Garratt	Built by Neil Simkins, 1986

Rolling stock
One 5-vehicle articulated set with covered guard's compartments
One open bogie freight wagon, used mainly for coal
One former 2 ft gauge tipper wagon transferred from harbour line

Liveries at the time of opening were dark green for locomotives and red for rolling stock. Boiler bands, domes, and other details are kept highly-polished, recalling those far-off Edwardian days when Great Eastern 2-4-0s ran along the single track branch to Wells-next-the-Sea. The line, by its very nature, lacks sophisticated lineside buildings, and it is perhaps a pity that (apart from bridges) so little of the former standard gauge infrastructure could be used. There are, nevertheless, one or two minor structures, including a wooden engine shed and lineside hut at Wells, together with a miniature water tank supported on a stack of unused sleepers.

Recent Developments on the Wells & Walsingham Railway

The Wells & Walsingham Light Railway has gone from strength to strength since its opening in April 1982. The line is now so popular that a second 2-6-0+0-6-2 Garratt locomotive was obtained in order to assist *Norfolk Hero*, which had hauled more than 450,000 passengers and covered 200,000 miles over a period of 24 years.

To help with the cost of £100,000, the railway received £38,000 from the Norfolk Coast & Broads Rural Development Programme, while practical help was provided by engineering students and one apprentice from the College of West Anglia at Kings Lynn. The assembly of the new Garratt and much of the engineering work was carried out by Richard Coleby and Jim Wickett (Rowland Engineering), while the boiler was constructed by Mervyn Mayes at Yaxham. The engine was assembled at Uniseed Engineering with the help of Mark Manning and his team.

The new Garratt locomotive was named *Norfolk Heroine* by the Countess of Leicester at an inauguration ceremony at Wells station on Saturday 16th October, 2010. Before christening the engine with champagne, Lady Leicester remarked that it was highly appropriate that the new locomotive would be named *Norfolk Heroine* in commemoration of Edith Cavell (1865-1915), the British nurse who was shot by the Germans in World War I. The daughter of a Norfolk vicar from Swardeston, Edith was working in Brussels as the Director of a nurses' training school when the Germans occupied the city, and in this capacity she became involved with an organization that helped British soldiers to escape from Belgium. This inevitably brought her to the attention of the Germans, and after a summary court martial on 7th October she was shot at dawn on 12th October, 1915. Her execution outraged public opinion and caused an international outcry against the Germans, and resulted in an upsurge in recruitment for the British army; the Kaiser later ordered that no more women should be shot without his permission.

Norfolk Heroine waits to depart from Wells with the afternoon train for Walsingham on Good Friday, 22nd April, 2011.   *Dr G.R. Siviour*

Appendix One

Promoters, Directors
and other Prominent Personalities

Thomas Coke, Earl of Leicester (1752-1842): The celebrated 'Coke of Norfolk', who inherited Holkham in 1776 and transformed the hitherto barren estate into an agricultural show piece.

Thomas William Coke, Earl of Leicester (1822-1909): Succeeded his father in 1842 and continued improving the estate; generally acknowledged as the 'founder' of the Wells & Fakenham Railway but it is conceivable that the whole project was initiated by local traders who, out of deference, would have taken their scheme to the Earl at an early date. T.W. Coke was nevertheless a major subscriber and without his support the line would not have been built; he took little obvious interest in the day to day operation of the line, but was probably well-briefed by Hall Keary.

Sir Samuel Morton Peto (1809-1889): Born in Woking, Surrey, Peto made his fortune as a railway contractor, in which capacity he was no doubt a brilliant organizer and a good employer. He always gave considerable thought to the spiritual welfare of rough, otherwise lawless navvies, and local historians have identified clear links between the progress of his railways and the spread of Baptist chapels. Unfortunately the great contractor tended to exert a strong 'political' influence on companies with which he was involved, and these influences grew as Peto's own wealth and prestige increased. Perhaps unintentionally, he was directly responsible for the Wells & Fakenham's problems vis-à-vis the Eastern Counties Railway, and having created this problem he seems to have made little attempt to rescue the smaller company.

Peto was associated with numerous lines, including the Norfolk Railway, the East Suffolk Railway, the Oxford Worcester & Wolverhampton Railway, the South Eastern Railway, the London Tilbury & Southend Railway, the Eastern Counties Railway and the Metropolitan District Railway. Peto usually worked in conjunction with Edward Ladd Betts, trading as Messrs Peto & Betts. The firm went bankrupt following the failure of bankers Overend & Gurney in 1866, and Peto never recovered his lost prestige.

Hall William Keary: A Wells & Fakenham Director and Lord Leicester's estate manager. He was apparently one of the Wells & Fakenham's most committed supporters and usually chaired public meetings of the company.

Joseph Southgate: A coal and corn dealer of Wells, and like Hall Keary one of the most committed Wells & Fakenham supporters; he may have been the first to suggest the scheme, but as a mere trader he would not have been able to act without the Earl of Leicester.

Richard Till: Chairman of the Norfolk Railway and a Director of the Wells & Fakenham company - in which capacity he evidently felt himself at the centre of the Wells & Fakenham/Eastern Counties Railway imbroglio, and tried his hardest to solve the problem.

George Berkeley: An experienced engineer, though much of his work was overseas on foreign or colonial lines such as the Marseilles Extension and Great Indian Peninsula Railways; the Wells & Fakenham was a very minor project in comparison, and Berkeley is unlikely to have spent much time in North Norfolk.

Horatio Love: Chairman of the Eastern Counties Railway from 1856, and first Chairman of the GER, Love made only small concessions towards the Wells & Fakenham; he negotiated with Richard Till during the months before opening, but would not honour the 46 per cent operating agreement arranged by Morton Peto.

Appendix Two

Signal Boxes and Signalling

Signal box	Levers	Notes
Wells-next-the-Sea	45	
Walsingham	19	
Parkers Siding	5	Ground frame
Fakenham North	37	39 levers after 1928
Fakenham South	25	Abolished 1928
Ryburgh	25	Saxby & Farmer frame
Broom Green	–	Abolished 1880s
County School	44	Saxby & Farmer frame
North Elmham	20	
Dereham North	25	
Dereham Central	50	
Dereham South	27	Later 32 levers
Yaxham	26	
Thuxton	18	
Hardingham	21	Abolished 1968
Kimberley	–	
Wymondham South Junction	42	

Note: Most Wells branch signal boxes had McKenzie & Holland frames.

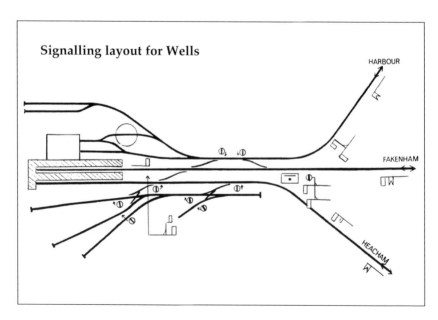

198

Sources and Bibliography

Valuable insights into the early history of the Norfolk Railway, the Wells & Fakenham Railway, and the West Norfolk Railway were obtained from the *Times*, the *Railway Times* and other contemporary newspapers and journals - which frequently printed Director's reports verbatim for the benefit of potential investors. Other primary sources included the relevant Acts of Parliament, the *Journal of the House of Commons*, the House of Lords Journal and the minute books of the companies concerned. This material was supplemented by annual reports and financial statements appearing in *Bradshaw's Shareholders' Manual* - which also yielded useful information on Boardroom changes throughout the 19th century.

Information on individual Directors was culled from the *Dictionary of National Biography*, or in certain cases from gravestones and church monuments. Other sources for the early periods included the *Railway Magazine*, the *Great Eastern Railway Magazine*, and *The Locomotive Magazine*. For more recent periods, GER, LNER and BR public and working timetables gave details of train services, distances and working arrangements, while topographical information was obtained from a variety of sources, including 25 inch Ordnance Survey maps, *Kelly's Directories* and RAF navigational charts.

Personal recollections were also of immense help, and the author would like to extend special thanks to Roy Francis, and to Ray King who checked the Mid-Norfolk Railway section. Help with photographs and other illustrations came from the Lens of Sutton Collection, Edwin Wilmshurst, G.R. Mortimer, Canon Charles Baynes, Alan Taylor, William J. Sutton, H.C. Casserley, Dr G.R. Siviour, John Hendy and Adrian Vaughan.

The following books and articles, many of which are long out of print, may contain extra information for those seeking further details of Norfolk railways, or Norfolk local history in general.

Cecil J. Allen, *The Great Eastern Railway*, Ian Allan (1955)

E.L. Ahrons, The Locomotives of the GER, *The Locomotive Magazine* Vols. 7-18, 1901-1912

David J. Bosher, 'Norfolk Postscript', *Railway Magazine* Vol. 126, February 1980

Michael Crofts, 'Minimum Gauge to Walsingham', *Railway Magazine* Vol. 129, June 1983

N. Crump, *By Rail to Victory*, LNER (1947)

W.A. Dutt, *The Little Guide to Norfolk* (1902)

W.R. Jenkinson, 'The Predecessors of the Great Eastern Railway', *Great Eastern Magazine* 1913-15

Michael Crofts, 'Articulated Miniature', *Railway Magazine* Vol. 132, November 1986

A.W. Purchas, *Some History of Wells-next-the-Sea* (1965)

G.W. Potter, 'The Great Eastern Railway in West Norfolk', *Railway Magazine* 1910

R. Murman, 'Plan of the Month: Wells-next-the-Sea', *Railway Modeller* Vol. 32 April 1981

Railway Invigoration Society, *Can Bus Replace Train?* (1977)

Alan Summers, 'Maunsel Parva to Wells', *Railway Modeller* Vol. 24 February 1973

E. Tuddenham, 'A Journey to Wells-next-the-Sea', *Railway World* Vol. 26 March 1965

Iain C. Scotchman, The Dereham Branch, *Great Eastern Journal* No. 20 (1980)

Alan Summers, 'East Barsham Tunnel & Viaduct', *Great Eastern Journal* No. 107 (2001)

Alan Summers, 'The Harbour Branch & Quay Tramway, Wells', *Great Eastern Journal* No. 103 (2000)

Stanley C. Jenkins, *The Lynn & Hunstanton Railway*, Oakwood Press (1987, enlarged second edition 2011)

Stanley C. Jenkins, *The Lynn & Dereham Railway*, Oakwood Press (1993)

Stanley C. Jenkins, 'The West Norfolk Branch of the GER', *British Railway Journal* No. 35 (1991)

Stanley C. Jenkins, 'The West Norfolk Junction Railway', *Great Eastern Journal* No. 109 (2002)

R.S. Joby, *Forgotten Railways of East Anglia*, David & Charles (1977)

Donald I. Gordon, 'The Lynn & Dereham Railway', *Railway Magazine* Vol. 102, 1958

Donald I. Gordon, *A Regional History of the Railways of Great Britain Vol. 5*, David & Charles (1968)

J.F. Gairns, 'The Norfolk Lines of the LNER', *Railway Magazine* 1929

C.B. Carter, 'LNER Coach Cascading in the 1930s', *British Railway Journal* No. 12

M.R.C. Price, 'From Fakenham with the Grain Train', *Railway World*, September 1974

Index

Accidents, 13, 21, 71, 81, 128, 137, 139, 153
Aerodromes, 74 *et seq.*
Aldeburgh, 39,149
Armoured trains, 53, 58, 73, 74
Barnard's cutting, 192
Barsham, 21, 37, 51, 73, 141
Beeching, Dr Richard, 169, 173
Berkeley (or 'Berkley'), George, Engineer 17, 21, 25, 197
Bidder, George Parker (1806-1878), Engineer 13, 14, 83
Binham Priory, 9
Blakeney, 11, 165
Borrow, George 109
Broom, Green, 36, 127, 128, 129
Burnham Market, 30, 31, 165
Burnham Thorpe, 10, 153, 157
Carrow Road football ground, 87
Castle, Barbara, 173
Cavell, Edith (1865-1915), 196
Church Lane crossing & siding, 95
Clacton, 39, 179
Coastal shipping, 17, 28, 158
Coast defence batteries, 75
Coke, Thomas, (1752-1842), 9, 197
Coke, Thomas William (1822-1909), promoter, 17 *et seq.*, 40, 197
Coleman's siding, 141
County School, 36, 37, 68, 126 *et seq.*, 173, 175, 182 *et seq.*
Cromer 21, 35 *et seq.*, 39, 71, 163
Dereham 11, 12, 14, 37, 67, 68, 111 *et seq.*, 174, 175, 177, 179 *et passim*
De-staffing of stations 109,174
Dumpling Green, 109
East Anglian Railway, 11, 14, 29
Eastern & Midlands Railway, *see Midland & Great Northern Joint Railway*
Eastern Counties Railway, 10, 14 *et seq.*, 19, 24, 26, 27, 29, 30
Eastern Union Railway, 11, 29, 77
East Norfolk Railway, 35 *et seq.*
East Suffolk Railway, 149
Eaton level crossing, 87
Egmere Road level crossing, 143, 145
Erasmus, Desiderious, 142
Everitt's siding, 145
Fakenham, 14, 15, 21, 36, 67, 68, 71,133 *et seq.*, 174 *et seq.*
Floods, (1912), 51
Floods, (1953), 163, 165
Floods, (1968), 174
Goods traffic, 67, 68, 81, 85, 107, 111, 125, 127, 128, 137, 143, 149, 151, 168, 175, 177, 185
Great Eastern Railway, creation of, 29, 30
Hardingham, 14, 37, 67, 68, 99 *et seq.*, 174, 175, 179, 183, 185
Hetherset, 87 *et seq.*
Hoe level crossing, 123
Holkham, 9, 17, 28, 31, 40, 165
Home Guard, 73
Hudson, George, 26
Hunstanton, 30, 37, 39, 41, 59, 65, 68, 71, 163, 165, 168, 173
James, William, 10
Keary, Hall William, promoter, 17, 18, 24, 25, 29, 197
Ketteringham crossing, 89
Kett's Rebellion, 89
Kimberley Park, 12, 14, 37, 68, 94 *et seq.*, 173, 174, 179
Leicester Lime Co. siding, 147
Liveries, 33, 49, 59, 61, 63, 159, 195
Love, Horatio, 197

Lynn & Dereham Railway, 11 *et seq.*
Macmillan, Harold, 169
Marples, Ernest, 169
Midland & Great Northern Joint Railway, 35, 36, 133, 139, 169
Mid-Norfolk Railway, 183 *et seq.*
Motive power, 15, 20, 32 *et seq.*, 44, 47 *et seq.*, 59, 62 *et seq.*, 72, 73, 76, 81, 93, 151, 159 *et seq.*, 163
Nationalization, effects of, 159
Nelson, Horatio, 10, 153, 193
Norfolk County School, 36, 127
Norfolk Railway 11, 13 *et seq.*, 17 *et seq.*, 24, 26, 29, 32, 77, 83, 91
Northall Green, 123
North Elmham, 15, 37, 68, 123 *et seq.*, 172, 174, 175, 177 *et seq.*, 181, 183,
Northern & Eastern Railway, 10
Norwich, 10, 77
Norwich & Brandon Railway, 10 *et seq.*, 77, 90, 91, 95
Norwich Thorpe, 75, 77 *et seq.*
Norwich Trowse, 81 *et seq.*
Norwich Victoria, 77, 81
Parker's siding, *see Coleman's siding*
Peto, Samuel Morton (1809-1889), 13,17,18,19,24,30,197
Pilgrimage traffic, 71, 142, 149, 158, 159, 163
Railway Mania, 11
Rolling stock, 16, 61, 63, 67, 69, 70, 161
Ryburgh, 15, 37, 67, 68, 129 *et seq.*, 168, 174, 175, 177, 179
Salthouse 165
Signal boxes 81, 83, 85, 87, 89, 91, 95, 97 *et seq.*, 101, 105 *et seq.*, 119 *et seq.*, 128, 129, 133, 137, 143, 151
Signalling, 33, 83, 125, 128, 141, 147, 157, 168, 198
Slipper Chapel Halt, 71, 142
Southgate, Joseph Springhill (or Springhall), promoter, 17, 18, 21, 23 *et seq.*, 29, 197
Spinks Lane, station at, 87
Station architecture, 77, 78, 85, 87, 91, 95, 97, 99, 103, 105, 107, 111, 114, 123, 127, 130, 131, 135, 137, 142, 143, 149
Steam railcars, 61, 65, 69-70
Thuxton, 13, 14, 37, 68,103 *et seq.*, 173 *et seq.*, 179
Tickets & fares, 59, 163
Till, Richard, promoter 17, 18, 24 *et seq.*, 197
Tunnels, 21, 37, 141
Valentine, John Sutherland (1813-1898), Engineer, 31
Viaducts & major bridges, 21, 83, 134, 141
Waddington, David (1810-1863), 26, 30
Walsingham, 19, 28, 37, 68, 71, 140 *et seq.*,190 *et seq.*
Watts Naval Training School, 127
Wells & Fakenham Railway, 17 *et seq.*
Wells & Walsingham Railway, 191 *et seq.*
Wells-next-the-Sea, 7, 49, 51, 67, 68, 70, 146 *et seq.*, 191 *et passim*
West Norfolk branch, 30 *et seq.*, 41, 47, 59, 65, 68, 70, 147, 149, 159, 161, 163, 165
Wighton Halt, 70, 145, 192
World War I, 51 *et seq.*, 58
World War II, 77, 78, 89, 131, 132
Worthing 123,125
Wroxham Line, 36, 47, 58, 65, 67 *et seq.*, 125, 127 *et seq.*, 163
Wymondham, 68, 89 *et seq.*, 169, 174, 175, 177,
Wymondham to Forncett line, 41, 47, 51, 63, 67, 91, 93
Yarmouth, 39, 67, 74
Yarmouth & Norwich Railway, 11, 77
Yaxham, 14, 37, 67, 68, 105 *et seq.*, 173 *et seq.*, 179, 185
Zeppelin raids, 53, 58, 74